'Dr Feyisa Demie's book identifies some excell‹
city schools and provides "what works" evide
policymakers to use to address educatioı

**Christabel McLean, former headteacher and locaı auтnoriтy scnooı
improvement adviser**

'This important book moves from a widespread review of evidence to the
essential work of improving schools and outcomes in one large London
authority. By focussing on areas of undoubted success for disadvantaged
children, students from ethnic minorities, and additional language
learners, Dr Demie offers measurable ways forward for successful
education. Others take note.'

Professor Stephen Gorard, Durham University

'A timely and important book that provides positive messages and a rich
evidence base to inform and guide school leaders, teachers and policy
makers. It should become essential reading for all concerned to address
the equity gap in student achievement with well founded research and
evidence based approaches.'

**Pamela Sammons, Emeritus Professor, Department of Education,
University of Oxford, and Emeritus Fellow Jesus College**

For Margaret, Kulani and Ibsa, with love

Educational Inequality

Educational Inequality
Closing the gap

Feyisa Demie

 is an imprint of

First published in 2019 by the UCL Institute of Education Press, University College London, 20 Bedford Way, London WC1H 0AL

www.ucl-ioe-press.com

British Library Cataloguing in Publication Data:
A catalogue record for this publication is available from the British Library

ISBNs
978-1-85856-879-9 (paperback)
978-1-85856-903-1 (PDF eBook)
978-1-85856-904-8 (ePub eBook)
978-1-85856-905-5 (Kindle eBook)

Typeset by Quadrant Infotech (India) Pvt Ltd
Printed by CPI Group (UK) Ltd, Croydon, CR0 4YY

Cover design by emc design ltd

Contents

List of figures and tables

List of abbreviations

ASDAN	Award Scheme Development and Accreditation Network
AST	advanced skills teacher
CAT	cognitive ability test
CPD	continuing professional development
DCSF	Department for Children, Schools and Families
DfE	Department for Education
EAL	English as an additional language
EEF	Education Endowment Foundation
EMAG	Ethnic Minority Achievement Grant
ESOL	English for speakers of other languages
EU	European Union
EYFS	early years foundation stage
FSM	free school meals
FSP	foundation stage profile
FSW	family support worker
GCSE	General Certificate of Secondary Education
HMI	Her Majesty's Inspector
HLTA	higher-level teaching assistant
ICT	information and communications technology
IEP	individual(ized) education plan
INSET	in-service education and training
KS1	Key Stage 1
KS2	Key Stage 2
KS3	Key Stage 3
KS4	Key Stage 4
LA	local authority
LSA	learning support assistant
NAO	National Audit Office
NQT	newly qualified teacher
NFER	National Foundation for Education Research
NLE	national leader of education
NPD	national pupil database
NQT	newly qualified teacher
NVQ	National Vocational Qualification

Ofsted	Office for Standards in Education, Children's Services and Skills
PP	pupil premium
PPF	pupil premium funding
PPG	pupil premium grant
PPR	pupil performance review
PSHE	personal, social, health and economic education
RWM	reading, writing and mathematics
SAT	standard attainment test
SEAL	social and emotional aspects of learning
SEN	special educational needs
SENCO	special educational needs co-ordinator
SFR	statistical first release
SLE	specialist leader of education
SLT	senior leadership team
SMT	senior management team
TA	teaching assistant

Case study schools: Type and age range

School code	Type	Age – lower	Age – higher	Gender
A	Primary	4	11	Mixed
B	Primary	4	11	Mixed
C	Primary	3	11	Mixed
D	Primary	3	11	Mixed
E	Secondary	11	18	Mixed
F	Secondary	11	18	Mixed
G	Primary	3	11	Mixed
H	Secondary	11	18	Girls
JE	Primary	2	11	Mixed
O	Secondary	11	16	Mixed
RE	Secondary	11	18	Girls
SJ	Primary	4	11	Mixed
SS	Primary	3	11	Mixed
V	Primary	3	11	Mixed
Y	Primary	3	11	Mixed

Key Stages year group ranges

Key Stage 1	Years 1 and 2. A typical 7-year-old is expected to achieve level 2B+
Key Stage 2	Years 3 to 6. A typical 11-year-old is expected to achieve level 4+
Key Stage 3	Years 7 to 9. A typical 9-year-old is expected to achieve level 5+ _[handwritten: Aged 11-14.]_
Key Stage 4	Years 10 and 11. Measured using percentage of 5+ A*–C including English and maths

Note on terminology

Disadvantages

The Department for Education has a broad range of criteria for identifying disadvantaged pupils. The DfE uses the term 'disadvantaged' of pupils who are entitled to pupil premium funding. They include:

- children eligible for free school meals,
- children in families on a low income,
- looked-after children, and
- Traveller children.

(DfE, 2014; NAO, 2015)

In this book 'disadvantaged pupils' refers to pupils from low-income backgrounds who are eligible for free school meals. This differentiates between pupils eligible for FSM and those who are not. More importantly, it allows us to use the free school meals national data collected as part of every school census over the period.

Pupil premium

The pupil premium is additional funding given to publicly funded schools in England to raise the attainment of disadvantaged pupils and close the gap between them and their peers. In the 2018/19 financial year, schools received £1,320 for each eligible primary-aged pupil and £935 for secondary-aged pupils. A total of £2.42 billion was allocated for primary and secondary pupils, looked-after children and service children. This covers 1.86 million pupils in England.

About the author

Dr Feyisa Demie is an Honorary Fellow at the Durham University School of Education, and head of research and adviser for school self-evaluation at Lambeth LA. He has worked extensively with local authorities, government departments, schools and school governors for over 25 years in the use of data and research to raise achievement. As an education adviser he works with schools covering all phases of assessment, from foundation stage to GCSE. Feyisa has developed a comprehensive data service for schools, comprising individual school profiles and contextual and value-added reports, as a means of providing detailed, confidential data to help schools to monitor performance and improve their processes and outcomes. He runs school-focused training programmes, and an annual national school-improvement conference for headteachers, teachers, governors and policy makers at UCL Institute of Education to share good practice in schools.

Acknowledgements

This book is based on research conducted by the author over 25 years into what works to raise achievement in schools. It would not have been written without the interest, help, encouragement and collaboration of many people. Chapters 4 to 6 in this book are based on previously published articles and research reports. All the extracts and quotations in these chapters are used with the kind permission of Christabel McLean and Kirstin Lewis. Where this is the case their source is referenced in the introduction of each chapter. Where I am not the sole author, the co-authors to whom I owe a debt of gratitude are listed. All journals and their editors who published articles of mine that are used in the book, the referees who commented on my papers, and those who edited this book are also owed a great deal of thanks.

The author would like to thank the headteachers, teachers, parents, pupils, school governors and school staff of the case study schools who took part in the various activities, including the case study interviews, focus groups and questionnaire surveys. Unfortunately, promises about confidentiality prohibit us from naming them here. The schools were coded and given pseudonyms.

Grateful thanks also go to many people at UCL IOE press, particularly Dr Gillian Klein for her help and encouragement, for taking an active interest in the book and for spending much time reading and editing the draft.

Finally, for a long time Anne Taplin, Rebecca Butler, James McDonald, Andy Hau and Robert Tong of the Schools' Research and Statistics Service at Lambeth Council have helped in data collection and analysis. Dr Kirstin Lewis and Christabel McLean have helped with research into what works in schools, and have commented on much that I have written. I cannot easily express how grateful I am for all their help over many years.

The views expressed in this book are those of the author and not to be taken as the views of the London Borough of Lambeth or Durham University or other institutions mentioned in the book. I accept full and sole responsibility for any mistakes or unintentional misrepresentations in reporting the findings.

Chapter 1

Introduction

1.1 The gaps in achievement at school

The hard question that faces educational policy makers today is not how to raise achievement, but how to tackle educational inequality. A well-established body of research evidence shows that inequality in educational outcomes has grown for some groups over the last three decades, and that a large number of children are underachieving at school. Yet policy makers do little to tackle it. Of particular concern is the growing inequality in educational outcomes for some disadvantaged groups, such as Black Caribbean, White working-class and Pakistani pupils on free school meals (Andrews *et al.*, 2017; Demie and McLean, 2015a, 2015b, 2017a, 2017b; Hutchinson *et al.*, 2016; Cassen and Kingdon, 2007; Cassen *et al.*, 2015; Strand, 2014). The attainment gap between children eligible and not eligible for free school meals is apparent at the age of seven and at the age of eleven. Generally, pupils eligible for free school meals have lower rates of progress (see DfE, 2014).

A similarly large gap is reported in US studies. The data shows that the achievement gaps between Black and White students and between Hispanic and White students in the USA have generally narrowed in recent years. However, there are still large disparities between these groups (Berliner, 2009). Williams (2003) argues that educational inequality between White and minority students continues to perpetuate social and economic inequality in the USA. International studies also conclude that the most disadvantaged pupils tend to perform the worst (see Duncan and Magnuson, 2005; Behnke *et al.*, 2010; Mensah and Kiernan, 2010).

The reasons for the underachievement of disadvantaged pupils and some minority ethnic groups are wide-ranging and complex. In recent education literature, research confirms a number of barriers to learning, in schools and beyond the school gates, that need to be taken into account and, if possible, addressed. They include poverty, negative parental attitudes to education, lack of parental involvement in children's schooling, lack of targeted support, curriculum barriers and low levels of literacy in the disadvantaged community (Demie and McLean, 2016). These findings are supported by a survey of headteachers, teachers and governors in schools in an inner-London local authority, which asked 'What are the main barriers to learning for disadvantaged pupils in your school?' The results of the survey provide useful data on barriers to learning in schools and give a clear picture of the views of the respondents. The survey identified, in addition to the barriers listed above poverty, lack of parental involvement, parental numeracy issues, lack of funding and pupils' low aspirations (see Figure 1.1).

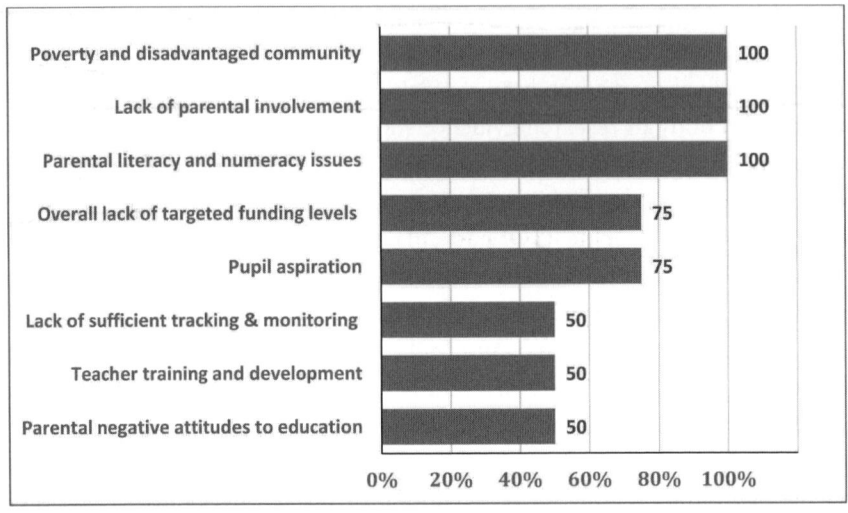

Figure 1.1 Barriers to learning for disadvantaged pupils. The percentages represent the respondents to a school survey who agreed that the named factor is a barrier. From Demie, 2018a

A number of studies have attempted to explain the many factors associated with low achievement and the barriers to learning for disadvantaged and ethnic-minority pupils. UK and international evidence suggests that disadvantaged pupils at school face a number of problems, including poverty across generations, lack of parental engagement and negative attitudes towards education (Mongon and Chapman, 2008; Demie and McLean, 2015b). There is a consensus that poverty, and home and community factors, impact the academic achievement of students and contribute to the achievement gap. Despite average overall improvements in test scores, large differences in educational achievement according to socio-economic status persist, with family income and status by far the most significant indicators of success in the school system (Mongon and Chapman, 2008). The attainment gap widens at each key stage as children pass through the education system, with pupils eligible for FSM falling behind their peers.

Studies by Mongon and Chapman (2008) reveal gender and ethnic background to be important factors, with girls performing better than boys in all ethnic groups. Earlier studies show that the attainment difference is due more to socio-economic factors than to other differences. The research also reveals that inequality in education outcomes has grown for some disadvantaged groups, including White working-class, Black Caribbean and Pakistani pupils on free school meals (Demie and McLean, 2016). In particular, White working-class boys who qualify for FSM do worst of all except Travellers. Indeed, White British pupils from low-income families consistently emerge as the lowest-achieving ethnic group whatever the socio-economic dimension (entitlement to FSM, parental occupation, neighbourhood deprivation, etc.) (Cassen and Kingdon, 2007; Strand, 2008). It is important, however, that these findings are not interpreted as indicating that it is only the attainment of White British pupils from low-income families that is of concern. Clearly, the effect of poverty on learning dominates the outcomes (Andrews *et al.*, 2017; Demie and McLean 2015, 2017; Hutchinson *et al.*, 2006; Cassen and Kingdon, 2007; Cassen *et al.*, 2015; Strand, 2014) and is the greatest cause for concern.

Other factors than poverty do affect outcomes, such as lack of parental engagement, and negative attitudes towards education. Hutchinson *et al.* list them as 'limited language, restricted vocabulary; poor attendance; mobility – many moves between schools; poor nutrition; low aspirations; low expectations; narrow range of opportunities outside school; lack of role models, especially male role models; lack of self-confidence and self-esteem; poor social skills; and inadequate support from teachers and teaching assistants' (Hutchinson *et al.*, 2016: 29–30). Schools have difficulty in engaging with 'hard to reach' parents from disadvantaged communities where children receive little support at home. This can be frustrating for teachers, as they want to build strong relationships with all parents. Research shows that many parents feel that they don't have the skills, education or knowledge to support their children in their learning. Detailed case studies are needed of successful schools that are closing the achievement gap.

1.2 Effective strategies to close the achievement gap: Evidence from the literature

Debate on the role of the school in closing the achievement gap is not new. Coleman *et al.* (1966) pioneered research in the USA and Rutter *et al.* (1979) in the UK on the effectiveness of schools in raising standards, and accepted that much of the difference in pupil outcomes is due to school intake characteristics and family social background, the neighbourhoods where pupils live and the types of schools attended (Mortimore and Whitty, 1997; Sammons, 1999; Gorard, 2000). School effectiveness research has consistently shown that only about 8–15% of the attainment difference between schools is accounted for by what they actually do; the rest is attributed to intake variations, including home background (Sammons, 1999; Strand, 2010). Gewirtz (2002) reported that other school improvement researchers have highlighted that 'while schools can and do make a difference, what they can achieve is "partial and limited, because schools are also part of the wider society, subject to its norms, rules, and influences" (Mortimore 1997: 483). ... And a study by Thomas and Mortimore ... concluded that: "Once background factors have been accounted for, the variation in pupils' total examination scores attributable to schools is 10 per cent" (Thomas and Mortimore 1996: 26).' Research by Strand (2010) in an Inner London LA suggests an effect of 12% once socioeconomic background is taken into account.

Clifton and Cook, citing a study by Rasbash *et al.* (2010) that explored the role that schools can play in tackling the general link between educational achievement and family income, noted that academic studies 'generally find that about 20 per cent of variability in a pupil's achievement is attributable to school-level factors, with around 80 per cent attributable to pupil-level factors' (Clifton and Cook, 2012: 4), such as the wider family environment, the neighbourhood where they live and the school attended. Ofsted pointed out that 'factors beyond the school gates and in the communities where pupils live can have a detrimental impact on their achievement. Schools can do much to improve outcomes for disadvantaged pupils but only so much' (Ofsted, 2014). ASCL (2014) also suggested that 'the problem ... is not of schools' making ... they cannot solve it by themselves', and pointed out that the factors influencing low attainment are beyond the control of individual schools: they cannot overcome the wider problem of poverty and disadvantage. Other studies confirm that schools do make a difference (e.g., Mortimore, Sammons *et al.*, 1988; Sammons, 2007; Strand, 2010). They also highlighted that social and economic factors and family background affect pupils' attainment and progress. Mortimore's recent research (1999: 300) endorses previous school effectiveness and school improvement studies that show that school can make a difference but 'the effects of poverty cannot be dismissed as irrelevant just because some schools in disadvantaged areas are able to promote exceptional progress'.

I argue that while many of these factors influencing achievement are beyond the direct control of schools, it is a mistake to assume that schools cannot be part of the solution. It would be wrong to undermine the strong role that schools – as institutional pillars of our society – can play in a child's life. This book encourages schools to engage actively with the externalities their pupils face and work alongside these factors rather than ignore them. Such engagement could facilitate an education system that is able to cope with pupil diversity, and is inclusive to its core. The reasons for the underachievement of disadvantaged pupils are indeed complex, but a body of research is beginning to show that schools can make a significant difference, albeit within certain limits (see Demie and McLean, 2013; Demie and Lewis, 2008, 2010a, 2010b; Mongon and Chapman, 2008; Ofsted, 2009a, 2009b; Cassen and Kingdon, 2007).

A number of schools serving disadvantaged communities demonstrate powerfully that poverty should not be an excuse for low attainment (Demie and McLean, 2014; Demie and Lewis, 2010a, 2010b; Mongon and Chapman, 2008; Ofsted, 2009). For example, Mongon and Chapman's (2008) study records encouraging signs of improvement in the ways in which schools are addressing the underachievement of disadvantaged pupils. They found that these are schools with strong leadership and strong systems, where headteachers do not accept poverty as a reason for failure. They have high expectations of their students, and several headteachers said they had come from low-income backgrounds themselves, and claimed working-class roots. A number of the headteachers in the study had been in post for some years; they spoke about the importance of building a deep respect for the community they served. The headteachers encouraged and valued the active involvement of parents and the community in their children's education, and adopted strategies to overcome some of the barriers to achievement, such as effective use of staff, targeted support, mentoring, and the development of an inclusive ethos and curriculum that met the needs of disadvantaged pupils.

Sharples *et al.* (2011), in a review of international evidence of classroom strategies that were effective in raising the achievement of pupils from disadvantaged backgrounds, identified school leadership, quality of teaching, the effective use of data to identify underperforming groups, initiatives to raise aspirations, and parental engagement. They argued that the quality of teaching was among the most important factors to make a significant difference.

Demie and McLean's (2015a, 2015b, 2016) research also identified factors that are proving successful in closing the gap in their case study schools, such as strong leadership, high-quality teaching and learning, an inclusive curriculum, parental engagement, the effective use of data to identify underachieving groups, the effective use of outstanding teachers to teach intervention groups, the redeployment of support teachers who have a good track record in raising achievement, the effective use of pupil premium funding to challenge poverty, and the effective use of pupil voice and feedback.

Ofsted research into what works in outstanding case study schools has identified similarly effective strategies in raising achievement and closing the gaps in schools. These included:

> rigorous monitoring of data and its effective use in feedback, planning, support and interventions[;] ensuring access to the highest quality teaching[;] providing strong and visionary leadership [and] working with ... parents to increase engagement and raise expectations.
>
> (Ofsted, 2013: 31)

Ofsted commented that these schools prove constantly that disadvantage need not be a barrier to achievement.

Similar findings were reflected in a report from the former Department for Children, Schools and Families, 'The extra mile: How schools succeed in raising aspiration in deprived communities' (DCSF, 2008). It too uses a case study approach and cites dynamic leaders who set a 'can do' culture, strong systems for quality assuring the curriculum, teaching and pupil progress, and creative recruitment measures, specifically, recruiting staff from the local community. It highlights extra measures targeted at the most disadvantaged pupils, including outreach work with local families and strategies to persuade children to associate school with learning that is fun, interesting and action-packed. Yet, a more recent report published by Ofsted, 'Unseen children: access and achievement 20 years on' (2013), suggests that although the English education system has undoubtedly improved in the past 20 years, there remains a large minority of children who do not succeed at school or college and become less and less visible as they progress through the system, and that a disproportionate number of these children are from disadvantaged backgrounds. Furthermore, the Organisation for Economic Co-operation and Development (OECD) has highlighted the association between low family income and poor educational outcomes as a particular weakness of the English educational system. It argues that 'We ... cannot have a world-class education system until we solve this problem' (Ofsted, 2013: 4).

Rea, Hill and Sandals (2011) also reviewed the research evidence of effective school-level specific intervention strategies used by school leaders to support disadvantaged pupils who were underperforming. These included early intervention and targeted learning support, one-to-one tuition and catch-up provision, targeted parental engagement including raising aspirations and developing parenting skills, developing confidence and self-esteem through pupil voice, and empowering student mentors. A dedicated champion, who was also a member of the school leadership, co-ordinated a support programme that encouraged engagement in sport, music, school trips and other activities. One-to-one tuition was provided by the school's own senior staff, so no time was wasted in getting to know one another. It fostered confidence and ensured that strategies used in tutoring sessions mirrored the work taking place in regular lessons.

The Sutton Trust and the Education Endowment Foundation (EEF) commissioned research into 'what worked and what failed' in school improvement in schools and produced the Teaching and Learning Toolkit (Higgins, Katsipataki, Villanueva-Aguilera *et al.*, 2016; EEF, 2019). The aim of the toolkit is to provide an accessible summary of international research on the effectiveness of a range of strategies schools could use to raise the attainment of disadvantaged pupils. In this context, their findings revealed a number of effective school-based interventions and targeted support that have impact in raising achievement (EEF, 2019). These include effective feedback, metacognition, reading comprehension strategies, peer tutoring, early intervention, one-to-one tutoring, homework (in secondary school), mastery learning, phonics, and small-group tuition. Of all the activities identified in the toolkit, effective feedback had the largest impact on student outcomes. The impact of these intervention strategies is well supported by extensive and moderate evidence from schools (see EEF, 2019). Evidence from the EEF also suggests that setting or streaming has a negative impact and is harmful to a student's chances of academic success, particularly for disadvantaged children.

The DfE commissioned the National Foundation for Education Research (NFER) to conduct research into what worked in schools that have improved the academic results of their disadvantaged pupils. The DfE survey (Macleod *et al.*, 2015) asked schools to select the most effective intervention strategies they had used to raise the attainment of disadvantaged pupils. The evidence from the survey suggests that schools had used a range of strategies, most of which focused on teaching and learning. A key driver to closing the gap was improving the quality of teaching across the school. Quality first teaching was prioritized, with inputs on differentiation, progression and success criteria. The biggest areas of focus were marking and feedback, and giving pupils time in the school day to improve their previous work and address next-step targets. Extra funding was focused on the needs of individual pupils. Other strategies that were widely used included paired or small-group additional teaching, improved feedback between teachers and pupils and one-to-one, peer-to-peer tutoring, a new homework strategy, extending school time, additional resources, and new speaking and listening programmes. Most schools also initiated trips to cultural venues, additional teachers, and social and emotional strategies.

On the whole, the strategies adopted by the largest number of schools are also those identified as most effective in the Sutton Trust–EEF Teaching and Learning Toolkit (Higgins, Katsipataki, Villanueva-Aguilera *et al.*, 2016). However, metacognition and collaborative learning, although identified as highly effective in the Toolkit, were less popular among the schools surveyed for this research. However, improving pupil aspirations, setting/streaming, and improving the classroom/school environment are not well supported by evidence of effectiveness in the Teaching and Learning Toolkit; improving attendance, continuing professional development (CPD) and improving engagement in the curriculum are more effective.

A well-established body of research evidence shows that a long-standing achievement gap remains between FSM pupils and non-FSM pupils, despite the national pupil premium initiatives to help schools to close the gap through targeted support and interventions (Ofsted, 2014; Demie and McLean, 2016).

The research evidence shows that there are now a number of schools, serving disadvantaged communities, that demonstrate that poverty should not be an excuse for low attainment (Demie and McLean, 2015a; Demie and Lewis, 2010a, 2010b; Mongon and Chapman, 2008; Ofsted, 2009).

> Leaders of more successful schools emphasise the importance of 'quality teaching first'. They aim to provide a consistently high standard, through setting expectations, monitoring performance, tailoring teaching and support to suit their pupils and sharing best practice.
>
> (Sharp *et al.*, 2015: 8)

A body of research has found that good teachers are especially important for pupils from disadvantaged backgrounds. For example, the Sutton Trust confirms that 'for poor pupils the difference between a good teacher and a bad teacher is a whole year's learning' (Sutton Trust, 2011: 2). There is clearly a growing synthesis of evidence of what works to raise the achievement of all pupils. The key challenge, then, is to find out what strategies schools can use to make a difference to the achievement of certain groups, in particular disadvantaged pupils from low-income backgrounds and ethnic-minority pupils.

Overall, the literature shows that policy makers and schools need more evidence of 'what works' and need to look closely at why some schools do well against the odds. Research of the kind set out in this book, that focuses on 'what works' in practice, challenges the perceived notions of underachievement in schools and provides positive messages.

1.3 The aim and structure of the book

This book is rooted in the field of school improvement, which has witnessed rapid growth since about 1990, and aims to provide evidence of good practice in schools that are closing the achievement gap. It argues that educational inequality matters and looks to answer certain questions in some detail:

- What does education policy tell us about inequality in education?
- What does the empirical evidence tell us about the achievement gap?
- What is proven good practice for closing the gap in educational inequality?
- What are the implications for policy and practice?

The book seeks to provide answers to these and other questions. Drawing on empirical evidence using KS2 and GCSE data from the National Pupil Database (NPD), case studies, focus groups and interviews with headteachers, teachers, school staff, policy makers, parents, pupils and governors, I chart the road to improvement and to tackling inequality in education. The book draws on studies I have been involved in over 20 years with local authorities, government departments, schools and governors as a researcher, school self-evaluation adviser and CPD trainer.

I believe that the importance of this book lies in the richness of its research data, which illuminates inequality in education. It aims to offer a vivid account of what works in tackling educational inequality. I hope it will make an significant contribution to theoretical knowledge, policy and practice, and will challenge policy makers and school leaders on their current practice.

Each chapter takes a theme, such as what the longitudinal data tells us about attainment in education, patterns of inequality in education by social, ethnic and economic group, or what works to raise achievement and close the inequality gap, and considers the implications for policy and practice. Although it focuses on the school sector in England, it also draws on relevant experience elsewhere. It seeks to reach conclusions on what is, and is not, effective in addressing educational inequality. 'Effective' is defined as what can reasonably be expected to be achieved in a given situation. It is a book about what has been found to work. The notion of 'what works' will avoid crude assumptions and adopt a nuanced understanding of causality.

Chapter 1, the **Introduction**, reviews the literature on what has been shown to close the achievement gap. It explores why educational inequalities in the UK persist. It argues for the need of evidence of 'what works' in raising achievement and closing the achievement gap so as to rise to the challenges of tackling educational inequality.

Chapter 2 explores **Inequality in education and the empirical evidence**. It asks: 'What is the empirical evidence for educational inequality?' Drawing on longitudinal KS2 and GCSE national pupil database (NPD) data, it examines the attainment pattern by social and ethnic background and regional variation, to measure the impact of past government policies on educational inequality and attempts at closing the achievement gap. The following chapters will explore some possible answers.

Chapter 3 discusses **case studies of schools**, to identify good practice.

The next two chapters draw on the major studies in which I have been involved over the last 25 years that sought to identify what works in raising achievement in schools. I have reworded certain sections of the texts and rearranged some of the quotations from teachers, school governors and parents to ensure that the evidence for each success factor is in one place. I decided which publications to include from my corpus of work so that readers can see what was identified as raising the achievement of ethnic minorities and disadvantaged pupils, and narrowed or even closed the gap between their attainment and that of their peers.

Using the published research I have been involved in, **Chapter 4** discusses school strategies in closing the achievement gap for **disadvantaged pupils**. It details the findings from the case study schools that effectively raised the achievement all pupils, including the disadvantaged children. The success factors proved to be the provision of strong school leadership, effective teaching and learning, the use of data for monitoring and tracking pupil progress, the provision of targeted support and interventions through pupil premium funding, observation of the effectiveness of the governing body, and the effective use of pupil voice and feedback. Each of these success factors was explored in detail in the research, to determine exactly what schools were doing to provide education of the very highest quality.

Chapter 5 discusses **good practice in raising the achievement of ethnic minority pupils and closing the gap with their peers**. It considers success factors such as partnership with parents, notably Black African and

Black Caribbean parents, delivering an inclusive multicultural curriculum, building strong links with the local communities, commitment by leadership and staff to equal opportunities and resisting racism, effective use of a diverse multi-ethnic workforce, celebrating cultural diversity, and effectively supporting pupils for whom English is an additional language. It draws on my studies of good practice and on surveys that explored in detail what schools are doing to ensure they provide the optimal quality of education. I also consider the findings of several new, unpublished studies.

Chapter 6 focuses on **raising the achievement of pupils for whom English is an additional language**. It discusses assessment approaches, attainment and strategies for raising the achievement of pupils with EAL through effective use of high-quality EAL teaching, monitoring and tracking the progress of EAL pupils, and targeted support using EAL teachers, EAL teaching assistants and learning mentors.

Chapter 7 draws conclusions and considers the implications of what we have learned from this 25 years' work about addressing educational inequality and tackling disadvantage for the attention of the following stakeholders:

- schools
- central government
- local government and multi-academy trusts
- practitioners who use data and research
- research communities.

Chapter 2

The achievement gap: The empirical evidence

This chapter examines what the data tells us about the standard of achievement of all pupils in English schools at the end of KS2 and GCSE, by ethnic background and disadvantage factors.

Two methodological approaches are used. First, we examine the gap in educational achievement between ethnic minorities and the majority group in England. Second, we look at the achievement gap between disadvantaged pupils and their peers, to gain further insight into the effects of social background and inequality in education.

2.1 Demographic trends in England

This research considers evidence from schools in England, one of the more ethnically, linguistically and culturally diverse countries in Europe. The 2017 census shows that there were 8.1 million pupils attending 24,372 schools (including nursery schools, state-funded primary schools, state-funded secondary schools, special schools, pupil referral units and independent schools). Of these, 69% were White British, followed by White Other at 6%, Pakistani 4%, Indian 3%, Black African 3%, Bangladeshi 2% and Black Caribbean about 1%. The census data also shows that 31% of the school population are from Black and ethnic-minority groups, 18% speak English as an additional language (EAL) and 14% of pupils are eligible for free school meals (FSM).

There are regional variations in the numbers of pupils. Data by region from the latest school census is presented in Figure 2.1. Across England the numbers varied widely from a low of 390,063 in inner London to nearly 1.3 million in the South East.

The census data shows that the number of disadvantaged pupils in England is very high but has fluctuated over the years. This issue is increasingly important given the number of disadvantaged pupils in England during the last decade. In 1998 there were 1,428,121 and this was down to 1,079,500 in 2017 (DfE, 2017f).

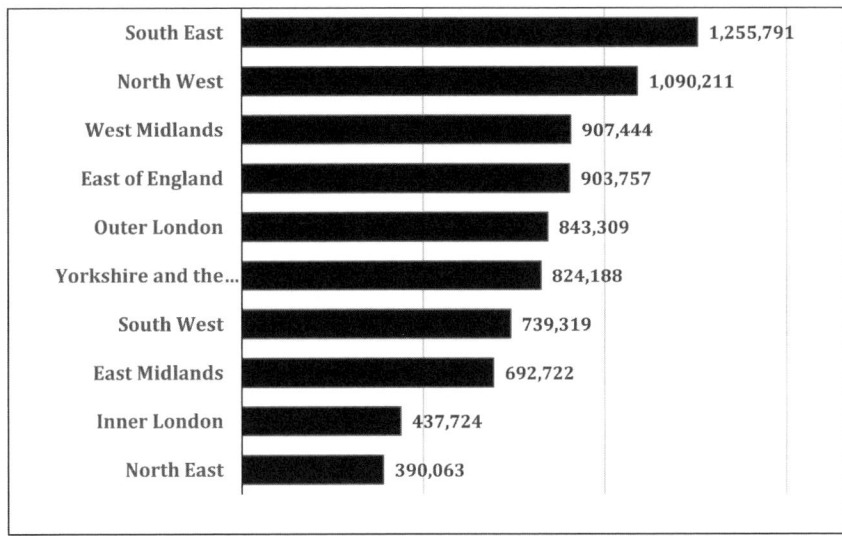

Figure 2.1 Number of pupils in schools by region, 2017. From DfE (2017f)

However, the National Audit Office (NAO) suggests that recent measurements exclude some disadvantaged children. For example, 'if a parent doesn't register their child for free school meals then they won't show up in the figures. The Department's (DfE) last estimate was that about 160,000 eligible pupils had not registered in 2013' (*Full Fact*, 2015). It is suggested that 'this rate will [increase] with the introduction of free school meals for all children aged four to seven. Pupils receive the meals regardless of whether they're registered, but not registering means the school doesn't receive Pupil Premium funding for that child' (ibid.). It is also suggested that 'some low-income pupils aren't [recognized as] eligible for free school meals' (ibid.). Another DfE survey suggests that there are around 200,000 pupils aged 4–15 who appear to be entitled to, but not claiming, FSM, which may be the main reason for the apparent decline in numbers. The survey data shows that in particular 'pupils living in a less deprived area, pupils attending schools with a lower school FSM rate, pupils from families with higher status occupations …, pupils living in a family with higher parental qualifications, and pupils of Chinese ethnic origin … have lower likelihoods of claiming FSM' (Iniesta-Martinez and Evans, 2012: 1).

Despite this worrying lack of reliable data, there are now over a million pupils between the ages of 5 and 18 years in England who are eligible for free school meals, and about 14% of the school population in England and Wales are classified as disadvantaged (DfE, 2017b). But disadvantage is very unevenly distributed in England and varies widely across the regions, ranging from 10% in the South East to 23% in Inner London; the figures are 18% in the North East, 16% in Yorkshire and Humber, the North West and the West Midlands, 13% in Outer London and the East Midlands, 12% in the South West and 11% in the East of England (DfE, 2017c, 2017d).

2.2 The national curriculum assessment data and measure of performance

The strength of the research is its data source of the national pupil database (NPD). The NPD is a pupil-level database that matches data on pupil and school characteristics to pupil-level attainment. The number of pupils who completed GCSE in summer 2014 was 558,432 and of those who completed KS2 in 2012 544,220. The data on state schools is accurate and has a number of key features. First, this census dataset of information about the population of all pupils in state schools is more helpful, for a variety of analyses, than a dataset based on just a sample of schools, as it provides a much richer set of data on school and pupil characteristics. The dataset includes information on the language spoken at home, ethnicity, free school meals, gender, and results at key stages 2 and 4. Second, data has been drawn from DfE statistical first releases (SFRs), although some statistics have been calculated by myself directly from the NPD files. The lists that the SFRs draw on to collate data on achievement are given in the references (NAO, 2015).

It is important to note that in the English education system, pupils aged 5 to 16 years old are taught the national curriculum. It covers subjects such as English, mathematics and science. There are four key stages, KS1, KS2 (primary), KS3 and KS4 (secondary). At the end of each key stage, assessments are undertaken. Until 2015, pupils in key stages 1 to 3 were given levels ranging from 1 to 8. In key stages 1 and 2, results are reported for reading, writing and maths. Thus a typical seven-year-old is expected to reach level 2B, an eleven-year-old (end of KS2) level 4, and a fourteen-year-old level 5. At the end of KS4, pupils take General Certificate of Secondary Education (GCSE) exams. These are the main qualifications attempted by pupils at the end of compulsory schooling at the age of 16, and consist of examinations in the curriculum subjects the pupils have been studying. The measure of performance used in this book is the percentage of pupils gaining level 4 or above at KS2, in reading, writing and maths, and for GCSE it was the national measure of the percentage of pupils gaining five or more good GCSEs including English and maths (5+ A*–C). However, in

2016 the measures used to discuss attainment changed, and a new version of the national curriculum assessment was introduced that removed the attainment levels. Instead, tests and teacher assessments are available for reading, writing and mathematics, as follows:

- Working at greater depth or above expected standard
- Working at the expected standard
- Working towards the expected standard
- Below the expected standard.

2.3 The achievement gap of ethnic minorities and inequality in education

2.3.1 The standard of achievement of ethnic-minority pupils: The evidence at KS2 and GCSE

The 1990s and 2000s saw a dramatic improvement in the proportion of pupils completing their compulsory schooling with five or more GCSE higher-grade passes including English and maths.

In England more pupils have been achieving 5+ A*–C grades year on year, from 20% in 2000 to 61% in 2017. This is an improvement of 21% over the period, suggesting a remarkable transformation. The key question is, Which students made such an improvement?

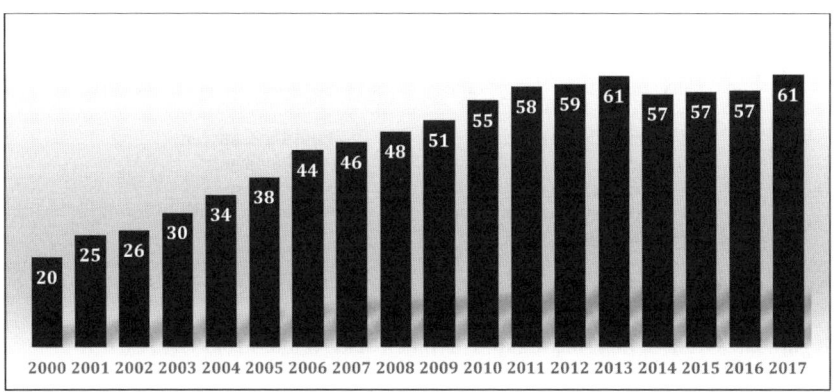

Figure 2.2 Percentage of pupils achieving 5+ A*–C at GCSE, including English and maths. From DfE, 2017c, 2017d

As Figures 2.2 and 2.3 illustrate, the proportion attaining this key benchmark rose by almost half in the decade up to 2017. A striking finding is that members of every main ethnic group are more likely to attain five higher grades than ever before. This is an important achievement that demonstrates that levels of attainment can be improved for every ethnic group. The data in Figure 2.2 also reveals that there are considerable differences in attainment between different ethnic groups: this suggests that pupils of different ethnic origins do not experience equal educational opportunities. African-Caribbean, Pakistani and Bangladeshi pupils are markedly less likely to attain five higher-grade GCSEs than their White, Chinese and Indian peers.

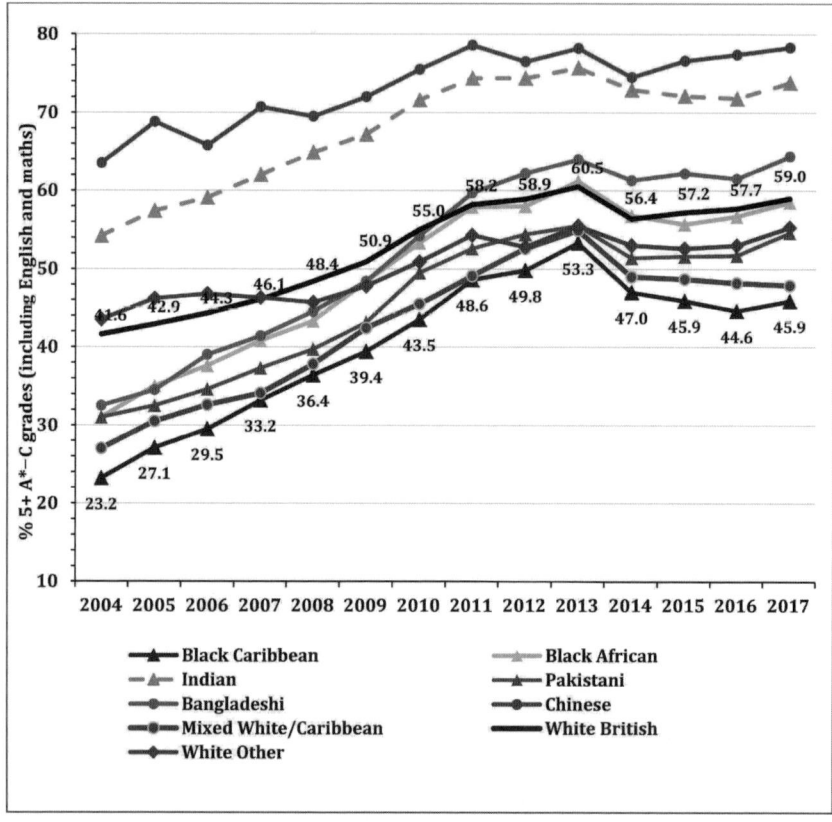

Figure 2.3 GCSE achievement gap by ethnic background. From DfE, 2017d

It is difficult to ascribe the above pattern of improvement to education reform alone, but previous research confirms how significant the government policy measures are in raising standards (Demie and McLean, 2015a, 2015b). However, not all ethnic groups shared equally in the overall improvement in attainment at the 5+ A*–C level. As we argue next, government policy measures have also had a negative impact: they have increased inequalities between different ethnic groups. Table 2.1 shows the KS2 and GCSE results for each group at national level. The main findings from this data show that at KS2 75% of Black Caribbean pupils achieved level 4 and above compared with 80% for England as a whole. Similarly at GCSE, 46% of Black Caribbean pupils achieved 5+ A*–C including English and maths compared with the national average of 54%. However, nationally there are marked differences in performance between different ethnic groups. Broadly speaking, Chinese-, Indian- and White-heritage pupils are the highest-achieving groups at GCSE, followed by Black African and Bangladeshi. Black Caribbean and Pakistani are the lowest-achieving groups. The national data in England also suggests that Black Caribbean underachievement in education is real and persistent, and Black Caribbeans remain the consistently lowest-performing group in the country. The real concern is that the difference between their educational performance and that of other groups is larger than for any other ethnic group.

As at GCSE, Black Caribbean pupils are the lowest-achieving group at KS2 (see Table 2.1). This is not surprising, as previous studies came to similar conclusions (Demie, 2001; Gillborn and Mirza, 2000; Gillborn and Gipps, 1996). Perhaps the most important new finding from the national data is that there is now some evidence that Chinese-, Bangladeshi- and Indian-heritage pupils are improving more rapidly and narrowing the gap with White pupils. However, Black Caribbean pupils have not improved enough to narrow the gap (see Figure 2.3). Like findings from previous studies, the data highlights a particular disadvantage experienced by Black Caribbean pupils in the English education system (Demie, 2001; Gillborn and Mirza, 2000; Gillborn and Gipps, 1996). To date it has been difficult to draw from research generalized conclusions on Black Caribbean educational achievement, but the new national data is at least helpful and confirms that Black Caribbean children have not shared equally in the increasing rates of achievement at KS2 and GCSE (see Table 2.1 and Figure 2.3). These findings have important implications for strategies of raising achievement. The findings make it at least easier for researchers to examine the differences in performance between pupils from different ethnic groups and for practitioners to identify appropriate strategies to tackle perceived problems.

Overall the national data supports the previous finding that the gap between the highest- and lowest-achieving ethnic groups is growing, and that Black Caribbean-heritage pupils are achieving on average significantly below the level of other main ethnic groups at KS2 and GCSE (Table 2.1).

Table 2.1 KS2 and GCSE performance by ethnic origin in England (%)

Ethnicity	KS2 L4+ (reading, writing and maths)				GCSE (5+ A*–C including English and maths)			
	2012	2013	2014	2015	2012	2013	2014	2015
Bangladeshi	77	76	81	82	62	64	61	62
Black African	73	75	78	81	58	61	57	56
Black Caribbean	69	70	73	75	50	53	47	46
Chinese	84	85	88	88	77	78	75	77
Indian	83	83	86	87	74	76	73	72
Pakistani	69	71	75	77	54	56	51	52
Mixed White/Black Caribbean	71	72	75	77	53	55	49	49
White British	75	76	79	81	59	61	56	57
White Other	68	68	71	73	53	56	53	53
All pupils	74	75	78	80	59	59	53	54

Source: DfE, 2015a, 2016a.

2.3.2 Gender and ethnic background

Table 2.2 repeats the pattern established earlier, in which girls tend to outperform boys at each key stage (see Demie, 2001 and Gillborn and Gipps, 1996). Overall, girls achieve higher averages than boys by a noticeable margin. This is true for African, Caribbean and White British pupils at all key stages. It also confirms that for Black Caribbean pupils the gap in performance between boys and girls is higher than for Black African and White British pupils, suggesting the lower achievement of boys. Overall, these findings question some of the previous studies that argued that only Black boys, and not girls, faced inequalities. The data in Table 2.2 confirms that both girls and boys of Black Caribbean heritage were lagging behind White British boys and all three groups were some distance behind White girls.

Table 2.2 KS2 and GCSE performance in England by gender and ethnic background (%)

Ethnicity	KS2 L4+ (reading, writing and maths)			GCSE (5+ A*–C including English and maths)		
	Boys	Girls	Gap	Boys	Girls	Gap
Bangladeshi	80	84	4	61	69	8
Black African	78	83	5	54	64	10
Black Caribbean	71	80	9	44	56	12
Chinese	85	90	5	71	83	12
Indian	85	89	4	71	77	6
Pakistani	74	79	5	51	59	8
Mixed White/Black Caribbean	73	80	7	49	59	10
White British	78	84	6	56	66	10
White Other	70	75	5	50	59	9
All pupils	77	83	6	56	66	10

Source: DfE, 2015a, 2016a.

2.4 Disadvantaged pupils' achievement gap and inequality in education in England

2.4.1 The attainment of disadvantaged pupils: The KS2 and GCSE evidence

Poverty is certainly a major factor influencing the performance of disadvantaged pupils (see Cassen and Kingdon, 2007). The free school meals variable is often used as a proxy measure of the extent of social deprivation in the pupils' backgrounds and has been linked to underachievement (see Gillborn and Youdell, 2000; Demie, 2001). Figure 2.4 shows a significant gap, with only 38% of pupils on free school meals gaining 5+ A*–C, compared to 65% of those who were not. Overall, the findings from the national data confirm that pupils eligible for free school meals did considerably less well than their more affluent peers in England (see Figure 2.4).

The attainment gap between children eligible and not eligible for free school meals is also apparent in the age 11 KS2 national tests in the average marks for reading, writing and maths. At the end of primary education in 2017, 43% of eligible pupils achieved the expected standard, whereas 64% of pupils who were not eligible achieved at this level (Table 2.3). It is not just achievement that is affected: pupils eligible for free school meals generally have lower rates of progress (see DfE, 2014).

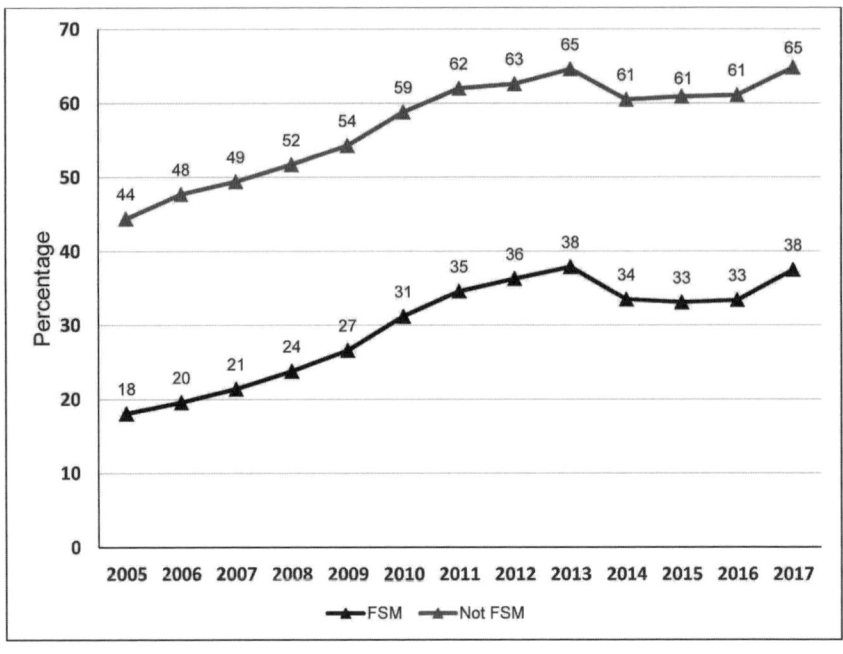

Figure 2.4 The achievement gap in England between pupils eligible for free school meals (FSM) and non-FSM pupils: % achieving 5+ A*–C including English and maths, 2005–2017. From DfE, 2017d, 2015a: Table 10a, SFR06/2015; DfE, NPD 2016, 2017). (The 2016 and 2017 GCSE FSM data for 5+ A*–C including English and maths is from the NPD (2016) and NPD (2017). The DfE has not published this indicator as SFR since 2016.)

Table 2.3 Disadvantaged pupils'[1] KS2 and GCSE performance in England, 2005–2017

	KS2 performance 2017 (RWM level 4+)				GCSE performance in England (5+ A*–C including English and maths)			
	All pupils	FSM	Non-FSM	Gap	All pupils	FSM	Non-FSM	Gap
2011	67	49	71	–22	58	35	62	–27
2012	74	59	78	–19	59	36	63	–27
2013	75	60	79	–19	61	38	65	–27
2014	78	64	82	–18	57	34	61	–27
2015	80	66	83	–17	57	33	61	–28
2016	53	35	57	–22	58	33	61	–28
2017	61	43	64	–21	61	38	65	–27

[1] Disadvantaged pupils are those in receipt of free school meals.

Source: DfE, 2011, 2015, 2016, 2017d.

2.4.2 The achievement of disadvantaged pupils by gender

Table 2.4 repeats the pattern established earlier, whereby girls tend to outperform boys at every key stage (see Demie, 2001; Gillborn and Gipps, 1996). Overall, the results at different key stages indicate that girls achieve higher averages than boys by a noticeable margin. This is true at all key stages. It also confirms that the gap in performance between boys and girls is wide, suggesting that boys underachieve. Generally, these findings question some of the previous studies that argued that boys, but not girls, face inequalities. The data in Table 2.4 confirms that disadvantaged girls and boys were lagging behind the national average.

Table 2.4 KS2 and GCSE performance of disadvantaged pupils in England by gender (%)

	KS2 RWM level 4+ by FSM eligibility and gender				Pupils achieving 5+ A* to C including English and maths			
Year	Boys FSM	Girls FSM	All pupils FSM	All FSM and non-FSM	Boys FSM	Girls FSM	All pupils FSM	All FSM and non-FSM
2011	44	54	49	67	31	38	35	58
2012	54	64	59	74	32	41	36	59
2013	56	65	60	75	34	43	38	61
2014	59	68	64	78	29	38	34	57
2015	62	70	66	80	29	37	33	57
2016	32	39	35	53	29	38	33	57
2017	39	47	43	61	33	42	38	61

Source: DfE (NPD, 2016b, 2017c).

2.4.3 The attainment of disadvantaged pupils by ethnic background

Tables 2.3–2.6 indicate that there is a marked difference in KS2 and GCSE performance between pupils eligible for free school meals and the more economically advantaged groups in schools. At the end of primary education, the difference between pupils eligible for FSM and those who are not is significant: about 46% of Black Caribbean eligible pupils achieve level 4+, whereas 57% of pupils who are not eligible achieve this level. The GCSE data also shows a significant gap, with only 37% of pupils on free school meals gaining 5+ A*–C, compared with 51% of those who are not. Overall, the findings from the national data confirm that Black Caribbean pupils eligible for school meals did considerably less well than their more affluent peers: the gap at GCSE is 14%.

Table 2.5 KS2 and GCSE performance in England by ethnic background, 2017 (%)

	KS2 level 4 (reading, writing and maths combined)			GCSE 5+ A*–C including English and maths		
	FSM	Non-FSM	Gap	FSM	Non-FSM	Gap
Bangladeshi	59	66	7	62	70	8
Black African	54	65	11	52	65	13
Black Caribbean	46	57	11	37	51	14
Chinese	66	77	11	77	85	8
Indian	58	72	14	61	79	18
Pakistani	49	57	8	47	60	13
Mixed White/Black Caribbean	44	60	16	31	55	24
Mixed White/Black African	50	66	16	43	64	21
White British	39	65	26	31	64	33
White Other	45	57	12	54	62	8
National	43	64	21	37	65	28

Source: DfE, 2017d; DfE (2017c).

There are also striking differences within the main ethnic groups when the data is analysed by eligibility for free school meals. Table 2.5 shows that at GCSE, 31% of White British pupils eligible for free school meals achieved 5+ A*–C, compared with 64% of pupils who were ineligible. The White British difference is higher, with a gap of 26 percentage point at KS2 and 33 at GCSE. However, the gaps for Chinese, Bangladeshi, Pakistani and Black African pupils at KS2 are narrower. This is despite more of these pupils than White British being on free school meals. This finding underlines the importance of treating with scepticism any measure of school performance that does not allow for the influence of background factors such as social class and deprivation. Social class data is particularly significant for the analysis of the performance of White British and Black Caribbean pupils in addition to other factors of disadvantage. As we have argued, our analysis is not complete because of the lack of data on social class. Care must be taken in generalizing the results of White British pupils, particularly, from this study to a wider context. Clearly, further research in school populations outside London is required. Overall, the evidence from analysing free school meals (FSM) data is that:

- Black Caribbean and White British children eligible for FSM are consistently the lowest-performing ethnic groups of children from low-income households.
- The attainment gap between children eligible for FSM and the remainder is wider for Black Caribbean, White British and Mixed White and Black Caribbean than for any other ethnic group.
- The gap widens even more at the end of secondary education for White British and Mixed White and Black Caribbean pupils.
- Chinese and Indian disadvantaged pupils tend to significantly outperform the White British majority.

It is a matter for concern that the gap widens rather than narrows during schooling for Black Caribbean, White British and Mixed White and Black Caribbean children more than for any other ethnic group. This indicates the failure of the English education system to address those pupils' needs and to establish fairness for all.

Table 2.6 GCSE achievement gap of disadvantaged pupils by ethnic background and FSM (%)

	2011	2012	2013	2014	2015	2016	2017
White British	29	31	32	28	28	28	31
Mixed White/Black Caribbean	34	36	38	32	31	32	31
Mixed White/Black African	44	45	49	42	43	43	43
Indian	57	58	61	56	55	55	61
Pakistani	43	47	47	42	42	41	47
Bangladeshi	56	59	59	56	56	55	62
Black Caribbean	38	40	42	37	32	34	37
Black African	47	48	51	46	46	46	52
Chinese	74	68	77	68	74	75	77
FSM – all	35	36	38	34	33	34	37
Non-FSM – all	62	63	65	61	61	61	65
All pupils	58	59	61	57	57	57	61

Source: DfE, 2017d; DfE, 2015, SFR06/2015.

Table 2.7 KS2 performance of pupils eligible for FSM

	2011	2012	2013	2014	2015	2016	2017
Bangladeshi	63	74	72	76	80	52	59
Black African	56	66	68	72	75	46	54
Black Caribbean	52	61	62	66	67	35	46
Chinese	77	83	87	84	85	67	66
Indian	64	73	71	78	75	47	58
Pakistani	52	63	65	68	72	39	49
Mixed White/Black Caribbean	51	62	63	64	67	34	44
Mixed White/Black African	57	64	66	70	71	42	50
White British	46	56	58	61	63	32	39
White Other	52	61	57	60	64	38	45
FSM – all	49	59	60	64	66	35	43
Non-FSM – all	71	78	79	82	83	57	64
National – all	67	74	75	78	80	53	61

Source: DfE, 2017d.

2.4.4 The attainment of disadvantaged pupils by region

Using the empirical data from the 2017 NPD, the achievement of Key Stage 2 and GCSE pupils was examined according to the region of England they live in (Table 2.8).

The analysis of the achievement of Key Stage 2 and GCSE pupils by region revealed wide variations in performance and in the achievement gap (see Table 2.8 and Figures 2.5 and 3.7). Key data show that at KS2 Inner and Outer London have the highest density of disadvantaged pupils in England, and yet disadvantaged pupils perform better there than they do in other parts of the country (Table 2.8 and Figure 2.5). Fifty-eight per cent of disadvantaged pupils in Inner London achieved expected levels or better at KS2. Overall, the KS2 data confirms that disadvantaged pupils do not perform as well as their peers, and the gap in achievement between disadvantaged pupils and their peers is high in many regions. The Inner London figure, however, shows a smaller gap.

Table 2.8 KS2 and GCSE performance of disadvantaged pupils by region, 2017

Region	KS2 L4 (reading, writing and maths) (%)			GCSE (5+ A*–C including English and maths) (%)		
	Non-FSM	FSM	Gap	Non-FSM	FSM	Gap
North East	69	46	–23	63	32	–31
North West	65	43	–22	64	35	–28
Yorkshire and the Humber	62	39	–23	63	34	–29
East Midlands	62	39	–23	63	32	–31
West Midlands	63	42	–21	62	36	–27
East of England	64	38	–26	65	34	–31
London	70	54	–16	69	50	–19
Inner	71	58	–13	67	53	–14
Outer	70	50	–20	69	46	–23
South East	65	39	–26	66	32	–34
South West	63	39	–24	64	33	–31
England	65	43	–22	65	37	–28

Source: DfE, 2017d.

2.4.5 The attainment of disadvantaged pupils in England by local authority

The GCSE data also revealed that disadvantaged pupils from all regions were achieving below the national average for achievement at GCSE (Table 2.8 and Figure 2.6). Disadvantaged pupils living in the South East attained 26 percentage points below the national average. The East Midlands, the South West and the North East showed the biggest gap in achievement between disadvantaged pupils and the national averages (Table 2.8). Perhaps significantly, there is a far smaller percentage of disadvantaged pupils in the regions with the largest gaps than in Inner and Outer London. There does appear to be a correlation between the density of the disadvantaged pupil population and their success at GCSE.

However, the data shows overwhelmingly that disadvantaged pupils are underachieving in all regions of England (Figures 2.5 and 2.6). The performance of disadvantaged pupils varies greatly across different local authorities in England, however (see Figure 2.5). In 2017, 43% of pupils eligible for free school meals at the end of Key Stage 2 attained the expected standard in reading, writing and maths, compared with 64% of all other pupils (Table 2.8). In that year, 70% or more of the pupils eligible for free school meals in ten local authorities attained the benchmark level at the end of Key Stage 2. Attainment gaps were smaller than average in all these authorities. All ten of these higher-performing local authorities were in London, and against this measure of attainment the four most strongly performing authorities were Camden, Hackney, Newham and Lambeth.

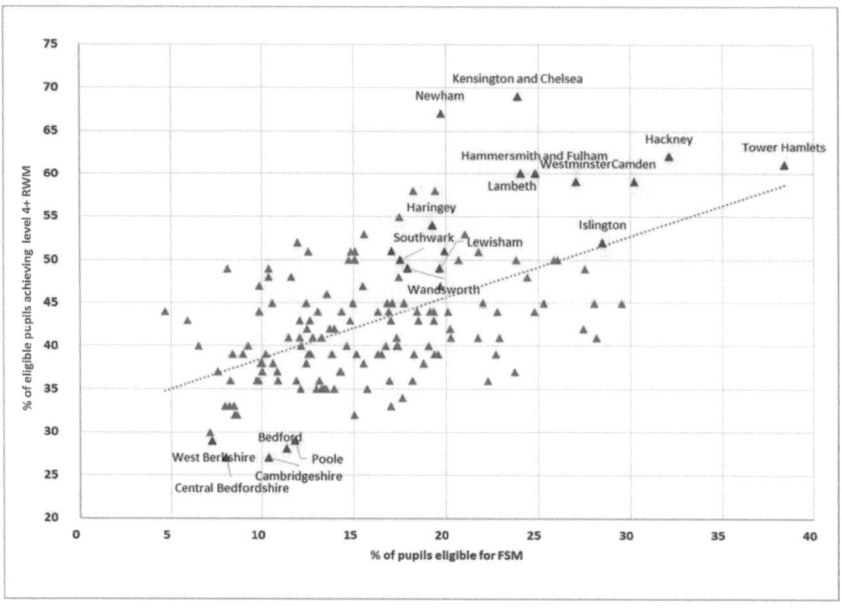

Figure 2.5 KS2 performance in England by LA and FSM (level 4+). From DfE, 2017d

There are also larger variations in attainment at GCSE (see Figure 2.6; DfE, 2017c, 2017d). In 2013, 41% of pupils eligible for free school meals nationally gained five or more GCSEs at grades A*–C including English and mathematics, compared with 68% of all other pupils. In that year, there were 27 local authorities in which 45% or more of the disadvantaged cohort achieved the GCSE benchmark. The majority of these local authorities were in London, exceptions being Luton, Slough and Birmingham. The attainment gap between disadvantaged pupils and their better-off peers was also lower than the national average in all except two of these local authorities (Slough and Bromley). By contrast, there were ten local authorities in which the benchmark GCSE attainment of disadvantaged pupils was 26% or less. The local authorities that performed most weakly against this measure were Barnsley, Portsmouth and South Gloucestershire.

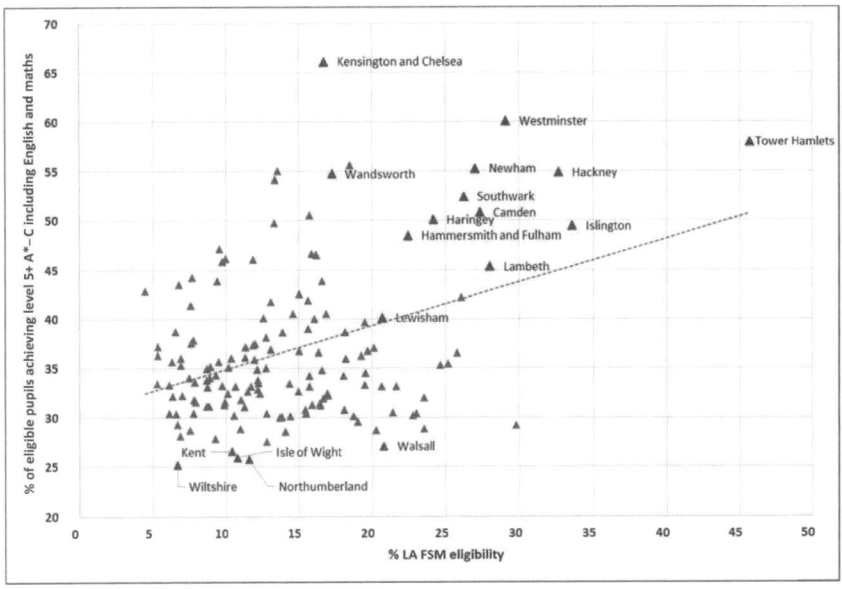

Figure 2.6 GCSE performance in England by LA and FSM (5+ A*–C including English and maths). From DfE, 2017c; DfE (NPD) 2017

The notable performance of London's more disadvantaged pupils compared with local authorities elsewhere is borne out by statistics. Figure 2.6 shows the difference in FSM pupils' performance by local authority. If we look more broadly at the 25 top-performing local authorities in terms of GCSE attainment for low-income pupils, the data confirms that disadvantaged pupils in London LAs do better than their peers at national level and in other local authorities. In Kensington and Chelsea the percentage of pupils on free school meals achieving 5+ A*–C including English and maths is 66%, compared with Wiltshire (25%), Northumberland, the Isle of Wight and Kent (26%), Walsall (27%), Reading (28%) and the average in England of 38% (see Figure 2.6; DfE, 2017c, 2017d). The five strongest-performing authorities, in rank order, are Kensington and Chelsea, Westminster, Tower Hamlets, Redbridge and Barnet.

There are a number of reasons for the vast improvement in the achievement of disadvantaged pupils in London compared with those elsewhere in England. The LAs firmly believe that disadvantage has multiple causes and that the challenges faced by young people in the most deprived areas cannot be ignored, or left at the school gates. The London boroughs have therefore taken a wide range of approaches to providing additional support to schools in areas of high socio-economic disadvantage, starting with many initiatives such as London Challenge (a government initiative to raise standards in London schools) and school partnership schemes and working with other local authorities to sustain school improvement.

2.5 Conclusions

This chapter asks the key question, 'What is the empirical evidence for educational inequality in England?' Drawing on longitudinal KS2 and GCSE data, we have examined in detail the achievement pattern and evidence, by ethnic background, EAL and disadvantage, to show the impact of government policy over the past decades on educational inequality. The national data suggests that the pattern of comparative underachievement in some ethnic groups through English schooling is strong and persistent. There is evidence that:

- Chinese, Indian, Bangladeshi and African pupils tend to significantly outperform the White British majority.
- Black Caribbean, Pakistani and Traveller and Gypsy children tend to underperform. Moreover, worryingly, the gap in Black Caribbean achievement actually increases rather than narrows as a child progresses through compulsory education.

The empirical evidence confirms that disadvantaged pupils' underachievement in education is real and persistent and that they are consistently the lowest-performing group in the country. It shows that:

- Black Caribbean, Traveller and White British children eligible for FSM are consistently the lowest-performing ethnic groups of children from low-income households.
- The attainment gap between children eligible for free school meals and the remainder is wider for Black Caribbean, Traveller, White British, and Mixed White and Black Caribbean than for any other ethnic group.
- The gap widens, particularly at the end of secondary education, for White British and for Mixed White and Black Caribbean pupils.
- Chinese and Indian disadvantaged pupils tend to significantly outperform the White British majority.
- 'At the current rate of progress, it would take a full 50 years to reach an equitable education system where disadvantaged pupils did not fall behind their peers during formal education to age 16' (Education Policy Institute, 2017; see also Hutchinson *et al.*, 2016).

The next chapter looks in detail at what works in addressing educational inequality, with particular focus on:

- closing the achieving gap for disadvantaged pupils
- raising the achievement of ethnic-minority pupils
- raising the achievement of pupils who speak English as an additional language.

Chapter 3

The case study schools

3.1 The context of the case study schools

This chapter considers evidence from schools in one local authority ('the LA') in Inner London. The local authority is one of the most ethnically, linguistically and culturally diverse boroughs in Britain. About 85% of pupils are from ethnic-minority groups. African pupils form the largest ethnic group with 24% followed by Black Caribbean with 17%, White British 15%, mixed race 13%, White Other 8%, Portuguese 6% and Other Black 6%. There are also a small number of Indian, Bangladeshi, Irish, Pakistani and Turkish pupils in the schools.

The ethnic composition of the LA's school population has changed considerably over the years: White British and Black Caribbean numbers are falling while Black African, White Other and mixed-race pupils are increasing (see Figure 3.1).

The social and cultural diversity noted in the schools is echoed in the languages the students spoke – around 150 in all. For almost half the students (47%) a language other than English was their main language. The most common were Yoruba, Portuguese, Somali, Spanish, Twi, French, Ibo, Ga, Krio, Tagalog and Luganda. A large proportion of the bilingual pupils needed support in English language.

3.2 The case study schools

The case study schools serve some of the most deprived wards in the LA. Many pupils come from economically disadvantaged homes. The number of pupils taking up free school meals is about 34% across all schools in the LA, ranging from 19% to 65% (Demie and McLean, 2015b). Student mobility is high; students join and leave the school at irregular times. Over half the pupils are from homes where English is not the first language. The number of pupils with a statement of special educational needs is below average but the number who have learning difficulties is very high. The students come from a wide range of minority ethnic groups and speak more than 50 different languages. The school populations mirror the communities in which the schools sit. Most pupils come from African, Caribbean, Portuguese and White British backgrounds and a significant proportion are of mixed heritage. Despite challenges in terms of the level of deprivation in the area, the overwhelming impression the schools create is of confidence and cohesiveness. The schools are exceptionally inclusive. They promote community cohesion and ensure pupils understand and appreciate others from different backgrounds and have a sense of shared vision, fulfilling their potential and feeling part of the community. Through the school curriculum, the pupils explore the representation of different cultural, ethnic, linguistic and religious groups in the LA and the UK.

Clearly, diversity is a strength that should be, and is, reflected in all aspects of schooling. What these statistics clearly demonstrate is that to succeed in raising levels of educational sattainment, we must raise the attainment of ethnic-minority and disadvantaged pupils.

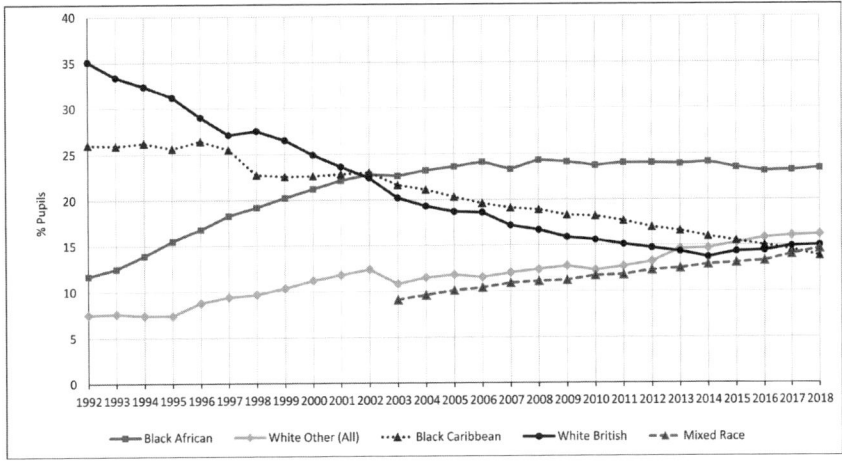

Figure 3.1 Changes in school population in the LA by main ethnic group, 2000–2018. From Demie, Butler, Tong *et al.* (2018)

3.3 Research methods

This is a qualitative study of these schools. It examines the success factors driving school improvement and raising achievement for all groups of pupils. It is similar to other studies that look at examples of schools that provide an environment in which underachieving groups flourish, but the present study reflects the perspective of the pupils, using detailed case studies to illustrate how policy and practice help to raise the achievement of pupils and identifying what works (Demie and McLean, 2007, 2015a; Demie and Lewis, 2010a, 2010b, 2010c; Mongon and Chapman, 2008; Ofsted, 2009a, 2009b). Three overarching research questions guided this research:

- What does the data tell us about raising achievement?
- What factors successfully drive school improvement?
- What are the implications for policy and practice?

The research provides evidence-based answers to these questions, drawing on the practice, experience and ambitions of schools in challenging circumstances. The case study schools, which all serve disadvantaged communities, had all been identified by Ofsted at some point in their past as 'requiring special measures' or 'having serious weaknesses'. However, eleven schools have been graded 'outstanding' in recent inspections, and their pupils have consistently high levels of achievement.

The research into the LA's schools comprised data analysis, a questionnaire survey, case studies of selected schools, and focus group interviews. The case studies were supported by a qualitative study of the strategies used by the school to raise achievement. The methodological framework is summarized below:

Data analysis The study drew on the analysis of a range of data that was collected centrally as part of statutory returns, including KS2 and GCSE attainment data, to examine the achievement of Black Caribbean pupils in the case study schools and to note changes over time. Table 3.1 shows that the selected case study schools serve some of the most deprived wards in the authority; the proportion of pupils taking up free school meals averages about 26%, ranging from 9 to 65%. There are high numbers of mobile pupils. Over half the pupils are from homes where English is not the first language. Table 3.1 also shows that the attainment of all pupils has been exceptionally high. Of the pupils in the case study schools 87% achieved the expected standard at KS2, compared with 80% nationally. From 2006 the case study schools have consistently had results that are above the national average. At GCSE, 60% of the case study school achieved 5+ A*–C including English and maths, compared with 57% of the national average (see Table 3.2).

The case study schools defy the association of poverty with low academic outcomes and enable children from disadvantaged families to succeed against the odds. They refuse to use a child's disadvantaged background as an excuse for underachievement. Overall, the case study schools data shows that from their generally low starting points, pupils reach exceptionally high standards.

Table 3.1 Background of case study schools

Case study schools: primary	Background				
	Ethnic minorities (BME) (%)	Black Caribbean (%)	Black African (%)	FSM (%)	EAL (%)
School C	88	20	33	23	46
School B	90	21	27	31	43
School G	79	18	18	26	40
School A	93	26	22	33	33
School SJ	60	14	14	10	15
School SS	59	15	9	9	20
School Y	73	11	16	17	42
School V	94	9	43	57	69
School JE	87	21	20	26	32
All case study primary schools	80	17	22	26	40
LA	84	14	22	25	52
National	31	1	4	17	19

Case study schools: secondary	Ethnic minorities (BME) (%)	Black Caribbean	Black African	FSM	EAL
School F	78	13	19	14	35
School D	78	18	16	20	37
School E	85	23	19	23	41
School H	98	30	37	23	45
School O	96	19	32	56	65
School RE	96	13	46	13	55
All case study secondary schools	94	20	29	24	46
LA	82	17	25	26	47
National	30	1	4	13	19

Sources: Demie, Butler, Tong *et al.* (2018); DfE, NPD performance data for 2015.

Table 3.2 KS2 and GCSE performance in the case study schools

Case study schools: primary	Pupils reaching the expected standard in reading, writing and maths (%)						
	Black Caribbean	Black African	FSM	Non-FSM	EAL not fluent	EAL fluent	All pupils
School C	100	89	100	90	100	100	93
School B	63	85	76	80	55	100	78
School G	95	85	96	93	91	100	94
School A	100	100	100	90	93	100	93
School SJ	80	78	50	73	57	100	70
School SS	83	80	100	89	33	100	90
School Y	100	88	100	91	100	100	93
School V	100	75	92	69	100	100	79
School JE	64	100	87	84	78	100	85
All case study schools	88	85	90	86	78	100	87
LA	84	75	77	86	67	95	86
National	81	75	66	83	n/a	n/a	80

Case study schools: secondary	Pupils achieving 5+ A*–C including English and maths (%)						
	Black Caribbean	Black African	FSM	Non-FSM	EAL not fluent	EAL fluent	All pupils
School F	52	43	56	73	0	77	70
School D	49	30	38	56	43	53	51
School E	42	41	33	49	0	42	45
School H	50	49	41	57	43	52	55
School O	33	66	50	56	45	77	54
School RE	88	88	85	83	0	84	84
All case study schools	49	61	46	64	39	67	60
LA	43	57	42	62	37	65	57
National	46	57	33	61	n/a	n/a	57

Source: Demic, Butler, Tong *et al.* (2018); DfE, NPD performance data for 2015.

Focus groups Parent, pupil, governor and headteacher focus groups were convened to ascertain their views on strategies that worked to raise achievement and to identify whether their views mirrored those of the participants in the case study interviews.

Case studies Detailed case study research was carried out to study the strategies used to raise achievement and narrow the gap. A structured questionnaire was issued to headteachers, teachers, parents and pupils, to gather evidence on what worked to raise pupils' achievement. The aim was to triangulate the voices of the various stakeholders in the children's education. The questionnaire explored the school curriculum, the quality of teaching and learning, how the school monitors pupils' performance, how it supports and guides pupils, school links with parents, parents' and pupils' views about the school and its support systems, race and ethnicity in the curriculum, the quality of school leadership and management, and the availability of the competence and materials to use the existing flexibility within the curriculum to make subjects more relevant to pupils' own experiences and to reflect their cultural heritage. The final visit focused mainly on gathering more evidence about the case study schools, parental engagement, and diversity in the school workforce.

Eight primary and six secondary schools were selected for the case study (see Table 3.1). The schools were chosen as examples of different types in the local authority that have relatively high numbers of pupils on free school meals, from ethnic minorities, and who have EAL. They were selected according to the following criteria:

- an above-average proportion of students who are eligible for free school meals
- an above-average proportion of students who have EAL
- an above-average proportion of students from ethnic-minority groups
- a good or outstanding grade in their most recent Ofsted inspection
- exceptionally good results, high standards and sustained KS2 or GCSE improvement.

As part of the research, various members of school staff and parents were interviewed in order to gain a range of perspectives on the main practices in the schools over a given period. These included: headteachers and deputy headteachers; class teachers; EAL teachers and special educational needs co-ordinators; teaching assistants and learning support teachers; family support workers; governors; and pupils. Each of the case study schools was visited as part of the research every year between 2010 and 2017.

In all the case study schools we visited we carried out classroom observations, with the main aim of understanding how schools and teachers recognize and value diverse cultures and heritages, and how children respond in lessons where this is the case. The classroom observations focused on teachers' interactions with Black Caribbean, Black African and minority ethnic children, disadvantaged pupils and interactions between diverse groups of children. The findings that emerged from the data analysis, focus groups and case studies follow.

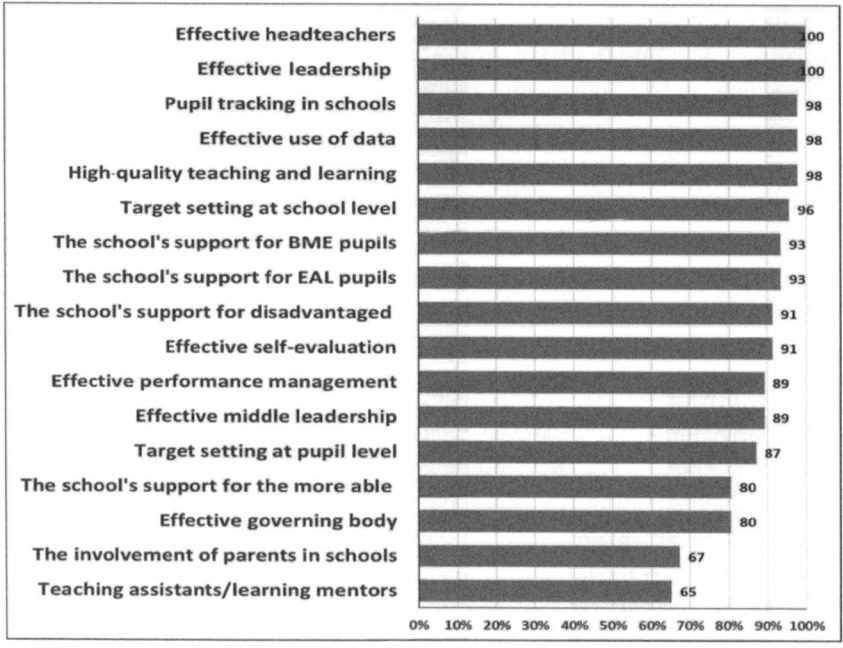

Figure 3.2 Factors that contributed to improved school KS2 and GCSE results (% of respondents who considered that factor important). From Demie, 2018a

Questionnaire survey A school survey was undertaken in 90 schools to collate the views of headteachers, teachers, governors, school improvement advisers, parents and school staff on what they perceived as the reasons for the improvement in educational outcomes in schools at KS2 and GCSE, in order to identify examples of good practice. We posed the question, 'How much do you feel the following factors contributed to your school's improved educational performance at KS2 and GCSE?', and asked the respondents to rate the level of impact by ticking one of five boxes, denoting 'strongly agree', 'agree', 'don't know', 'disagree' and 'strongly disagree'. An additional question in the survey invited respondents to 'describe the most important factors that you feel have contributed to improved results and to give examples of good practice'. The survey showed that many factors contributed to improved KS2 and GCSE results (see Figure 3.2).

The main findings of the survey indicate which factors the respondents rated as having the greatest impact on raising pupils' achievement. From the survey data, we have identified 14 key factors that we believe underpin the raising of the achievement of all pupils and the closing of the achievement gap:

1. strong school leadership
2. high-quality teaching and learning
3. effective governing bodies
4. effective use of data
5. effective use of pupil voice
6. targeted interventions and support
7. effective support for ethnic-minority pupils
8. effective support for pupils who speak English as an additional language
9. parental engagement
10. links with the community
11. use of a relevant and inclusive curriculum
12. commitment to equal opportunities
13. diversity in the school workforce
14. celebration of cultural diversity.

The findings of the survey have led us to identify explanatory factors that we believe have aided the educational improvement in the LA's schools. Some of these factors are explored in detail in the next chapter.

Chapter 4

Closing the achievement gap for disadvantaged children

4.1 Introduction

This chapter explores the key strategies used by the case study schools to narrow the gaps for disadvantaged pupils. It presents some of the major findings, also reported in local publications over the last 20 years (Demie, 2005, 2017a, 2017b; Demie and McLean, 2015a, 2015b, 2016, 2017a, 2017b; Demie and Lewis, 2010a, 2010b, 2010c, 2010d).

The overall performance discussed in Chapter 3 suggests not only that the case study schools have narrowed the gap between disadvantaged pupils and their peers but that some have closed it. There are several reasons for the vast improvement in the achievement of these pupils compared with those across the LA and, indeed, England. In the interviews we asked headteachers and teachers, 'What strategies does your school use to raise the achievement of pupil premium pupils?' The research identified the following success factors in raising achievement and narrowing the gap: outstanding, visionary school leadership, effective teaching and learning, effective use of data, targeted support and interventions by using pupil premium funds to challenge poverty. These practices are discussed below.

4.2 Strong leadership

One of the main reasons for excellent performance in the case study schools is strong leadership on equality and diversity. There is general recognition that the role of leadership is central to improving schools (Day, Sammons *et al.*, 2009; Day and Sammons, 2014; Leithwood *et al.*, 2006a, 2006b). The literature on effective school turnarounds repeatedly points to the importance of effective leadership, and there is evidence that talented leadership is one of the strongest explanations for the success of schools performing beyond expectations in settings of severe poverty (Harris and Chapman, 2008; Day and Sammons, 2014). Day and Sammons (2014) describe the core practices of leaders in successful schools. They actively set direction, develop people, and engage in organizational redesign. They create the conditions that allow improvement that is sustainable, and they develop and adjust their practices according to the needs of the organization.

The past 15 years have witnessed a remarkably consistent, worldwide effort by educational policy makers to reform schools by holding them publicly accountable for improving students' performance in national tests. For school leaders the main consequence of this policy is the pressure to show how their work contributes to such improvement. It appears that this pressure is not due to scepticism about the value of good leadership but rather to 'prove' that it is of key importance.

The outstanding leadership of the case study schools sets clear direction and creates a positive school culture. A proactive school mindset supports and enhances the staff's motivation and commitment to fostering school improvement and promoting success in schools in challenging circumstances. Staff are empowered and supported to fulfil the aims of the school. These school leaders understand the importance of culture. They have built institutions in which people believe and with which they identify, and to which they are loyal. The evident value of their work is highly motivating.

The school leaders are national leaders of education (NLEs) of most of the case study schools, who identify, train, designate and deploy specialist leaders of education (SLEs), developing a school-led workforce of middle and senior leaders to provide school-to-school support. Common characteristics of the leadership of these school leaders are:

- The ambition that each child will acquire the particular skills they need to reach their potential and lead a successful life.
- The ability to remove barriers to pupils' learning and provide a culture of achievement, with a can-do attitude. Central to their work are high expectations and the provision of intensive support for the pupils to meet them.
- Valuing the diversity of pupils' backgrounds and circumstances.
- Monitoring pupils' progress by ethnicity and social background. They monitor the details of learning, the pupils' work, marking, record keeping, teacher assessment, quality of teaching and learning, and the progress made by individual pupils and collectively by each class. Pupil tracking is rigorous. The data gives senior staff the confidence to challenge assumptions about and attitudes to the pupils' performance.
- Seeing parental engagement as vital to the school's drive to raise achievement. They have developed genuine partnerships beyond the school to encourage parents' support for learning and new learning opportunities.

Evidence suggests that the dimension of leadership that matters most for pupil outcomes is leaders' professional development of their staff. The case study headteachers are also attentive to their own learning: 'Shaping one's own professional vision and providing the leadership necessary to enrol others in the pursuit of a shared educational vision requires informed thought' (Stoll and Fink, 1996). Leaders need to stay current in order to have credibility with their staff and to build up-to-date networks. The cluster arrangements in which these schools are working offer opportunities for school leaders at all levels to further their leadership roles. A review carried out by Robinson *et al.* (2009) identified eight dimensions of leadership practices and activities linked to student outcomes. Of all the factors identified, headteachers leading and actively participating in professional learning and development had the greatest impact on student outcomes, an effect double that of the next most important, which was planning, co-ordinating and evaluating teaching and the curriculum.

Many of the school leaders have successfully turned around schools deemed to be inadequate or 'requiring special measures' to become judged later by Ofsted as 'outstanding'. Some have gone on to replicate this success across schools within a federation, and as national support schools they support, challenge, coach and direct. Other case study schools, which were recognized as 'good', improved continuously to become outstanding in all areas.

One such school is School F (an all-through school), where the principal has developed a clear vision of every student as able to achieve and a culture in which individuals at all levels enjoy a degree of autonomy in relation to their own work. The possibility of bringing knowledge, skills and creativity to bear in resolving problems and pursuing opportunities is extended to students as well as staff.

The principal is passionate about every child's sense of 'being known' by the school and of being valued as an individual. As he observed:

> 'Overwhelmingly our children know that they are known and their needs are secure. That's the basis that liberates them to be good learners, more confident and optimistic. Outcomes follow from getting these things right. Increasingly it's about the whole child. If we can give this to our children regardless of their background then we are doing a good job.'

One of the reasons for the school's dramatic improvement over the last decade is the promotion of a dynamic and decentralized approach to leadership. Giving staff authority while supporting them to develop the best possible way of going forward is a feature of the distributed leadership at School F. Clarity about roles and responsibilities is evident at every level. The deputy principal characterized the leadership team as 'cohesive ... it is not negatively competitive, it is cohesive'.

She said of the next tier of leadership:

> 'Progress with middle leaders has improved capacity considerably, and subject and year leaders became Directors of Learning. We changed the name three years ago because both groups focus on learning and progress. We wanted to give them more autonomy. It is about staff taking responsibility for outcomes ... everyone is clear about their roles and everyone is supported!'

There is also a shared vision for excellence at School RE, where Ofsted found that:

> Leadership and management are outstanding. The Headteacher and senior leaders lead by example, creating a positive climate where staff and students work closely together with shared aims and expectations. The Headteacher's vision for the school is shared at all levels.

However, the leadership has identified an ongoing challenge for the school's pupils eligible for pupil premium funding and their families:

> 'The key challenge we face is one of aspiration. The school deprivation indicator is in the highest percentile, as is our FSM eligibility. Forty-eight per cent of the pupil population is eligible for pupil premium funding. Few pupils have been exposed to higher education and career opportunities outside their immediate environment. Many pupils also face the difficulty of living in the inner city, with limited opportunity for extracurricular activities. Our EAL and ethnic minority percentage is in the highest quintile. Many parents do not have a tradition in, or understanding of, the UK school and higher education systems, creating a sense of "inaccessibility" to both pupils and their families.'

The leaders of the case study schools constantly seek ways of reaching out to parents and the community and go out of their way to recruit teaching assistants and support staff who live locally. They represent a wider age range than the teachers and speak various community languages, which helps in communicating with the parents. Discussions with these staff members in School RE reveal that they believe they have an in-depth knowledge of the children they support as they see them in the playground, at lunchtime and in after-school clubs, as well as in the classroom.

One of the key features of leadership common to all the case study schools is the facilitation of the personal and professional growth of staff. The commitment to enabling staff members to participate in the leadership process has encouraged their motivation and involvement. A teaching assistant at School A said of their headteacher: 'She trusts us, all her faith and confidence she has in us. She lets us get on.' Another commented: 'I have never been to her with an idea for a job and she has said it wouldn't work. She always lets you try it out.'

The roles and responsibilities of School A's staff have been reviewed to bring them into line with the intervention strategies designed to meet the needs of pupil premium pupils. New posts have been created, of parent partnership leader and pupil guidance and support leader, and they have become members of the senior leadership team. Their understanding of the local context in which children and families live and their empathy are great sources of support to the school community:

> 'Parents may have had a very difficult experience themselves with school and we have to let them know that we are there for them as well as for the kids. We are a small school and this helps. We look at the social and emotional aspects, and how this impacts on their children's academic progress. We focus on how they are getting on with life and their next steps. Pastoral care is very important – the mixed backgrounds of staff all helps – we all work together and bounce ideas off each other.'
>
> (Pupil guidance and support leader, School A)

The staff at School RE share a vision for each child to acquire the particular skills they need to reach their full potential and lead successful lives. The ethos of the school is centred on achievement and the quality of students' learning experiences. There are high expectations of all students and the staff will not accept social deprivation or English not being their first language as excuses for underachievement. They consistently challenge the students to do well. A deputy head leads the strong behaviour management policy, which supports learning and consistency in behaviour management.

RE School's leaders hold very high expectations of what can be achieved. As a result, whole-school targets for students' progress are translated into ambitious yet realistic targets for individual pupils. The leaders have substantially reviewed the use of data over the course of a year so that the data presented is exceptionally helpful and is used by all staff to ensure accurate analysis and monitoring of progress towards targets at all levels.

The school's planning is well focused, and built on an excellent understanding of its strengths and areas for improvement. Rigorous self-evaluation is informed by regular monitoring of the school's work. Ofsted judged the school to be outstanding in all areas and reported as follows:

> The work of this outstanding school is underpinned by an atmosphere of high expectations and care for the individual. The new Headteacher has built well upon the high achievement evident when the school was previously inspected to raise students' GCSE and A-level attainment further. … There is a relentless pursuit of excellence by the Headteacher, senior leaders and governors. Leadership is outstanding at all levels and has established a climate where staff readily share expertise and monitor the impact of their work.

Staff and students benefit from the headteacher's inspirational leadership. His commitment to ensuring that all students excel is underpinned by a strong sense of moral purpose that is shared by the teaching and associate staff. The staff and students we interviewed are fulsome in their praise of the school's leadership.

Innovatory leadership is a feature of **School Y**. Although it is recognized as an outstanding national support school and a consistently high-achieving school, its headteacher is not complacent and is constantly looking at ways of ensuring that every child reaches their full potential. He has a strong belief that all pupils, whatever their starting point, can achieve. The school monitors pupils' progress by ethnicity and social background, and the details of learning, pupils' work, marking, record keeping, teacher assessment, quality of teaching and learning and the progress made by each pupil. Pupil tracking is rigorous. The leadership team has courageously decided to use its most skilled and experienced teachers to teach groups of underachieving children, in order to accelerate their progress. The headteacher explains his strategy as follows:

> 'I took my strongest teachers out of class in each of the phase teams EYFS, Year 1/2, Year 3/4 and 5/6 and each is picking up intervention groups. I have spent quite a lot of money upgrading small rooms, making them enticing for children by decorating, putting in spotlights, whiteboards – these rooms are even more enticing than the classrooms. Our children are not seen as

second-class citizens being shunted off … they also have some of the most popular teachers and therefore are envied rather than looked down on. Despite our best intentions most children know why some children are taken out of class, but now they are with a special teacher who is universally loved and they are going into an attractive environment.'

Having an expert teacher take out groups of pupils who need more help frees the class teacher to accelerate the learning of the other pupils, including those of high ability.

Such decisions come at a cost, but the headteacher has some creative ways of using available funding and resources to make the strategy sustainable by incorporating some well-specified, well-supported programmes of extensive professional development for volunteers, teaching assistants and School Direct staff. The headteacher explains:

'We have got two School Direct students that we have trained to our specification. We train them in the "School C way". We tell them how we would like them to teach using our Teaching Toolbox and they observe exemplary quality first teaching. We then observe them and ensure that they are up to our standard. Our current School Direct staff are virtually as good as any class teacher. This further frees up class teachers to teach groups of six or seven pupils.'

Accepting the leadership of a school in very challenging circumstances and deemed by Ofsted to require special measures requires extraordinary abilities. The headteacher who took up post in 2000 at **School O** signalled the start of an impressive journey of improvement, which saw the school's achievement at GCSE rise from 11% in 2000 to 73% nine years later.

The headteacher is uncompromising in her view that the focus of the school is to ensure achievement for all. There is zero tolerance of poor behaviour and an unremitting belief expressed to staff that 'disruptive behaviour should not be allowed to damage the education of our pupils'. The school has clear sanctions in the event of inappropriate behaviour. The head's first priority on arrival was to tackle persistent underachievement in the school and support the teachers by establishing and maintaining good discipline. Alongside discipline runs an approach of care and encouragement for pupils and staff, supported by extensive staff CPD and training programmes. It is no surprise to see that expectations and academic standards keep on rising, and the upward trends at GCSE continue.

This transformation has been due to outstanding and inspirational leadership, as recognized in the Ofsted inspection report:

'The outstanding leadership of the Headteacher and her leadership team has been instrumental in continuing the very successful drive for improvements in achievement, quality of teaching and the behaviour and safety of students since becoming an academy. All staff are highly ambitious for the students. As a result, all students make exceptional progress in their personal development and academic achievement.'

The key to maintaining School O's excellence is the powerful culture of high expectations, based on a shared commitment to meeting pupils' often complex needs. The tone is set by the school's headteacher and governing body. Staff are trusted and valued, expectations of all pupils' social and academic achievement are high and the school is deeply embedded in the life of the area it serves.

The headteacher is well regarded, both by the local community and by national policy makers, for her success in raising achievement in the face of extraordinarily challenging circumstances. In this school, poverty is not an excuse for poor performance and teachers are very effective at challenging the children to achieve to the best of their abilities. They see the children's circumstances as an opportunity for change, not an excuse for underachievement. In the words of the headteacher, 'Anybody who says children from around here cannot achieve is badly letting down local children and communities. We challenge stereotypes about the area served by the school by asking questions such as, Why can't a school behind Brixton be a good school? Why not let children in the area have their dream? We have strong values and high expectations that are applied consistently. ... We are constantly reviewing ourselves, reflecting on why we are here, our vision, our ethos. Our spiritual connections are strong – the belief in the agenda goes beyond the contract, there is a moral obligation to get this right.'

Ofsted concurred with the school's evaluation of itself:

The school's view about its own performance is robust and accurate. It is well informed by an excellent improvement plan that has clearly measurable outcomes. The plans for improvement are monitored regularly, progress is carefully reviewed and any required changes implemented quickly. The management of teaching and its impact on learning are outstanding. School leaders' judgements on the quality of teaching are very accurate, informed by extremely rigorous checks by senior and middle leaders. ... Middle leaders have a very well-grounded understanding of how to improve the learning opportunities for students. They very effectively review the performance of their subject areas to ensure that the quality of provision remains high for all students. Training for all staff is highly personalised and based on an accurate analysis of need. All staff speak very highly of the quality of the training provided by the school, which is tailored to the stage that individual staff have reached in their career development. Systems for managing staff performance are extremely rigorous and salary progression only occurs when merited by good performance. Senior leaders have taken very robust action to challenge student underperformance. This is in line with the high aspirations set for the students, summarised in the school motto 'Attitude Determines Altitude'. This approach has been very successful in ensuring that where progress has faltered, underachieving students quickly catch up with their peers. Students' spiritual, moral, social and cultural development is a real strength of the school. The school monitors very effectively the performance and well-being of the small number of students who receive aspects of their education in other settings. School leaders are robust in addressing any instances of bad behaviour. The effectiveness of this action is seen in the continued decline in the number of exclusions, which is significantly below the national average.

An assistant headteacher gave us an overview of why she thought this was an outstanding school, saying, 'This is the best case of a school that has improved and has sustained this improvement that I have been involved in.'

School JE is another school that was 'causing serious concern' to the local authority for many years before the current executive headteacher was appointed. It was her exemplary leadership that led it to become outstanding in all areas. The leadership has been able to remove barriers to pupils' learning and provide a culture of achievement with a 'can-do' attitude. Central to the team's work are high expectations and the provision of intensive support so that pupils are enabled to achieve to the best of their abilities.

The following quote sums up Ofsted inspectors' views of the school:

This is an outstanding school. Achievement is outstanding because the motivational leadership of the Executive Headteacher and senior leaders and managers has secured outstanding teaching. Parents and carers highly value the progress that their children are making. Pupils enjoy lessons and make outstanding progress because they are inspired by the interesting variety of activities offered to them.

The executive headteacher became acting headteacher of **School JE** in 2007, from being a deputy headteacher of another primary school. She recalls that, with so many issues to address, and the enormity of the challenge she faced, she decided to tackle the physical environment first, as a signal to all that improvement was on its way:

> 'We applied to NatWest for funding. We persuaded them to come and see our playground and they awarded us £100,000 saying it was the worst they had seen in the country! Parents were asked to help design the best playground for their children. The parents and children formed a working party with the governors. We all visited schools with really good playgrounds and this focused us on what was possible. The children felt valued and the parents felt that something was being done about the school.'

The headteacher then embarked on an intensive programme of monitoring teaching and learning:

> 'The programme involved classroom observation, work scrutiny and drop-ins. Eighty per cent of lessons were graded inadequate. We recruited some new teachers from local schools, including an advanced skills teacher (AST), and we started the process of change. I modelled lessons together with the AST to share good practice with the teachers.'

This practice of rigorously monitoring teaching and learning continues; even the most competent teachers receive pointers on how they can improve their teaching:

> 'When we observe lessons we always give teachers steps to improve, even if they are outstanding. We still observe all our outstanding teachers.'

Despite there being several newly qualified classroom teachers at **School JE**, the leadership have no qualms about the school's capacity to sustain its outstanding provision. All newly qualified teachers (NQTs) are observed at interview, and if successful they are appointed to the school and paired with outstanding teachers:

> 'I have seen the potential in our NQTs who have to be at least "good" first of all and then we build on that.'

The rigorous monitoring of teaching and learning ensures that everyone is clear about the school's high expectations for the achievement of all its pupils. The headteacher explained:

> 'Each term staff are given a monitoring schedule so they are well aware of what the focus for monitoring will be each term, i.e. lesson observations for teachers and TAs, planning, monitoring of children's workbooks, including the "effective marking" system.'

The senior management team includes a business manager, a premises manager, three assistant headteachers, the head of school and the executive headteacher (who is a national leader of education). Rigorous performance management and high-quality professional development of staff, including coaching and whole-school training, have contributed to the school gaining a CPD Award from the Institute of Education. The executive headteacher believes that this has empowered staff to 'step up' when she is not in the school. As she says, 'They can operate without me being here. They are confident in doing so.'

When asked why the school has succeeded against the odds, she replied:

> 'I just believe that every child is good at something and it is our job to tap into this and extend it. Our belief is every child can achieve but it is up to us to find out how to bring it about. Some achieve through music, sport, reading or maths, wherever their interests lie.'

Ofsted inspectors recognized the excellence of the distributed leadership and management at **School JE** in the following extract from their report on it:

> The Executive Headteacher, together with senior leaders and managers, provide outstanding leadership. They are very well supported by leaders and managers at all levels and by members of the cohesive staff team. An ambitious vision and accurate evaluation have resulted in rapid and sustained improvements in achievement, attendance, teaching, behaviour and the curriculum

since the previous inspection and demonstrate the school's secure capacity to improve further.

Rigorous monitoring of teaching and learning and an ambitious vision that every child will succeed has been the key to the dramatic improvement of **School G**, which was described as a 'sink school' when the headteacher took up post two weeks before it was inspected by Ofsted in 2002. It was removed from special measures after only four terms, having made good progress in addressing all the key issues. The headteacher was described as providing 'excellent leadership'. He said he knew the school was going to be a challenge when he accepted the post:

> 'Pupils looked neglected and needy, not materially, but in terms of their self-esteem, their confidence and their self-worth, they had poor attitudes to learning and poor behaviour, attendance levels were very low and there was inadequate provision for pupils with EAL and SEN. Staff were bruised and battered and had been neglected, morale was low, teachers' expectations of pupils' achievement and behaviour were low; there was no deputy headteacher and an ineffectual leadership team, the overall quality of teaching was poor and there was a high rate of staff absence and long-term sick leave.'

The headteacher's main priorities were to:

> 'deal with restructuring the leadership team and appoint a deputy and to be tight and highly prescriptive and put in place structures and systems to establish a climate for learning, e.g. behaviour management strategies, staff communication, set the highest expectations, curriculum planning, monitoring and the checking and relentless evaluation that what we had put in place was being implemented and impacting on the children. I had to crack the culture of dependency on the headteacher and ensure that there was collective responsibility. It was also vital to improve the learning environment.'

The headteacher monitored learning rigorously by examining children's workbooks weekly. He and his deputy modelled excellent teaching strategies and demonstrated to staff how to manage the children's behaviour. Tough decisions were taken as they tackled issues of poor performance and the long-term absence of some members of staff. The headteacher confronted all obstructions to the achievement of his vision for the school in an honest and forthright manner. He modelled a professional approach for staff and developed leadership roles at all levels by providing a bespoke professional development programme.

The motivation to improve the life chances of some of the most deprived children in the country stemmed from the headteacher's own working-class background:

> 'I come from a working-class background myself; my parents worked as a mechanic and in a shoe factory and my granddad down the pit. My family valued education and learning. Education was my chance to do something they didn't do. I've clawed my way to where I am now. My lesson is that perseverance pays off.'

The headteacher is a strong and persuasive role model for the pupils. He has played a key role in raising the aspiration of the many disadvantaged communities he serves. Back in June 2008 the school was recognized as an organization of outstanding strength and capacity and was selected to become a national support school by the National College for School Leadership. Through its work as a national support school, highly skilled members of staff from across the federation provide outreach support, coaching and mentoring to schools experiencing serious difficulties. They have retained this status for some years now and continue to provide expert advice and intervention to other schools experiencing difficulties; some demonstrate significant impact. The executive headteacher has delegated the operational leadership to 'heads of schools' within the federation of five schools and two children's centres. He recognizes the need for and mutual benefits of collaborative working in driving and securing school improvement. The executive headteacher's style, described by School G's head of school as 'brave and community-focused', is what makes him an outstanding leader: 'He revels in it, he doesn't shy away from the early conflict and he is straightforward in a no-nonsense, impassioned way.'

The leadership of the school was described by Ofsted:

> Highly qualified, exceptionally talented, inspirational leaders and managers at all levels are extremely ambitious for the pupils, and uncompromising in their drive to improve this school and others in the federation. They are determined that education in the school should be first rate, 'World Class'. Whilst supporting other schools, and growing at a rapid rate, the school has improved its outstanding practice and raised further pupils' achievements since the previous inspection. Faculty, year group and inclusion

teams include staff from schools across the federation. They have high levels of responsibility and are held to account for pupils' progress. Together with senior leaders, they are innovative and share and develop their considerable leadership expertise through robust self-evaluation and frequent checks on the quality of teaching.

School V provides yet another example of outstanding leadership, which has taken the school from twice being subject to special measures to becoming outstanding in all areas. Leaders, staff and governors are fully committed to supporting the drive for the highest levels of achievement and personal development for every pupil. Teamwork is extremely strong. Everyone's contribution is valued and morale is high. The executive headteacher and the head of school have set out a clear agenda for the development of the school. They are positive role models, and both lead by example. Support for teaching is very effective, with excellent systems in place to monitor the impact of teaching on the pupils' achievement. Able middle leaders contribute effectively to the process through lesson observations, regular analysis of pupils' work and by sharing best practice with colleagues. All of this has ensured that the teaching is outstanding.

School V is in a federation partnership with members, who share the common vision of 'Achievement for All', while retaining the individual character of each school. The executive headteacher has had a long association with School V, having led the school out of special measures for the first time, in 2002. He was invited to develop a federation with School V when it was put into special measures for a second time in 2009. As the experienced and highly regarded headteacher of another primary school and a national leader of education (NLE), he used his prior knowledge of School V to identify some talented key members of staff to form a new leadership team. He stated, 'The leadership structure might look top-heavy with a head of school and three assistant headteachers, but they all have clearly identified roles and make a strong supportive team'. To further strengthen the leadership and build capacity at School V he moved a SENCO and a Key Stage 2 manager from another primary school in the federation. Clearly the hard federation has had a bearing on School V's capacity to sustain improvement, not least because of the availability of additional financial and human resources. The retention of staff has also been secured, as opportunities for promotion are increased via the federation.

The leadership's initial task at **School V** after the federation was formed was to clarify the school's priorities for everyone. As the school was still being monitored by HMI, the executive headteacher used Ofsted evaluation criteria. The key issue for the headteacher is to establish priorities for improvement using Ofsted criteria. The staff bought into the need for change, recalls the executive headteacher:

> 'It drove the momentum for change. ... A combination of new projects brought in and certain things that were not contributing to achievement were lost or pushed out. Some of the existing good practice, such as pupil progress meetings which are an embedded part of the practice here, and the very strong English and maths leadership just needed the space to put their plans in place.'

It is no secret that leadership teams face a serious challenge when they try to bring the staff on board and get them committed to change. Without full commitment, long-lasting improvement will not be established. A critical factor in School V's current success is undoubtedly the exemplary leadership skills of the executive headteacher. He made his ambitious vision explicit to all those connected with the school and embedded a culture of excellence.

The current head of school was formerly the maths co-ordinator, and has been pivotal in ensuring that children achieve the highest standards, not only in maths but in all areas of learning. His passion for the future success of every pupil is supported by his constant efforts to improve outcomes for them. His goal, which he has achieved over successive years, is to ensure that by Year 2 every child is able to read, to write independently, and to show a mastery of number appropriate to their age or better. Despite attainment levels on entry to the nursery being well below average, the implementation of rigorous literacy and number programmes ensures that no child slips through the net.

School V is now at the forefront of leading-edge practice through research-based learning and development. The leadership is committed to disseminating good practice locally, nationally and internationally, and this commitment extends to making some of its master's curriculum and assessment programmes commercially available. At a conference attended by delegates from thirty countries, School V was the only primary school asked by the OECD to give a presentation about the successful implementation of its educational policies.

What these outstanding case study school leaders have in common is an unshakeable belief that all children can achieve their best, no matter what their background, language or circumstance. They have created a climate of excellence that is conducive to growth and where the emphasis is on innovation, consultation, teamwork and participation. This is confirmed by a selection of Ofsted inspection reports on the case study schools, which suggest that leadership in schools is critical and has a powerful influence on the achievement of students. The Ofsted inspection comments also confirm the common threads in leadership and management that have the power to transform the schools:

> Inspirational leaders and managers are determined to ensure pupils receive a 'World Class Education'. They are highly ambitious for each child to acquire the particular skills they need to achieve their potential and lead successful lives.
>
> The headteacher, together with senior leaders and managers, provides outstanding leadership. They are very well supported by leaders and managers at all levels and by members of the cohesive staff team. An ambitious vision and accurate evaluation have resulted in rapid and sustained improvements in achievement, attendance, teaching, behaviour and the curriculum.
>
> The headteacher is determined and relentless in his focus on improvement. This is driven by his passionate belief that all students, irrespective of their circumstances, are entitled to the best possible education.
>
> The headteacher has created a very strong team of staff who share her high expectations and aspirations. Together with governors, they have established a vibrant learning community in which all pupils thrive and flourish, academically and personally.'
>
> Leadership and management are outstanding because leaders have accurately analysed pupils' assessment information and put effective strategies in place to ensure that pupils' progress is accelerated at every key stage.
>
> Evaluation of the school is rigorous and accurate. They monitor teaching regularly and accurately, and there are many training opportunities for teachers to improve their expertise.

Leithwood and Louis (2012: 3) sum up the case: 'To date we have not found a single documented case of a school improving its student achievement record in the absence of talented leadership.'

4.3 Excellent teaching and learning

Another key factor in raising achievement is the high quality of teaching and learning; this, too, was evident in the case study schools. In just over a decade, London schools were transformed from being the worst for children from low-income communities to attend, to being a leading example across the world of improving outcomes for such pupils. At the heart of London's many educational problems had been its inability to attract and retain high-quality teachers. The ability and skill of their teachers is the most important school-based factor for pupil learning and attainment (DfE, 2010; Barber and Mourshed, 2007; Slater *et al.*, 2009; Day, Stobart *et al.*, 2006). Meta-analyses indicate that while 50% of the variation in student achievement is attributable to their prior cognitive abilities, around 30% is attributable to teaching variables. What teachers do in the classroom matters more than non-teacher factors such as class size and school organization (Atherton, 2011; Hattie, 2009). If research can be used to impact positively on teaching, it can demonstrably contribute to school improvement. This is further supported by the McKinsey report on education systems. It claims, 'There is no more important empirical determinant of student outcomes than good teaching' (Barber and Mourshed, 2009: 27). Sammons (2007) has also drawn attention to the centrality of teaching and learning. She observes (p. 29), 'It has been argued that the quality of teaching and expectations has the most significant role to play in fostering students' learning and progress', and identifies a number of characteristics of effective teachers:

- They teach the class as a whole;
- They present information or skills clearly and animatedly;
- They keep the teaching sessions task-oriented;
- They are non-evaluative and keep instruction relaxed;
- They have high expectations for achievement (give more homework, pace lessons faster and create alertness);
- They relate comfortably to students (reducing behaviour problems).

(ibid.)

In addition, effective teachers:

- Emphasise academic goals;
- Make goals explicit and expect students to be able to master the curriculum;
- Organise and sequence the curriculum carefully;
- Use clear explanations and illustrate what students are to learn;

- Ask direct and specific questions to monitor students' progress and check their understanding;
- Provide students with ample opportunities to practise;
- Give prompts and feedback to ensure success;
- Correct mistakes and allow students to use a skill until it is over-learned and automatic;
- Review work regularly and hold students accountable for their work.

(ibid.)

Our research shows how the quality of teaching and teachers' expectations played a key role in the case study schools. The pupils' attainment on entry to these schools is typically below the national average. The level of home support that the schools can expect is low, not because of lack of parental aspirations or concern but because many parents lack the ability to help. Accordingly, the schools focus on developing basic skills and providing an enriched curriculum to enhance pupils' social and cultural capital (Bourdieu, 1987).

Knowing the challenge of raising standards in inner-city schools, the headteachers are rigorous about who they appoint, and ensure that all the staff receive the best possible continuing professional development (CPD). Many headteachers prefer to 'grow their own' teachers. At **School Y**, for instance, the headteacher is skilled at spotting potential teaching talent. He explains his approach to recruiting new staff:

> 'Some of our teaching assistants are on one-year contracts. Every time we get a new TA vacancy we advertise in the *Guardian*, inviting people to apply for a TA post for a year. The people we are seeking would not want to stay longer because they are looking to become teachers. We have some high-quality people who apply and some of them we put through the School Direct route. I will talk with new staff and explain and demonstrate how it is done and take them through the Toolbox. This applies to TAs as well as teachers. We show them how to use whiteboards, talk partners and targeted questioning, etc. They also have opportunities to observe each other. … They are fast learners – that's why I have chosen them.'

The deputy headteacher added her own perspective on how the adept use of 'volunteers' – people aspiring to become teachers – benefits the school:

'They often become TAs and we get to "grow our own". They absorb good practice and we get to see aptitude so we would look, over eighteen months, to see someone progress from volunteer to TA to a School Direct candidate.'

The headteacher is passionate about coaching teachers (and those aspiring to become teachers) in new teaching strategies as the means whereby outcomes for children can be advanced:

'It's about humility – are you prepared to improve your teaching practice? If you are then we will give you the strategies to improve your teaching. Teaching is not rocket science: if you are prepared to improve then we can help you.'

Clarity about his expectations of staff and the support that is made available to those who take up the challenge of teaching at **School Y** is a feature of this headteacher's strong and visionary leadership:

'A major issue I think, nationally, is professional neglect. I recently did an Ofsted inspection outside London and the deputy said she only monitors teaching three times a year because the unions might object. I think that if you are clear about what you want and you are prepared to put in the resources, there shouldn't be a problem. I do not take any risks with staff, especially new teachers. I warn them at interview what they are going to get and the promise is that by the time it is over they will be a cracking teacher. Recruitment is where you get quality first teaching; you are minimizing risk.'

A similar process of carefully recruiting new teaching staff and then developing their professional skills, which are then extended to their teaching assistants, is in place at **School JE**. The executive headteacher explained:

'We employ graduates as teaching assistants (TAs) as much as possible and adults with a competent level of numeracy and literacy. We set targets for our TAs, linked to teachers' targets and to the pupils' targets. We observe them working with groups. We have the highest expectations of teaching assistants and they are valuable members of the school team. Our TAs attend a weekly whole-school INSET along with teachers. Many of our TAs go on to become teachers and when they have trained we ask them to come back.'

At **School RE** the quality of teaching is seen as crucial to raising pupils' achievement. The emphasis on quality teaching and student achievement is affirmed by the teachers. We interviewed the heads of the English and mathematics departments, who work closely together to gain greater insight into school achievement and teaching and learning throughout their departments. They feel they are well resourced and that this has had a positive impact on pupil outcomes.

> 'We feel our headteacher is listening to us when we say we need, for example, a bigger budget. The head has supported us in core subjects – made them the heart of the curriculum.'

> 'The fact of having an extra teacher in the maths department means we can have seven sets across a year group – much smaller classes. We also put the best teachers in the most appropriate classes to maximize achievement.'

> 'We let the girls know that it's OK to make mistakes in maths – it's part of learning. We come to school to learn.'

Ofsted inspectors noted:

> Teachers know their students and their abilities very well because their progress is tracked and monitored regularly. They use this information to plan work which challenges students and is matched closely to their earlier achievements, so that all groups of students make rapid progress. Students who speak English as an additional language make particularly strong progress in English and their other subjects. This is because of the closely matched individual support they are given beyond lessons and teachers' understanding of how to build steadily on their existing knowledge to take learning forward quickly.

School RE has a policy of early entry in Year 10 in maths. If pupils do well in maths, gaining an A or A* in Year 10, they can go on to do GCSE statistics. This allows them to increase the number of GCSEs they achieve and to prepare better for A-level maths. For students who will not get a C in maths 'we identify areas of weakness and give them close mentoring. They also have to come to maths club every Thursday; this is compulsory.' 'It is by focusing on the needs of individuals that the department achieves so well overall.'

The maths department uses a wide range of 'additional extras' to add value. All students receive a maths DVD to watch for revision. In the spring term a representative from EdExcel comes into school to work with groups who are on a borderline between C and D or between B and A. They are given hints on exam techniques and 'what they need to do to get the results'. In Year 11, the mock GCSE papers are scrutinized and topics that certain girls need to focus on are highlighted.

At the end of Year 10, the English teachers check who is behind in their course work and review who might be in danger of falling below a C grade, then give a great deal of extra time to support these students.

> 'We teach them to the highest possible expectation. We want them to keep their options open until the last minute. It's about our motto, "For the greater glory of God"; we want the students to believe that they can do anything.'

> 'It's about team work – sharing good practice. People want to help the students. It's part of the Catholic ethos. Sharing the belief that we are all part of a whole and understanding that each child is an individual loved by God for her talents. We want these girls to achieve the very best that they can.'

> 'The staff are aware that the key success for all pupils is ensuring that all the day-to-day teaching meets the needs of each learner rather than simply relying on interventions to compensate for teaching that is less good. Where more support is needed the school allocates the best teachers to teach intervention groups (for example all assistant headteachers support GCSE English). All teaching staff are aware of who is eligible for the pupil premium and this informs their planning. The school makes sure that support and the use of regular robust assessments allow teachers to give students effective and termly feedback.'

School F's talented and committed teaching staff are willing to share their expertise and have developed a culture and a learning environment in which skilled and deep questioning draws out and promotes the pupils' understanding. Pupils frequently lead parts of lessons, present their work and question each other and their teachers. The Ofsted inspectors observed:

> School leaders have placed a strong emphasis on raising the quality of teaching in all areas of the school and are passionate about involving the pupils in their learning. This is one of the main reasons why the quality of teaching has improved and is now outstanding.

Teachers and the other adults at School F encourage, support and declare high expectations for every pupil, and the pupils accordingly expect the best of themselves. Excellent support for pupils who have special educational needs is provided in class and within the resource base:

> Classrooms provide a safe and secure place where pupils are not afraid to speak out, or to learn by getting it wrong before they get it right. They check their ideas with a mark scheme, before their own work is returned and self-reviewed with increased skill and proficiency.

The teachers use their outstanding expertise to support pupils with learning English as an additional language; they are well qualified, experienced and knowledgeable. As a consequence, these learners' needs are met in lessons and appropriate targets for their literacy needs are regularly set. They make excellent progress during their time in school. When a new EAL pupil arrives at the school an assessment is carried out immediately and they are tracked carefully to monitor their levels of English and their progress. Pupils of higher ability are challenged by the pitch of work in the accelerated sets, which is matched to their needs. Ofsted noted:

> Teachers plan and adapt their lessons to incorporate a sharp match of tasks and interesting activities for all groups of pupils and are adept at stimulating interest about their subjects through the use of varied and different resources.

The teachers regularly check pupils' understanding during lessons and urge pupils to question and check their own and each other's understanding. The sharp and perceptive written and verbal feedback on how well pupils are learning helps them to improve even further. Ofsted said of School F, 'Excellent teaching and tailored support for pupils enable them to learn exceptionally well in all subjects.'

School F uses an innovative online homework system to track and monitor pupils' homework easily and effectively. The system makes it simple for teachers to set homework tasks; transparent and thorough reporting means that any teacher or other staff member can see at a glance the quantity and quality of work being set by individual teachers, departments or year groups. Students access their homework via an internet account. To help students who might not have ICT and internet access at home, the school library is open after school: it has a suite of computers that students can log on to to check their homework. Parents too can check and extend pupils' thinking beyond the lessons.

The teaching at **School O** continues to provide outstanding outcomes for students.

> Teachers and teaching assistants have very high expectations of all students. This leads to teachers planning learning activities which ensure students are enthusiastic about their learning. Teachers gauge the quality of students' work very well and set appropriate, but challenging academic targets.

According to Ofsted inspectors, the school has gone from strength to strength:

> The quality of teaching has improved significantly since the school became an academy. A significant feature of the outstanding teaching in the school is the excellent relationship that has been established between staff and students. Students collaborate exceptionally well in lessons to improve their learning. In a Year 11 lesson, for example, students were encouraged to support each other when comparing solutions to mathematical problems. This ensured they were not reliant on the teacher for their learning, and led to excellent progress in their knowledge and understanding. Teachers make very clear the standard of work and behaviour expected from all students. As a result, students participate very willingly in all their learning tasks and make outstanding progress. Teachers use their extensive subject knowledge very effectively to extend students' knowledge and understanding. Strong subject knowledge enables teachers to use a wide range of techniques to probe students' own subject knowledge, as seen in a chemistry lesson about electroplating where students' knowledge of electrodes was tested very thoroughly. Support for disabled students and those with special educational needs is extremely good. Teaching assistants are used very well in lessons to support students in their learning. They work closely with the class teachers in agreeing how they will support students. This was seen in a Year 10 art lesson where both the teacher and teaching assistant worked very effectively to challenge all students. The teaching assistant was focused on ensuring that the more able students were stretched to achieve their best work. The school has a highly effective reading and literacy programme. The numeracy programme is developing rapidly. Students whose literacy and numeracy are below expected standards are very ably supported

through specialised lessons and one-to-one mentoring, and make very rapid improvement.

In all the case study schools, the teachers operate in an environment of diverse learners and they facilitate the learning process of pupils who come from a wide variety of backgrounds and have various needs. They treat all students as individuals who have unique strengths, weaknesses and needs, rather than as generalized representatives of particular racial, ethnic or cultural groups. They employ a variety of teaching styles to respond to the needs of each learner and create an open classroom that values the experiences and perspectives of all the students.

Teachers view the diversity of their pupils as a real strength. A teacher at **School JE** said:

> 'The diversity of pupils is what makes this school special – they come from all over the world. They feel welcomed from the start and settle straight away because they feel valued. It's such a community school – parents are involved and they want to be part of the school. We celebrate diversity here, in class assemblies, the language of the month and international day. Children learn from each other and we make use of other teachers who might follow that religion or have the same language as our children. We draw on that and our pupils to support our teaching. We celebrate festivals so children and parents feel included.'

School JE's 'Values' programme is another feature that teachers identify as something 'special'. Now in its third year, it promotes friendship, appreciation, joy, hope, peace, love, unity, respect, humility, caring and co-operation. Teachers believe that the Values programme has significantly improved behaviour. Each value is introduced by the headteacher or head of school at assemblies, reinforced in circle times, in SEAL classes and through homework.

Ofsted inspectors judged the teaching and learning to be outstanding because:

> it leads to above average outcomes and fosters determination to succeed. Teachers have excellent subject knowledge, very high expectations and plan a range of activities that inspire and enthuse pupils in lessons. Almost all parents and carers feel that their children are well taught and pupils say that teaching is good. As one parent said, School JE is a fun, safe school where children come first and really learn. Teachers make excellent links

across subjects providing practical experiences to make learning more relevant to pupils and to develop curiosity. For example, a nature walk for Year 1 linked mathematical work on shapes with the identification of parts of a flower in science and with a story they were reading about an enormous turnip. Every opportunity is taken to promote learning, develop reflective thinking and independent skills and to teach collaborative skills. Very effective use of resources, including information and communication technology, along with excellent pace in lessons, ensures that learning is enjoyable.

School JE's teachers work extremely well together, sharing ideas on approaches to teaching topics and resources. The staff receive guidance in various ways and have a comprehensive induction programme that includes EAL strategies, behaviour management strategies, child protection, and supporting pupils with SEN. Newly qualified teachers receive excellent support for planning for differentiation from the inclusion manager, who also monitors their plans. Weekly staff meetings focus on developing aspects of the curriculum, teaching and assessment. This programme of professional development produces outstanding teaching.

Teamwork is also a feature of the various federations of schools. **School G** teachers join with colleagues from federation schools to develop consistently high-quality planning for a wide range of abilities. Teachers plan in teams with a team leader and around nine to 11 colleagues in equivalent year groups. A morning is set aside to meet and plan. The teachers are positive about the advantages of these planning meetings. The Year 6 team leader said:

> 'We value that teamwork because we know that people bring in different skills, securing quality first teaching. We ensure we match up people in planning sessions in terms of strengths and weaknesses.'

Teamwork extends to assessing pupils' work, and teachers value the opportunities afforded to them when they moderate pupils' work across the federation schools:

> 'We look at each other's books and anyone who is having difficulty challenging, say, more able pupils can learn from what colleagues have done. We do the same thing with peer observations and give each other feedback. Motivation is very high and people want to

get children to succeed – this comes from the senior leadership team [SLT].'

Ofsted inspectors noted how:

> Inspirational teaching methods and high expectations motivate pupils to achieve as well as they can. For example, Year 6 pupils responded extremely well to the challenge to apply their literacy skills by taking on the role of the 'Big Bad Wolf' and writing in defence of his actions towards the 'Three Little Pigs'. Thorough lesson plans set out what pupils are to learn and how they are to learn it. This is made very clear to pupils so that they know exactly what they need to do to achieve well. Activities are amended so that they are matched closely to pupils' interests and abilities. Through the evaluation of these plans teachers make sure that lessons over time build very effectively on what pupils have learned before and that all pupils have equal opportunities to excel.

Ever eager to provide additional challenge for gifted and able children in Year 6, teachers have established links with other secondary schools, as the advanced skills teacher (AST) in Year 6 explained:

> 'We have a strong link with the local secondary; it's almost like having another member of the faculty. In Year 6 we have an English session on Monday and maths on Tuesday and secondary teachers come in to take lessons with our higher-ability pupils working at level 6. This also helps transition to Key Stage 3.'

A commitment to ensuring that children develop the skills and acquire the knowledge to meet and surpass curriculum requirements means that **School Y** sets high standards and teachers are focused on helping the children to meet these standards. They are sensitive to the needs and learning patterns of each child and try to inspire them to recognize their own potential and work towards fulfilling it. Their belief that the most vulnerable pupils need the strongest teachers runs counter to the practice of taking children with behavioural issues, low self-esteem and SEN out of the class to work with a teaching assistant. An experienced, outstanding teacher, now a non-class-based phase leader and maths specialist who teaches small groups of pupils, explained why this practice works well at the school:

> 'It just doesn't work with a TA. It's the experience of teachers and their knowledge of how to motivate a wide range of pupils

with a wide range of needs that makes a difference. The TAs are extremely strong but they are not trained teachers. Teachers know how to break things down and how to change tack if it's not working, having a host of strategies and experience of what works. These children need to feel they are on a par with their friends. I make them know they are doing hard stuff – as hard as what is going on in the classes. It makes them feel equal, which is what we want.'

We asked whether this approach would work with inexperienced teachers, and she responded:

'If you started taking people out of class after only one or two years' teaching they may not feel they have the range of teaching strategies to be able to carry out the interventions. You have to choose the people wisely and you need experienced teachers – you also need to have the right space to use as an attractive teaching base.'

We observed this impressive teacher working with a group of seven Year 6 pupils. An air of excitement infused the lesson, which moved along briskly, the teacher drawing on pupils' responses to gauge their understanding. The teacher displayed their work on the whiteboard via a camera, inviting pupils to explain how they had arrived at their answers, marking any errors and then using them as teaching points. The school is using 'Learning Lines', which facilitates pupils' evaluation of their own learning, as they place themselves at some point on a line and identify any difficulties or 'pit experiences'. The teacher encourages pupils to reflect on the strategies they could use to get out of the pit. Trust between teacher and pupils, and between the pupils, has been built up to the extent that the children show no fear or shame about revealing their lack of understanding. As the lesson draws to an end, the teacher encourages the pupils and makes explicit how well they are achieving, saying:

'Our aim is to try and get you to level 4. We are all roughly about the same. The questions you are working on were level 4. If I came last September and asked you this question, you never could have done it, so you are making great progress!'

Outstanding teaching of early numeracy at **School V**, the daily teaching of phonics and reading in the early years foundation stage and in Years 1 and 2 give the children a firm foundation in basic skills. Involving teaching assistants in teaching phonics and mathematics enables children in Years 1 and 2 to make excellent progress, as they are taught in very small groups, with activities and resources that match their needs. The teaching assistants are well qualified and speak enthusiastically about the training they have received to teach phonics and mathematics:

> 'I had training in Jolly Phonics in another school, but not as intensive as the training I had here. Here it is a two-day course and we have constant catch-ups and updates.'

> 'We have peer-to-peer observations which are co-ordinated by the literacy co-ordinator. We have been doing it long enough now to know who to observe. … We talk about what we are doing and if you think you can learn something from the way someone else is doing it you ask if you can observe them.'

Another teaching assistant told us about INSET days that are run with other schools in the cluster: 'There's a selection of workshops in the afternoon. Individual CPD needs are taken into account.'

Ofsted judged the quality of teaching and learning at the school to be outstanding. The inspection report stated:

> High quality teaching has had a significant impact on the impressive rise in pupils' achievements over the last three years. Teachers create well-ordered and stimulating classrooms in which purposeful learning takes place. They have a calm and consistent approach to managing behaviour, which all pupils respond to well, including those who have emotional or behavioural difficulties. Pupils are in no doubt what is expected of them. … Teaching is particularly effective when adults ask pertinent questions to develop pupils' understanding. They get pupils started on well-tailored activities quickly and assess the quality of learning that is taking place thoroughly, correcting misconceptions and moving pupils to their next learning steps as soon as they are ready. … The use of additional staff in lessons to support individual pupils with specific needs or groups of pupils is very effective, so all pupils are purposefully engaged in activities and learning well. Work in pupils' books is marked well with clear next steps identified so pupils know precisely how to improve.

4.4 Effective use of data

One of the core elements of the case study schools' success in raising children's academic achievement is a robust focus on tracking and monitoring individual students' progress and their achievement in the widest sense. Schools and the LA are data-rich, the wide range of data including KS2 and optional assessments or tests for monitoring performance. GCSE examination data is rigorously analysed to identify areas for improvement and the support children or staff need, and to organize the deployment of resources accordingly. The schools have good systems for assessing and mapping the progress of all pupils, noting their ethnicity, and rating the bilingual pupils at individual and group level.

The case study schools use a range of other comprehensive benchmarking, contextual and value-added reports provided by the local authority. The LA, through its Schools' Research and Statistics Service, has established a strong tradition of providing performance data to schools and governors in their efforts to raise standards, by providing its schools with the following services since 1997 (Demie, 2013b).

1. School profiles
The Schools' Research and Statistics Service issues all its governors, headteachers and teachers with a document called 'School profile: Making figures speak for themselves'. The profile provides a comprehensive set of data to support governors and headteachers in developing their roles and exercising responsibilities for the strategic management of schools (Demie and Butler, 2018a; Demie and McDonald, 2018a).

2. Contextual reports for all key stages In addition to school profiles for primary schools, the team provides school-customized FSP, phonics, KS1, KS2 and KS4 contextual performance data reports to identify underachieving groups. The contextual reports are analysed by factors such as gender, ethnic background, fluency in English, eligibility for free school meals and mobility rate. Schools and governors use each contextual report to monitor progress over time, note the factors influencing performance, identify key areas of action to ensure improvement, set targets, and address issues when certain groups of pupils underperform (Demie and Butler, 2018b; Demie and McDonald, 2018b).

3. Value-added data The LA provides schools with KS1 to KS2 and KS2 to KS4 value-added reports. The LA regards value-added data as essential to enhance teachers' abilities to analyse effectiveness in terms of the progress their pupils have made and to enable them to take the steps needed to effect improvement. The reports are diagnostically valuable, and make it possible to track the progress of individual pupils (Demie and Butler, 2018a; Demie and McDonald, 2018b).

4. Training in the effective use of data The provision and use of data in the LA and schools are backed by extensive training of the schools' staff and governors by the LA's Schools' Research and Statistics team. The training is customized to each school's needs, so staff can look at the ways in which school performance data can be used for school self-evaluation and for raising achievement. Significant numbers of governors, headteachers and teachers have attended the training programmes, which have made them aware of any underachieving groups in their school and how good practice can be used to raise achievement. This training has led to a greater focus on issues that impact on school improvement and target setting. Headteachers, governors and teachers were asked how they rated the support, conferences, training programmes and good-practice reports provided by the LA:

> Almost all the respondents felt that the service and the information provided by the LA were either very useful or useful. General comments were positive and schools felt that all the reports were useful for their school improvement and self-evaluation and helped them to draw action plans and identify underachieving groups.
>
> (Demie, 2013b: 14)

> Research documents produced by the Schools' Research and Statistics Service are unique and well used by schools. Governors and teachers have been widely consulted to produce documents, which are a model of clarity. Data circulated to schools help to raise questions that pinpoint strength and weaknesses precisely. Governors, school staff and officers have received extensive training. Schools value the data and the work of the team in mediating it.
>
> (Ofsted, 2013)

> 'Data was used as a driving force for raising standards and was one of the key drivers of change and improvement between 1997 and 2016 in LA and schools.'
>
> (A headteacher)

> 'LA data and research support to schools enabled targeted support at school level and drilling down to individual pupil attainment.

Supported robust conversations at all levels including support and challenge.'

(A teacher)

'The school profile and key stage contextual reports are extremely useful, incredibly insightful and give me the ability to ask more questions on specific issues.'

(A governor)

'The work of the Schools Research and Statistics team is unique and has become a bible in many LA schools. The data provided to schools has helped in securing school improvement.'

(Chair of governors and Council lead member of education)

Data is made available across the schools and the LA and used to review the pupils' progress and set targets in the case study schools and other schools.

Meticulous assessment and pupil tracking therefore characterize the case study schools. Schools see 'the use of data as an essential part of school improvement and self-evaluation and [it] is used as one of the levers of change', according to a deputy headteacher.

All the case study schools use the data effectively. Evidence provided from case study research at **School O** confirmed that:

- Key stage data is gathered as early as possible and analysed carefully by gender, ethnicity and mobility, supplemented by other tests such as in English, mathematics or verbal reasoning.
- The schools extensively use KS2-to-GCSE value-added data to improve the attainment of individual pupils. The standards of year groups or the whole school are monitored and each pupil is plotted on a chart according to their KS2 point score or GCSE point score plus. The value-added charts offer the opportunity to probe the strengths and weaknesses within the group.
- Data is used as a baseline to monitor and review individual pupils' progress, especially to identify signs of underachievement or unusual potential and to help set targets for pupils and subject departments. Subject teachers and tutors use data and other assessment information to review the performance and expectations of pupils. Test results and teacher assessments are analysed to illuminate aspects of pupils' performance.
- The schools also use a range of comprehensive benchmarking, contextual and value-added reports provided by the local authority,

and national data. Data is made available across the school and is used to help review the pupils' progress and set targets.

- Teachers make use of data to evaluate the quality of provision and to identify and provide support for differentiated groups of pupils. At classroom or pupil level, data enables the school to highlight specific weaknesses of individual pupils, identify weaknesses in topics for the class as a whole, inform accurate curricular targets for individual pupils and provide evidence to support decisions as to where to focus resources and teaching. Heads of department use data to identify and target specific areas of improvement in their development plans.

The most common interventions the schools employed where data had highlighted issues to be addressed was providing additional support – including one-to-one support or booster groups – and making changes to the teaching programme or curriculum, such as more personalized or differentiated teaching to meet the needs of EAL pupils, pupils who have SEN, or pupils in targeted initiatives to improve their performance. Data is also used in the schools to review pupils' setting and teaching groups, and this has proved to help raise children's achievement. In the words of deputy headteachers:

> 'The school is good at assessing all pupils and teachers look at data carefully.'
>
> (Deputy headteacher, School O)

> 'Teachers use the data to review pupil performance, to have reflections and good conversations and to produce class profiles. This has been useful for assessment for learning and tracking individual pupils' performance. You cannot do without data.'
>
> (Assistant headteacher, School O)

> 'Data is critical for raising standards. It is useful to track pupil progress and identify strengths and weaknesses.'
>
> (Deputy headteacher, School O)

Teachers also acknowledged the effectiveness of data:

> 'Data has been a fuel that has kept the "engine for improvement burning".'

> 'Use of data raised the expectations of staff and pupils and makes you focus on what children are actually learning.'

'It has forced teachers to look at particular areas of attainment and decide what to do to help the children get to the next level.'

'The data provided by the school helps you to target groups of children for specific types of help.'

This is further supported by another assistant headteacher, who commented that data provided to teachers has been extremely useful 'to highlight specific weaknesses for individual pupils, identify weaknesses in topics for the class as a whole, inform accurate curricular targets for individual pupils and tailor teaching to the needs of targeted groups':

'The school is very successful in identifying and tackling barriers to learning for students from different cultural backgrounds and providing well targeted guidance and support.'

Our observations and evidence research of **School RE** confirmed that the use of a wide variety of data has promoted teaching and learning by clearly indicating areas for development, identifying underperforming groups, showing how to use staff and resources more efficiently, and closely monitoring the effectiveness of initiatives and strategies. The interrogation of data is a key feature of the pupil progress meetings (academic reviews) in the school. It helps the school to make wise judgements about the quality of teaching and learning and the impact of targeted interventions, and to plan further action to overcome barriers to attainment and progress.

The deputy headteacher is in no doubt that the focused use of data has raised teachers' expectations and introduced more challenges into their teaching. The teachers use the data to inform teaching strategies to determine specific interventions with individual children, such as extra support in maths or intensive EAL support. The teachers interviewed acknowledged the effectiveness of data and commented that:

'The data provided by school helps you to target groups of children for specific types of help.'

'It has forced teachers to look at particular areas of attainment and decide what to do to help the children get to the next level.'

The value of data is affirmed by an assistant headteacher in School RE, who told us that data provided to teachers has been extremely useful:

- to highlight specific weaknesses in individual pupils,
- to identify weaknesses in topics for the class as a whole,

- to inform accurate curricular targets for individual pupils, and
- to tailor teaching to the needs of targeted groups.

School RE's effective use of data to deliver well-targeted support was recognized in an Ofsted report that stated:

> The school is very successful in identifying and tackling barriers to learning for students from different cultural backgrounds and providing well targeted guidance and support. The high quality of the school's self-evaluation and review results from rigorous monitoring and analysis of performance at all levels. This helps the school to identify and prioritise areas for improvement such as developing the skills and roles of middle leaders and improving assessment for learning. … The school mid-term monitoring system plays an important role in securing positive value added for each student as there is targeted intervention for students requiring specific support.

All the people we interviewed were clear about the good practice described above. The successful use of data in School RE owes much to the headteacher's vision in setting up a strong data support service led by the data manager. The data manager is responsible for collating and monitoring trends and for analysis of how the school has performed in relation to similar schools and schools nationally. Comparisons are made between subjects using raw, contextual and value-added analysis. The rapid analysis of data by the school data service, heads of departments and teachers means that areas of weakness are picked up quickly and can become an immediate priority for targeted intervention. A core element of **School D**'s success in raising achievement is its robust focus on tracking and monitoring individual students' progress and achievement. The school has a well-developed management information and pupil-tracking system that meets the needs of the school. It allows evidence to be collected, analysed and evaluated, including detailed cognitive ability tests (CATS), KS2, KS3 and GCSE assessment data, and background data such as ethnic background, languages spoken, date of admission, attendance rate, eligibility for free school meals, EAL stage of fluency, SEN stage, mobility rate, years in school, which teacher's class attended, attendance record, types of support given, and postcode. The school continues to refine the data held in its information and data-tracking system, ensuring the datasets are simple, accessible, easy to understand and manageable. The systems can identify 'threshold' students and so trigger interventions. The use of red, amber and green to indicate actual as against expected levels of progress makes the student's attainment easy to grasp, which facilitates discussion with families. Families are regularly informed about their child's progress reports.

School D periodically updates its data and teachers estimate each student's progress towards targets. Students and staff have regularly updated grids, including the child's current attainments and personal targets, cohort list, detailed background, attainment and target data, classwork concerns, homework concerns, KS3 and KS4 mock results, and key stages current performance based on teacher assessment and school targets. Targets are based upon cognitive ability tests, Fischer Family Trust (FFT) estimates, and the school's additional challenging targets. Indicative grades are set for Key Stage 3 and GCSE. This data enables the school to identify what steps it needs to take to meet the needs of individuals, groups and the student cohort. It was clear that the teachers make effective use of data to evaluate the quality of provision and to identify and provide targeted support for differentiated groups of students. Analysis of the data highlighted that the interventions most needed were to provide one-to-one support and to give targeted, personalized or differentiated teaching to meet the needs of EAL students or SEN students so as to improve their performance. We saw such use of data and targeted support when we observed the mixed-ability class. The school also uses the data to review student-setting groups; this has helped to improve the students' attainment.

The use of performance data for school improvement is also a major strength of **School JE**. Data is used as a driver for raising achievement and is central for school self-evaluation and for drawing up action plans.

The case study schools have well-developed pupil-tracking systems of detailed phonics, FSP, KS1 and KS2 and non-statutory assessment data, followed by background data such as ethnic background, language spoken at home, EAL stage of fluency, SEN, mobility rate, free school meals, class attended, attendance rate and type of support. In addition, schools use LA data, Analyse school performance (ASP) and FFT for monitoring performance and setting challenging targets.

The successful use of data owes much to headteachers and heads of school. They are responsible for monitoring trends and results and analysing how their schools have performed in relation to similar schools and the national average. Comparisons are made in all curriculum areas and by groups of pupils. The senior management team supports and challenges teachers to raise the performance of every pupil. Teachers are held accountable for the results and progress of every pupil: this helps to sharpen the focus on raising achievement. They are expected to identify and monitor the progress of individual pupils who are underachieving. School JE is particularly proud of its approach to monitoring the individual performance of all pupils, and this is widely discussed at the meetings of the achievement committee and of the governing body. Schools use the data to identify individual strengths and areas in need of development:

> 'High-quality assessment data, tracking and target-setting procedures for individuals and groups of pupils are the key feature in our school.'
>
> (Head of School JE)

> 'We look at the LA data, RAISEonline and school-produced data very carefully to track individual pupil's performance and progress. Data leads us to the type of questions we need to ask. It has also helped us to set targets and plan strategies.'
>
> (Chair of governors, School JE)

> 'We have high expectations. We want most of the children to achieve three levels of progress. We also have children who can make four levels of progress.'
>
> (Headteacher, School JE)

> Progress of groups of pupils is carefully tracked and almost all groups make outstanding progress overall in this highly inclusive school.
>
> (Ofsted, School JE)

The chair of governors gave a detailed picture of school achievement and how the data is used in School JE. She confirmed:

> 'The school data shows a strong picture of achievement at School JE, including bucking the national trends around the achievement of boys, summer-born children, FSM and pupil-premium [PP] pupils and BME pupils in some year groups. ... At KS2 girls do better than boys in reading and writing, all ethnic groups do well and [there is] no gap between FSM and non-FSM. PP pupils do better than non-FSM.'

We believe that School JE is somewhat unique. It has a chair of governors who takes a forensic approach to the use and analysis of data, has a sound knowledge of national education policy development and issues, and has first-hand experience of working in the area. The governors discuss school performance at the achievement committee and with the headteacher and teachers. Our observations indicate that the governing body is excellent in challenging and supporting the headteacher, the head of school and the school management team (SMT). They monitor the impact of the school's work in raising achievement and hold the school leaders and managers to account through keeping up with the data. The governing body discuss what the data reveals about the school performance, including its intervention strategies and their impact on improving performance of particular groups of pupils. The discussion has led to some new challenging targets for the school. What is remarkable in this school is, as the chair of governors says:

> 'The data is read and used in the context and focuses on where the school could look to make further improvements. The school endeavours to go beyond outstanding.'

Interviews with the headteacher, the head of school, classroom teachers, inclusion managers, TAs and learning mentors confirm that the school is rigorous in assessing all pupils, and that teachers look at the data carefully. The school uses data to track pupil progress, set targets, identify underachieving pupils for further support, and inform teaching.

> 'Teachers make effective use of data to evaluate quality of provision and to identify and support for differentiated groups of pupils.'
>
> (Headteacher, School JE)

> 'There are excellent systems for monitoring the work of the pupils, identifying those who need additional help or extra challenge and then providing them with appropriate additional support.'
>
> (Inclusion manager, School JE)

> Careful use of data, rigorous monitoring in lessons and regular tracking ensure that any variance in progress is tackled quickly.
>
> (Ofsted, School JE)

School V has a well-developed pupil-tracking system. Consistent analysis and application of school data has promoted effective self-evaluation and high standards of teaching and learning. This informs professional discussions with governors, parents and staff, identifies pupils' achievement and determines the targets set for their learning, monitors the effectiveness of targeted support and interventions, and supports the allocation of staffing and resources. Staff have developed a good understanding of the range of data available and draw on the information to plan confidently for continuous school improvement.

The school is particularly proud of its approach to ethnic monitoring. It uses data to identify individual strengths and weaknesses in the school's provision so that target setting becomes more responsive to the children's needs. All the teachers monitor in this way and the data manager also factors in the data from the assessment of the stages of the pupils' English fluency. It was clear from our interview with the headteacher and from our classroom observations that teachers are using data in a number of effective ways to motivate their classes:

> 'Teachers are confident in the use of data and assessment information. The data is shared widely within the school. ... The school has been good in using our data to identify pupils who are particularly underachieving. The school looks very early on at the students who are underachieving against the FSP, KS1, KS2 results and this has led to a number of interventions or strategies where data analysis highlighted issues to be addressed in the school.'
>
> (Data manager)

> 'The most common interventions in the school as a result of looking at the data were changing a teaching approach, providing additional support including one to one, booster groups, tailoring teaching levels or the curriculum, mentoring and target setting.'
>
> (Headteacher and data manager)

> 'All pupils with EAL are assessed carefully using their stage of English fluency to ensure they receive appropriate support and are making the required progress.'
>
> (Teacher)

The strong focus on learning seeks to ensure that no one is left behind. Monitoring and tracking quickly identify the children who drop below the expected level, or appear to be at risk of falling behind, and their needs are targeted. The school uses data for tracking pupil progress, target setting, identifying underachievement, monitoring teachers' and other staff's performance, and for indicating the areas needing development and the groups who are underperforming. Data also informs best use of staff and resources and monitoring the effectiveness of the initiatives and strategies themselves. The headteacher captures the views in the school about using data that support the conclusions we reached in this study:

'Data is used as a driving force for raising standards and is central for the school self-evaluation process and target setting. The use of data at all levels by teachers also means that areas of weakness are picked up and can become a priority for early interventions.'

The strategies for raising achievement are characterized in all the schools by the intelligent use of assessment data to trace progress, set accurate targets and support the students who are slipping behind with targeted interventions. The teachers in all these schools expect every pupil to achieve their full potential. They use the data to pinpoint underachievement and target additional support. The senior managers, teachers and teaching assistants in the case study schools ask important questions to identify areas for improvement, such as:

- What does the social background of the pupils tell me about my school? How does the school compare with other borough schools, schools similar on measures of free school meals, pupil mobility, English as an additional language, level of fluency in English, attendance rate, summer-born children, and pupils with statements of special educational needs?
- What does the overall FSP, KS1, KS2 and GCSE school performance tell me about my school? Do we know why we are in this position? Are we happy to be where we are? Where do we want to be in one or two years' time, and how do we get there?
- What does the contextual attainment data tell me about the performance of the school compared with national and LA averages? Do we have any underperforming groups of pupils?
- How does the school compare with other borough schools and the national average in respect of performance at FSP, KS1, KS2 and GCSE, by gender, free school meals, ethnic background, attendance rate, mobility rate, and terms of birth and levels of fluency in English?
- What does the value-added data tell me about the children's progress?
- How many pupils appear to be achieving below the expected levels at the end of KS2 and KS3 tests and GCSE examinations?
- Are there any common characteristics among the pupils who appear to be achieving less well than expected? For example, is there a high proportion of pupils of one particular ethnic origin, or a high proportion of boys?
- What are the overall strengths and areas of development?
- What can we do to improve?

4.5 Targeted interventions to support disadvantaged pupils

Another key strategy the case study schools use is targeted intervention and support through effective use of the pupil premium. Careful targeting of the pupil premium has undoubtedly had a significant impact on raising achievement and closing attainment gaps for eligible pupils. Staff and governors share a strong commitment to do everything possible to remove any barriers that might hinder a child's development. Governing bodies are well informed and hold school leaders to account for raising standards. They use data to measure how pupils are achieving in relation to their peers in similar schools. They effectively monitor pupil premium funds to make sure they are having a real impact on raising standards. These outstanding schools are ambitious, respond to what they know to be good practice and ensure that their vision for improvement is clear, realistic and shared.

The pupil premium funding is most often used to pay for additional teachers and teaching assistants, who deliver one-to-one and small-group support, typically focused on English and mathematics. The funding is also used to enable eligible pupils to participate fully in after-school clubs and activities and to provide financial support for educational visits.

One reason for the success of our case study schools is the leadership's prompt and accurate pinpointing of pupils' specific needs so that low attainment can be tackled at once. They track the progress of these pupils meticulously and adjust the support provided according to their monitoring and evaluation.

School RE uses achievement data to check the effectiveness of interventions. Checking pupil performance against spending involves consideration of a wide range of data and evidence: achievement data, pupils' work, observations, and the views of pupils and staff. Effective monitoring means that interventions and approaches can be quickly amended and adapted if they are not working.

School RE's heads of maths and English reported that they use data extensively for lesson planning and targeting support:

> 'We track pupils over the term, fill in the Excel spreadsheet and identify key groups. Also I, with my deputy in the department, do a book scrutiny and give individual feedback to teachers. They look for constructive feedback. We do informal observations as a coaching tool.'

'Again in English we have six smaller sets across the year group in all years. This means that there are only 18 or 19 girls in the bottom set. We restructured the department with the help of the headteacher recently and this really helped with supporting students. We are very well resourced. We place a lot of emphasis on differentiation – even within ability sets.'

School F's carefully focused intervention and support for students in Year 7 continues, as necessary, through the school. For example, the innovative, effective support of the learning support team has a significant impact on pupils' progress. A learning support teacher (LST) and three learning support assistants (LSAs) are attached to each year group, providing consistency and continuity of provision. Many of the concerns about vulnerable pupils' transfer to secondary schools, and about those with emotional and behavioural difficulties, stem from their difficulties in dealing with the increased number of teachers they will need to engage with. An LSA described the advantages of School F's approach:

'In this school you have an LST and three LSAs to a year group, so we know pupils well. This really helps at transition. We are a constant feature of the lessons; even when they change teachers, we are always there. Pastoral care is included. We try to balance up pupils to the adults they get on well with, because we spend all day every day with them.'

The LA has a strong philosophy about working within the pupils' classroom lessons, not withdrawing any of them. It practises team teaching across the curriculum, using strategies such as visual aids, key words, and timing of activities, all of which are good for all pupils.

'We plan with the teachers, focusing on how will my child access this lesson, can we look at this activity in a different way?'

School F's excellent and well-coordinated approach helps staff to get to know the children and their families well, so providing much-needed stability and continuity. One LSA, who is also a qualified teacher, gave us examples of success stories for certain students she has supported:

'A statemented, autistic student with social/communication difficulties I have been working with over the years has achieved a GCSE in drama and is on target to get five more GCSEs. I meet regularly with his mum and he has received additional support from the local school autistic unit.'

'We also run a club at lunchtime for the autistic children because this is a difficult time for some of these children. They can come and play Connect 4, draw, etc. One child would only play with a car by himself but as a result of coming to this club he has learnt to interact and play with other children.'

'Another statemented student has completed the Duke of Edinburgh Award.'

(LSA)

The staff team focus on getting to know the child's whole family. The school, the family and the external agency strive to work together to support the child, and all give them the same message, which is, the team believes, 'particularly important with behaviour interventions'.

School F has set up an autism support group for the parents of children on the autism spectrum at the school. The parents are pleased with the progress their children are making and are keen to support the school. Students in Year 11 who have no support at home do fewer GCSEs and receive extra support. Thirty students targeted to achieve a GCSE C grade met every two weeks with mentors who push them along with their course work in a special mentoring programme. The LST observed:

'We are like the parents. … With this type of support you can push them to get over the C/D borderline. … We make timetables for revision, e.g. three two-hour slots a day, eating properly, going out to play. The sorts of things you would do with your own children. The learning support system here is so efficient. It is such a difference from my previous schools. It takes communication between support staff and the teachers to make it work. This impacts on the children.'

Also in Year 11, the 'Increased Flexibility' project enables students to attend local colleges for practical or vocational training. Students are able to work towards NVQ Level 1 or Certificate in Construction, which feed into school qualifications. There is great enthusiasm for this project, especially among boys who have gained entry to courses at a local college, following successful study experience.

By Year 10 and 11 some of the students want to be doing something more flexible, more practical than lessons. **School F** has links with various colleges in the local authority. The students go to college once a week to do, for example, car mechanics or childcare.

'These might be students who are always struggling at school but yet are the first to change a wheel on the college course! They are always on time for college, they like it, they get treated like adults, it's a more relaxed environment. It's a bit of a carrot and stick – going to college keeps them on track at school and many of them go on to college full-time at a later date. They catch up with their missed lessons in curriculum support time.'

(LSA)

Child A in Year 10 goes to college once a week for motorbike maintenance. He told us, 'I have always been interested in fixing bikes.' He said he does not feel overwhelmed with school work any more and that college has helped with his behaviour and attitude because he gets treated more like an adult at college. It will also help him with his future plans to join the army, which his head of year found out about for him. He added, 'I've had a lot of support here, I didn't do anything from Year 3 to Year 6 at primary school but here I've had an extra adult sat here helping me because I have dyslexia.' A member of staff said of Child A, 'The college course has had a big impact on him. We hope he gets into the army; it will be a way out for him.'

Child B is in Year 10. She has been to four primary schools, including a language unit. 'They picked twenty of us and explained what a college course was about. We had a booklet with different courses and I chose childcare. I go to a local college. I like it because I'm meeting new people in a different community. We get treated like adults too: school is OK if you are in Year 7 and 8, but it's relaxed at college. I've had a lot of one-to-one support here. If I get my five GCSEs I want to do sociology and health and social care because I want to be a nurse or a midwife when I leave school.'

Year 11 pupils are involved in the 'Going for Gold' intervention programme. 'Diamond' is for students targeted to achieve a minimum of five GCSEs at A*–C (everyone at the bottom end of the cohort). Gold is for the key marginals and platinum is for students on track to achieve a minimum of 5 GCSEs at A* including English and maths, raising the A/A* percentage of gifted and talented pupils.

The principal of School F summed up his thoughts on inclusion:

'I don't think you can have a successful, high-achieving school unless it's an inclusive school. In selective areas the success rates between those who just managed to pass the 11+ to get into a grammar school and then failed to thrive and those that passed easily varied widely. Inclusion costs; without pupil premium funding it would be disastrous. Whether we can sustain this in the future depends on the funding. Without it the most vulnerable pupils will suffer.'

School F also uses achievement data to check the effectiveness of interventions. Careful monitoring of pupil performance entails checking a wide range of data: achievement data, pupils' work, observations, and the views of pupils and staff. Effective monitoring means that interventions and approaches can be changed and adapted quickly if they are not working. The Ofsted report on the effectiveness of the school's strategies for supporting disadvantaged students confirmed that:

> The staff are aware that success for all pupils is ensuring that all the day to day teaching meets the needs of each learner rather than simply relying on interventions to compensate for teaching that is less good. Where more support is needed the school allocates the best teachers to teach intervention groups (for example, all Assistant Headteachers support GCSE English). All teaching staff are aware of who is eligible for pupil premium and this informs their planning. The school makes sure that the use of regular robust assessments allows teachers to give students effective termly feedback.

School RE recognized that many students lacked independent learning skills, and that this affected the possibility of their going to university. The school responded by setting up the 'Learning to Learn' programme. The Campaign for Learning promotes this programme as a process of discovery about learning. It involves a set of skills that teach children to be learners for life. At its heart is the belief that one can learn how to learn and that lifelong learners are likely to be happier, healthier, have better jobs, contribute more to society, and live longer and more fulfilled lives.

There is a weekly lesson in KS3 classes that promotes the five attributes of becoming a lifelong independent learner, namely resilience, resourcefulness, responsibility, reasoning, and reflective learning (the five Rs).

The focus in Year 7 is on how to learn on one's own, moving on to team learning, being a twenty-first-century learner, and communication skills. In Year 8 it is about being a peak performer, making the learning count and study skills.

The maths and science departments use Learning to Learn. In maths it is about being reflective.

> 'Our focus this year is to involve the heads of foundation subjects and see how [Learning to Learn] can be fitted into the foundation subjects and focus on which R [is suitable] for a particular year group. In art for example there is a reflective log of learning.'
>
> (AST)

> 'This all fits in with the leading learners because the older pupils link with the younger pupils with their learning. There are reading partners, identifying ways to learn better, pupils reflecting on their CAT score – "if I had done this I would have done even better". We are training leaders in learning to learn.'
>
> (AST)

Of school improvement strategies, the deputy headteacher said, 'In the last few years we have had an active focus on learning in school. This is consistent across the school.'

There is a sustained focus on ensuring access to the curriculum for every student, whatever their background, through scaffolding and differentiation. Teachers have an excellent understanding of where children are in their learning; they know the learning profile of each child and what interventions they might need. Pupil progression in curriculum areas is discussed at weekly team meetings.

Ofsted commented:

> All students make outstanding progress in a wide range of subjects including English and mathematics. Excellent achievement is based on students' quick acquisition of a wide range of valuable learning skills. These, which include the development of highly accomplished skills in literacy and numeracy, are central to the rapid progress they make in their learning.

Through weekly targets, teachers are focusing on the children's learning and constantly reviewing what they do in the classroom. 'Are they achieving?' asked one. 'If they are not it might come under the pastoral heading; we have a system of referral and have a dialogue with pastoral staff about our more vulnerable pupils.' Constant review is characteristic of all the LA's schools. In **School O** it begins at entry.

> 'After every six weeks the Directors of Learning and teachers look at the eight classes of Year 7. Maybe X amount are underachieving – this is what the teacher has done, this is what we are going to do to raise achievement, these are the resources.

Maybe we will give support before and after school: many pupils prefer this rather than in the lesson.'

(Deputy headteacher, School O)

School O also focuses on the gifted and talented pupils in the school. The Directors of Learning take account of children in this area and all gifted and talented pupils have their individual(ized) education plans (IEPs) monitored. Data is used to identify any gaps in the learning of gifted and talented pupils; the teacher, the pupil and the parents consider interventions to raise their overall achievement. To meet the needs of the gifted and talented pupils, the mathematics department is running different programmes, such as an after-school club to organize trips and prepare pupils for the UK Maths Challenge. One child attended a maths day, organized by UK Maths Challenge, which gave her the opportunity to meet pupils from other countries.

A strong part of the school's identity is the range of programmes ('academies') on offer to its pupils that extend the curriculum and develop skills beyond the classroom. The academies cover writing, drama, science, sport and film, for example. Pupils must apply for the academies by going through an interview process.

'The Writing Academy started well, in October 2008. The standard of entry is extremely high. So far the academy has worked on writing reviews and analysing video clips, and is now working on a school newspaper and a poetry competition. Journalists from established newspapers will visit the academy. Like all academies, it is a real opportunity to develop skills beyond the classroom' (School O, headteacher).

'The members of the New Science Academy have been making models and hot-air balloons and have also constructed a volcano. Science competitions have developed through the school: the Recycling Project has been a tremendous success. The scientists have planned the Fast Track project and a debating group to discuss contentious scientific issues. The academy has planned trips to Kings College in order to look at access to medicine-, science- and health-related careers' (School O, headteacher).

As part of its higher-performing school status, the school is a training school and has been developing school improvement training. 'We have trained 31 PGCE students; their experience was broad, they got trained in data analysis and a lot of them had experience teaching the middle band. This really makes their experience real' (assistant headteacher).

Some of the teachers have been doing master's degrees, undertaking, for example, 'in-house action research around the underachievement of Portuguese pupils and action research regarding the access of EAL pupils to Shakespeare in the curriculum'. 'We also offer foundation degrees in conjunction with Canterbury Christ Church University.'

'Many TAs and HLTAs benefit from this in-house training.' Many people are referred from the Stockwell Community Resource Centre to the school for a variety of training such as Family learning. 'They love coming here, it's like going to university!'

The care, guidance and support of vulnerable children who are experiencing difficulties are outstanding at **School H**. The school has effective and integrated support systems to ensure vulnerable students get the academic and pastoral support they need. As a result, students with learning difficulties make exceptional progress and no one is left behind. This scenario is confirmed by the students we interviewed, who rate the care, guidance and support the school provides as outstanding. More importantly, they involved parents and shared the planned support and interventions and the success stories. Parents are aware of the intervention strategies and greatly value knowing what is going on.

The staff at this girls' secondary school set out to identify the vulnerable children. They see each girl as an individual. A vulnerable pupil, according to the assistant headteacher, has 'a statement of special educational needs or English as an additional language, is on the Child Protection Register, is pregnant, disabled, has a serious medical condition, is known to be a gang member or involved in criminal activity, or has low self-esteem or a form of mental illness. It also includes girls whose family is experiencing breakdown, has been made homeless, is involved in drug or alcohol abuse, or who are not attending and feels they do not want to be part of the school community or any girls who are unhappy, unhealthy or unsafe, or who are not enjoying or achieving.' She listed the range of interventions and support that the school will offer to these vulnerable pupils:

- support with transfer from Key Stage 2 to Key Stage 3
- a pupil mentor
- help with forming friendships
- tracking of academic progress of all vulnerable children
- helping to ensure entitlement to free school meals
- giving access to advice on healthy eating, diet and exercise
- encouraging access to homework clubs and use of the library
- encouraging participation in extracurricular activities, house events and assemblies
- monitoring attendance and work with the Home–School Liaison Officer
- support with choosing GCSE options

- arranging individual interviews with Careers Officer
- providing a learning mentor support in Year 11
- support with moving from Key Stage 4 to the next stage
- regular communication and meetings with parents or guardians
- whatever is necessary to access outside agencies or in-school support as appropriate
- application of appropriate behaviour intervention strategies, education psychology reports, internal exclusion, and parental meetings as needed.

(Assistant headteacher, School H)

The school has strong support systems in place and goes the extra mile to support the children and ensure their needs are met.

'We carefully use data to identify underachieving students or struggling children or vulnerable students. Use of data enabled us to focus and to ensure their needs are addressed. We are a proactive team. We act quickly. Good records are kept for all year groups and in addition to this data; there is also a day sheet to record teacher comments. Teachers in our school are good in keeping records and entering useful information that help us to ask questions and take actions as required. This record book and teachers' comment are also passed to the year director to take action and ensure vulnerable pupils are well supported in class.'

(Assistant headteacher, School H)

Similarly, **School F**, another secondary school in the LA, used funds from the pupil premium grant to support the following strategies to close the achievement gap:

- pupil literacy programmes, including intensive interventions in Year 7 before school
- reduction of class size
- extracurricular small-group provision
- a TA team to improve the attainment of children who have English as an additional language
- numeracy programmes
- small-groups tuition
- Saturday interventions
- behaviour interventions
- digital technologies

- ensuring all homework is completed and pupils are offered appropriate support if they need it
- extending the range of enriching extracurricular activities to all pupils.

At **School Y**, pupils' progress is closely monitored in termly meetings with the SENCO and the class teacher, led by the deputy head. The views of phase leaders about how children are progressing are also considered and the effectiveness of the approaches used is evaluated. Data on the impact of interventions is recorded and shared with parents, staff and governors.

School Y's headteacher said this about the subject-specific interventions:

'What we know from our own experience of the School Y context, we take into account. The Sutton Trust toolkit is used to identify key approaches that come within our resources and what would work for us. Marking the children's workbooks is a priority. Our marking is manageable and teachers mark extremely well. Formative assessment is outstanding. Our TAs are actively involved in making observations of pupils' learning and recording them on Post-its, and this gives teachers feedback within the lesson.'

School V has achieved its ambition that every child will be able to read and write independently and have a command of number appropriate to their age. Support is targeted right from EYFS. Consequently, Year 1 phonics screening check outcomes are above the national average. Teaching assistants play a vital role in supporting children in small groups, individually in the early years and in both key stages. Roles are flexible: some TAs teach phonics or Number Masters,[1] take story time with the whole class and carry out administrative tasks. Others run breakfast and after-school clubs.

Improving its pupils' health has helped School V to win a place as one of the four pilot schools with high numbers of pupils who have FSM to receive sponsorship from Nike's 'Move It' programme, which provides physical activities (run by sports coaches) for all pupils in Years 5 and 6.

The school's intervention and targeted-support strategies are effective because they are driven by pupils' academic, emotional and social needs. As a result of high-quality teaching and learning and tailored, individual support for pupils, the school has closed the attainment gap. Ofsted noted:

The school is highly successful in closing any gaps in the attainment and progress of pupils. Those who are eligible for the pupil premium, for example, achieve at least as well as all other pupils in the school and better than similar pupils nationally.

Likewise, at **School E**, the overall package of support for eligible pupils is comprehensive, well integrated and responsive to their changing needs. The specialist literacy programmes, small-group support work in English and mathematics, and one-to-one tuition help students who speak English as an additional language, pupil premium and students who have SEN to make excellent progress in both English and mathematics. The school uses its best teachers to teach intervention groups so as to improve mathematics and English. Support staff, particularly teaching assistants, are highly trained and understand their role in helping pupils to achieve. The school provides a balanced programme of whole-school, targeted and specialist support that takes account of the needs of particular pupils. Take, for example, Child N:

> 'Child N is in Year 11. He is a looked-after child and had a difficult journey through school because of this. He receives special educational needs [SEN] support. He was with the same carer from the age of six but the relationship became strained throughout secondary education and both he and his carer requested an end to the foster placement. The child was placed in the care of first-time carers with a therapeutic background and was medicated in Year 8. But in Year 9, his behaviour deteriorated. He went missing from home and indulged in substance misuse. Because of poor attendance and on-going behaviour difficulties, he was referred to a learning mentor. His behaviour and attendance improved somewhat but he struggled in a mainstream setting. The Student Engagement Department brokered an alternative provision placement at Educational Excellence. His attendance, behaviour and attainment were closely monitored by a team who were instrumental in ensuring that Child N left Year 11 with an A*–G qualification. He gained an apprenticeship at the school, where he is developing key employment skills.' (School E)

Monitoring pupils' progress thoroughly and systematically underpins the school's continued success in raising achievement, through the quality of teaching and the students' involvement in their learning, to outstanding levels. The principal of School E said this about the pupil premium grant:

> 'If there are changes to the funding there would be unfavourable consequences. We will be finding it difficult to do what we have been doing. We will try our best around that but it's inevitable

that it will be difficult. Data doesn't tell the whole story: race, language, SEND needs to be taken into account in raising achievement.'

At **School JE** the pupil premium grant is used to deploy an additional classroom teacher so that the pupils thus funded are taught in focused teaching groups by well-qualified and experienced teachers who can address their learning needs. This strategy makes a real difference to the achievement of the pupils eligible for pupil premium funding (PPF). The headteacher explains that as the priority at School JE is quality first teaching, all teachers know which pupils are eligible for the pupil premium grant and have their own in-class tracking systems of looked-after, EAL and SEN pupils. Pupils' progress is closely monitored termly at pupil progress meetings with the SENCO and the class teacher, led by the deputy head. They consider the views of phase leaders about how children are progressing and evaluate what has worked and what has not. Data on the impact of interventions is recorded and shared with parents, staff and the governing body.

The headteacher described the members of the governing body as 'bright and sharp' and reported that they take an active interest in the pupils' progress. They ask for detailed evaluations of the impact of the interventions put in place to support pupils of all abilities.

In the knowledge that children's grasp of language and their skills in literacy during their early years is fundamental to their accessing the curriculum and making good progress, the school uses a plethora of literacy and mathematics interventions targeted mainly at pupils in reception classes and Years 1 and 2. Key Stage 1 is a particularly difficult phase for children in receipt of FSM and consequently there is emphasis on the development of social skills and communication skills in the reception class. Structured phonics teaching by a specialist read–write teacher, supported by two well-trained TAs, is very effective in improving literacy outcomes at Key Stage 1 and is eliminating risk factors for children from disadvantaged backgrounds.

The school has implemented other innovative and successful interventions, for example the 'Learning Line', which enables children to express themselves when they are struggling in class and to articulate how best they might find a way to move forward with their learning, as well as to recognize how much progress they have made within the lesson. Peer-tutoring, whereby children in Years 5 and 6 teach younger pupils, has been introduced. It builds self-esteem and is a great confidence-booster for both the 'pupil-teacher' and the 'learner'.

The headteacher reflected on why there is a need for interventions for PPG pupils higher up the school:

'Every time there is a gap in Years 5 and 6 we are picking up children who need pupil premium grant support. Parents tend to move out in Year 5 into the private-school sector, or families move out of London and we take in pupils from other schools into these year groups and very often they are working at below-average levels. We have Year 6 booster classes and Easter boosters with two members of staff taking children who are borderline level 4. After the summer half-term I place all my resources in Year 5. I will put all my strongest teachers to do intensive work in key areas for next year. I start early with smaller groups.'

The school's deputy headteacher is fostering a 'growth mindset' in children who are achieving a secure level 4 or level 5 in mathematics. She invites *any* child attaining this level to attend after-school booster classes in level 6 mathematics, which she runs. Research on the growth mind-set shows that pupils who believe they can grow their basic abilities have greater motivation, and higher achievement, than do pupils who believe their abilities are fixed. In a growth mind-set, people believe that their most basic abilities can be developed through dedication and hard work: brains and talent are just the starting point. This view creates a love of learning and a resilience that is essential for high accomplishment.

As a result of high-quality teaching and learning, targeted support, and use of pupil premium funding, 100 per cent of pupils achieved level 4 and above in reading and maths, and School JE has successfully closed the attainment gap. The school uses PPF extremely well, deploying the best teachers and employing extra staff to implement specific interventions. There is no difference in the school between the achievement of those in receipt of the fund and that of others, so any potential gaps in learning are closed.

In **School V**, the pupil premium grant has enabled the school to offer a range of curriculum-enrichment activities that have proved successful in developing children's confidence and boosting self-esteem while also improving standards in mathematics and Year 1 phonics and KS2 outcomes. There is one-to-one reading support, additional level 5 mathematics, small-group Springboard mathematics support,[2] English, mathematics and revision materials for Years 5 and 6, one-to-one phonics support and reading intervention, staff training on outstanding teaching, the release of teachers for pupil progress reviews sessions three times per year, and extended services including a wide range of after-school clubs. As a result of such support and outstanding provision, says the head of school, 'progress by FSM pupils in all subjects exceeded expectations and attainment is within age-related expectations. In particular the percentage of FSM children classed as "more able" is growing each year. By the end of Key Stage 2, the percentage of children achieving the higher level 5 in all core subjects is significantly higher than the national average.'

Pupil premium funding has been used to subscribe to Mathletics,[3] and this has contributed to the consistently improving standards in mathematics. Years 5 and 6 have an extended school day in the spring and summer terms; school begins with breakfast at 7.30 am and additional English and maths lessons begin at 7.45 am. Attendance is almost 100 per cent. Pupils have small-group lessons in grammar, writing and mental maths, and it is also a time for 'plugging the gaps' and 'going back to basics' (Year 5 teacher). From 9 am, Years 5 and 6 revert to the usual curriculum.

Further investment in reading has resulted in the Year 1 phonics screening check outcomes being above the national average. This has also been true for the end of Key Stage 2 outcomes: FSM pupils outperformed their peers nationally in reading, writing and mathematics.

In School V teaching assistants play a vital role in supporting children, in small groups and individually, in EYFS and in other key stages. Roles are flexible with some TAs teaching phonics, Number Masters, taking story time with a whole class and doing administrative tasks. Others run breakfast and after-school clubs. They know the children and families well. They gave examples of successful outcomes for individual children on FSM they had worked with:

> 'I worked with [Child K] from Year 1; he had slight cerebral palsy but that didn't impact on his general learning. He started off making huge letters when writing but his writing is now smaller and he's a top speller and his literacy is quite strong. He's now in Year 3 and attends after-school clubs.'

> '[Child L] came into EYFS from Colombia and didn't speak a word in English, or Spanish. He made noises and couldn't say any vowel sounds. His mother took him to visit a special school but he showed them his School V badge and his mum brought him back here. He was very timid. He is now in Year 2 and you can have a conversation with him, he is reading and he approaches adults. He never did that before. His mother is very happy, very involved in his homework.'

The school's talented, flexible and mature teaching assistants, many of whom live locally, represent a wider age range than many of the teachers and speak various community languages, which is a great help in communicating with parents. They also feel that they have an in-depth knowledge of the children they support, as they see them in the playground, at lunchtime and in after-school clubs, as well as in the classroom.

School V used pupil premium funding to deliver a wide range of intervention strategies to raise attainment in reading, writing, communication and mathematics. The school's intervention and targeted-support strategies were effective because they were driven by the children's academic, emotional and social needs. The classes we observed get lots of support from the class teacher, teaching assistants and learning mentors. As a result of high-quality teaching and learning, effective tailored individual support and effective use of PPF, the school closed the attainment gap; both PPF and non-PPF children achieved 100 per cent level 4+ in reading, maths and writing. Both groups also outperformed the national non-PPF average in each subject.

School Y's strategies for success in narrowing achievement gaps include engaging a diverse community of parents and carers, in partnership with the staff, in the provision of support for children's learning. The deputy head explained the school's approach:

> 'We work hard at building relationships, for example in engaging our Somali parents in the Family and Schools Together (FAST) programme. The difference it has made is amazing: now they say 'good morning' and are smiling at us, whereas they used to group together in the playground and not talk to us. During the ten-week programme they really got to know us and we worked together. Parents have time together and they also have time to talk with the headteacher and myself so they could ask us questions. It has really helped break down barriers. In the FAST programme you also get parents to run future sessions; parents are currently organizing this and are keeping it going. This has been down to our HLTA, who ran it the second time and organized it. She has a great relationship with parents.'

Parent workshops on phonics, reading and writing, and mathematics are a regular feature of the school's approach, and parents are invited to train as volunteer readers: currently there are 20. Training in phonics is provided for all the parents of children in the reception class and the school talks to them about the articulation of sounds and invites them to come into the school and observe a phonics lesson. They also offer parents the opportunity to see a mathematics lesson. The deputy head explained why this is important:

'We have done a lot with parents with the new mathematics curriculum, especially the calculation policy. We have put it on our website and parents come in and observe us teaching – they can help their children at home. Parents come from a wide range of backgrounds and experience and things keep changing, so we need to give them the support they need to help their children. We use our home–school agreement to talk with parents who are not supporting their child with their school work.'

Ofsted made the following comment when inspecting the school:

Pupils for whom the school receives the pupil premium make even more progress than the outstanding progress made by their classmates because additional support paid for by the funding, such as specialist small groups for English and mathematics, is highly effective in accelerating progress. Consequently, the gap between their attainment and that of other groups in school is narrowing rapidly. For example, in the latest published figures available, the gap in mathematics had closed, and the gap in reading was half that of the national gap, at just over the equivalent of one term.

This was confirmed by data that shows that both PPF and other pupils did very well. Both groups outperform the national non-PPF average in each subject. In addition, the gap in attainment in the school between PPF and others was narrower than pertains nationally.

School G has used some of its pupil premium funding to enable the school's teaching assistants to take part in the Institute of Education's 'Maximising the Impact of Teaching Assistants' programme. The headteacher explained why:

'We are changing the hours our teaching assistants work. At 8.30 am they will meet with each class teacher and plan the way they are working, although my objective is tied to my aim to extend their hours to 5.30 pm. It's about raising the teaching assistants' profile. There is no way they can turn up at 9 am and be prepared for the day ahead. We have to have them working more effectively. They will have new job descriptions which will focus on learning.'

The roles and responsibilities of the former learning mentors have also changed to reflect the significant roles they now play in removing barriers to learning. Now they are members of the senior leadership team; the inclusion manager explained the changes:

> 'The roles have changed, they have evolved. We now have a parent-partnership leader. We have written her a new job description. She has amazing relationships with parents and they feel they can say more to her than to me.'

There is now a pupil guidance and support leader, rather than a learning mentor:

> 'He works with children with behavioural and emotional difficulties. He trains the teaching assistants and works with staff, modelling and supporting staff to implement the behaviour policy.'

It is clear that pupil premium funding at School G has contributed significantly to staff development, deployment and training. Quality first teaching is the first priority, and therefore there is an ongoing need to support teaching and learning through staff training. Two teachers and one member of the support staff are undertaking MA-level study. All support staff have achieved National Vocational Qualification (NVQ) Level 3 and a teaching assistant recently qualified as a higher-level teaching assistant (HLTA).

School G aspires to support the families who are trying to overcome a multiplicity of challenges so that their children can thrive and reach their full potential. The Parent Partnership leader plays a key role in this, arranging parent workshops on, for example, 'understanding tax credits', 'eating on a budget' and 'back to work strategies'. She monitors attendance and punctuality. She explained the process:

> 'We have panels where we go through the report and see anyone with attendance falling below 95 per cent. I chat with parents about it and if it gets worse I'll arrange a more formal meeting with the chair of the governing body, the headteacher and the pupil guidance and support leader. As a small school we know families very well. Sometimes the family support worker [FSW] is involved if we know there are family problems. I grew up with the same background as our parents on the same multicultural estate. They see teachers as formal, they might feel they do not want to cross the line. I help them get their foot in the door ... bridging the gap. The next generation of parents coming up,

some are very scared of school. I had to take one young parent by the hand and lead her into the school to deal with her issues, she was in such a state.'

Overcoming the emotional and social barriers that both children and some parents experience is one reason why the school has invested PPF in developing the roles of support staff. The pupil guidance and support leader commented:

'Parents may have had a very difficult experience themselves with school and we have to let them know that we are there for them as well as for the kids. We are a small school and this helps. We look at the social and emotional aspects, and how this impacts on their children's academic progress. We focus on how they are getting on with life and their next steps. Pastoral care is very important, the mixed backgrounds of staff all helps – we all work together and bounce ideas off each other.'

He described the impact of his work on one pupil for the sake of an example:

'In Year 4 an FSM pupil had serious anger issues. He was in danger of not achieving his targets. He was one of seven children living in overcrowded conditions and his mother had cancer. He was so angry he used to smack himself. ... He was always in trouble and his older brothers gave him a hard time. He came to one of my behaviour groups. We identified situations that would get him into trouble, explored what anger is, like a bomb. I tried to get him to the point of choosing to make a change in his behaviour. I spoke to teachers about positive praise and how they could respond to him. I spoke to the teaching assistants about this boy and what we were doing for him. We started to build his self-confidence and in Year 6 he achieved level 4 or above in all subject areas. He came back to visit us from his secondary school the other day. He is doing well but his older brother is in trouble with the police.'

The HLTA at School G, who speaks French, Spanish and Portuguese and offers EAL support to pupils and families, observed, 'We are very strong; we are a family as a whole school. Everyone can depend on each other.' She gave the following examples of successful interventions with EAL pupils:

'The child arrived at the end of Year 5 with no English, although he was fluent in Spanish which he spoke at home. I met with the parents and supported the family, who wanted him to succeed. We provided one-to-one support and Spanish translation with a peer-buddy. By Year 6 he achieved level 5 in maths and level 4 in English.'

'Another child came from Brazil into Year 5. He had supportive parents and was excellent in Portuguese. The family situation was positive. He achieved level 4 in maths and English. We are a very inclusive school so the child would not have any hindrances.'

'A child came into Year 2 straight from Colombia. He could speak no English at all, but he is working at level 6 in maths and level 5 in English. Working with his parents was very helpful.'

School G offers adult literacy classes for parents and stages 1 and 2 ESOL classes, and crèche facilities are available for young children. The parent-partnership leader encourages parents to attend all meetings, and there is now a very good turnout at parents' meetings because of her friendly approach. Coffee mornings for parents of SEN pupils are also well attended; they offer a supportive environment in which to share experiences.

When asked whether the school could do without the pupil premium funding, which has enabled support staff to develop the skills to address the social and emotional needs of the children and families, she responded:

'Come and live in our world – a term or a year! Children would not have a successful future because we all make a difference. … If you don't look at the whole family but just at the child, you are going to have a seriously dysfunctional society.'

Ofsted noted that one reason pupils eligible for PPF make good progress is that they receive effective support from the teaching assistants:

The school have highly trained teaching assistants and they provide good support to pupil premium, English as additional language and SEN pupils. They deliver small groups of lessons as well as one-to-one support in class to help pupils to understand what they are expected to do. Consequently, these pupils make good progress at similar rates to their classmates.

We agree with Ofsted. Teaching assistants provide valuable support to all groups who need an extra boost in the classroom and this helps all the pupils to make progress at a similar rate.

4.6 Effective governing bodies

Over the last twenty years, the role of governing bodies and the part they play in school improvement and in raising standards has been of ongoing interest. Governors are at the heart of how a school operates and they are responsible for making sure the school provides a good-quality education for all pupils. Their priority is raising standards in the school and promoting effective ways of teaching and learning when setting the school aims and policies. They do this together with the headteacher, who is responsible for the day-to-day management of the school. In addition, they support and challenge headteachers by gathering views, asking questions and discussing what is best for the school.

Research has shown that there is a clear association between effective schools and effective governing bodies and that considerable benefits are enjoyed by the school, and in particular the headteacher, that has an effective governing body.

At **School JE**, the chair of governors believes that the single most important aspect of the governing body's work in raising achievement is their focus on data. She is very skilled at interpreting data, and was concerned that it appeared that this was true only of her and the leadership team:

> 'I wanted a wider group of people on the governing body to have an understanding of data. Now there are five governors who have this. We have built capacity.'

At **School V**, the chair of governors spoke appreciatively about the close-knit community and how the cultural capital brought by members of the governing body could enhance the curriculum offer:

> 'Families know each other very well. We are like the United Nations here. ... At the same time we have been able to exploit where we are located – right next to the South Bank, where through governors' connections the school can take advantage of visits. ... Not many schools can perform at the Royal Festival Hall and the Young Vic.'

School V's governors have a good understanding of the school's context, strengths and areas for development. They work closely with the senior leadership team and contribute significantly to school improvement. This is confirmed by the Ofsted inspection of the school, which states:

> The governance of the school is effective. Governors recognise that significant improvements have been made but are not

complacent – they are well informed and ask the school leaders challenging questions about the school's performance.

The assistant headteacher of **School O** and Ofsted also acknowledge the strengths of its governing body:

> 'In the case of this school, the role of the governors has been crucial. Their vision of what they want for the school has been clear all along the journey. Their development planning has been clear, lucid, simple and everyone has bought into it. They make decisions and explain why – they are transparent.'

> The governance of the school is outstanding. Governors support and challenge the school very effectively. Governors are fully involved in reviewing students' performance and setting the school's priorities through discussion of the school's views about how well it is doing, and its plans for improvement. They have a thorough understanding of the school's strengths and are fully aware of what the school needs to do to improve even more.

In **School RE** the evidence from our interview suggests that governance is of the same high quality as other aspects of school leadership. Governors know how achievement compares with that of other schools, for example through the new national 'dashboard' (a report that provides at-a-glance views of key performance indicators for education). They receive comprehensive, accurate and detailed information from school leaders and seek to ensure that any emerging weaknesses are addressed quickly. They understand the quality of teaching, and teachers only move up the pay scale if targets are met. They have set a strategic overview about the spending of pupil premium funding and, as part of their monitoring of overall performance, assess its impact on those eligible. Spending has supported a range of provision, including small class sizes, student mentoring and financial assistance to make sure that those eligible are fully included in visits and school activities.

In **School F** the interview with the chair of governors suggests that the governing body has an insightful and exceptional understanding of all aspects of the school's considerable strengths. This is further confirmed by Ofsted, which states:

> Governors are highly skilled and committed to continue to improve the school and have a clear and visionary 'eye' set on the future. Governors carry out their statutory duties at the highest level and provide a fine-tuned balance of providing strategic guidance

and an appropriate blend of support and challenge. Governors express great respect for the leadership team and work cohesively to drive forward the vision to create a fully inclusive, all-through school. They have an excellent understanding of school data and regularly use this to make comparisons with others nationally, and to raise questions within the school. Governors are passionate about how well pupils learn and intrinsically link this with the quality of teaching.'

At **School G** our interview and observations suggest that all members of the governing body work closely with the senior leaders in their pursuit of excellence to bring about the highest levels of achievement and personal development for students by the time they leave the school. They know that the school is very successful in comparison with other schools locally and nationally, and hold leaders fully to account. They are well aware of the school's strengths, including the high quality of teaching, and of its areas that need development. A parent governor with a child in Year 4 confirmed that she felt well informed about the school's performance:

'I know the school is doing really well; we look at the children's work, go on a learning walk around the school, and there are high standards of behaviour. The heads of school come to governors' meetings and report on progress. We look at how well they are performing against other schools, any dips or areas to improve, addressing issues where a year group might not be doing so well. Most people on the governing body are parents of children in the school. The school does really well at communicating with parents.'

In this school the governors are appreciative of the staff. The same parent governor said:

'The staff are really dedicated. They care about the children and they get involved; although this is a very large school they make it feel small for you, you never feel overwhelmed. I have never found that my son feels lost in any way. I have lived in this area a long time.'

Similar evidence has been observed about school governance in other case study schools. We would argue that the governance in the case study schools is outstanding and that governors play key roles by giving the school a clear vision and strategic direction, holding the headteacher to account for the educational performance of the school and its pupils and overseeing the financial performance of the school. Governors are very knowledgeable about the quality of teaching in their school, and about its strengths and which areas are in need of development. They use data to identify underachieving groups in order to provide targeted interventions and support. They are keenly aware of what is being done to reward good and outstanding performance and to address any underperformance. They make regular visits to check directly on key areas within the school and to analyse the impact of additional funding on the achievement of disadvantaged pupils. Furthermore, governors in the case study schools manage the school's finances extremely well and ensure that spending is linked to students' learning. They are very knowledgeable about how additional funding is used to support disadvantaged students, and those who are disabled or have special educational needs.

The support given to governors has been recognized by schools and Ofsted alike. Over the years the LA has played a key role in improving governance, sometimes having to remove ineffective governing bodies or replace chairs of governors in schools that were causing concern.

The school governors surveyed expressed their appreciation for the support they received from the LA:

> 'As a governor I've been very aware of the LA's desire to support us through School Improvement Advisory services, training, etc. Also I appreciate the termly meetings and other getting together for chairs and governors, keeping us in touch and giving us the chance to network. Governors know that they are an important part of the education business.'

> 'In our school we have managed to recruit excellent governors who have been rigorous in demanding higher standards. There is a relentless focus on school improvement by the LA, which has been the stand-out element of successes.'

> (School governor, School O)

In recognition of the increasingly important role of governors in the leadership and management of schools, the LA has for years offered a central training programme, informed by the training link governors' group, about the statutory duties and responsibilities of the governing body and national and local issues and needs. The LA believes the effective use of school data contributes towards a school's capacity to improve.

4.7 Effective use of pupil voice and feedback

The case study schools have established a culture in which all students have the opportunity to play an active role in the decisions that affect their learning and well-being. Research has shown that children who participate in decision-making enjoy enhanced self-esteem and motivation, gain important personal, social and organizational skills, and become familiar with group and democratic processes. At the organizational level, pupil involvement in decision-making leads to better relationships, more relevant and effective policies and better learning. We interviewed all groups of pupils during the research to find out about their attitudes to and views of their school and education. As part of pupil voice we explored the following questions with them:

- Do you enjoy coming to school?
- What do you like about your school; and
- What has helped you to do well at school?

The great majority of students in all the schools enjoy coming to school. They like their teachers and appreciate their kindness, the exciting activities they take part in and how teachers are helping them with their work, as expressed in the following quotes. In case study schools it is clear from one pupil's comment below that children's views are listened to and taken on board.

We asked the students in the case study secondary schools 'What do you like about your school and what has helped you to do well at school?'

'This is an outstanding school.'
'This is a good school – the teachers care.'
'Teachers in this school teach well and help you.'
'Every one helps and it's easier to learn.'
'It is socially diverse and a welcoming school.'
'The relationship we have with teachers – they are open and loving to their students.'
'Teachers help us get better at school.'
'The teachers really understand and help you with any problems you have, either with yourself or your school work, or problems outside school.'
'Teachers are good.'
'There are many good, kind children in our school and very intelligent pupils.'
'Teachers help us achieve what we need to achieve.'

'The school is high-achieving and the progress we make from where we started is very impressive.'

'Good support is available for students in our school. They go all the way to support you.'

'Teachers give extra help. We have a lot of help and revision support.'

'We are encouraged to aim high and we are supported to achieve it.'

'We celebrate our achievement at the Achievement Awards Ceremony and assembly.'

'Our school is ambitious and helps us to achieve our dreams. We all want to achieve both academically and in social life.'

'This school prepares you for life in addition to academic success.'

'The school is good in accepting new ideas.'

'Our school allows us to be active and be a good leader.'

'This school is a great school.'

'There are a lot of curriculum activities that motivate you in this school.'

'They take us from our comfort zone.'

'They give us opportunities to broaden our experience and travel to other educational places and institutions to learn.'

'They help us to achieve beyond expectations.'

'Our school ethos is based on Christian values. Our motto is "With love and learning".'

'School is a multicultural school. It is the school that values every culture, heritage and religion.'

'The school is good in breaking cultural differences and outstanding in community cohesion. They bring everyone together.'

'They are strict and firm.'

'The teachers are very good.'

'We all enjoy learning here.'

'Teachers are very good at teaching and making lessons fun.'

'Our school is an excellent place to learn.'

We asked the secondary school students what they would like to study at university. The Black Caribbean pupils were aspirational about their higher study:

'I would like to go to Oxbridge to study mechanical engineering and physics.'

'I like Oxbridge and Russell Group. I would like to study astrophysics.'

'I would like to study law and would like to go to Exeter University which is the best in this field.'

'I want to study medicine at Oxford.'

'I want to study English at Cambridge University. English is my favourite subject.'

'I want to study Arabic and would like to study at SOAS.'

'I was planning to go to Oxbridge or Imperial College to do chemical engineering.'

We asked the primary pupils similar questions including 'What do you like best about the school?' These were some of their replies:

'I like the school because you get educated better.'

'I like the school because you get caring teachers. They help us and they are kind.' 'You can go to the teachers if you have a problem.'

'I like teachers in our school.'

'I like this school because children respect teachers.'

'I like the school because we learn different subjects' music, arts, maths, history, literacy, PE and science.'

'I like it because people communicate, they are well behaved, respect each other, respect teachers and do as they are told.'

'We have good music and I play the violin.'

'I enjoy coming to school because the school gave me a good opportunity to be a peer mediator.'

'I love the teachers, they give you really fine work, and I love maths.'

Our question 'What is special about your school?' elicited the following:

'Our school is special because we have someone to play with – we have friendship buddies.'

'They ask us how we feel about stuff because everyone in the school is different.'

'Our school is special because everyone is diverse. It is a multicultural school and we love it.'

'Our school is special because we respect the environment.'

'We have a team meeting.'

'Our school is special because they always encourage us with outstanding behaviour.'

'The school is welcoming.'

'We have a great opportunity.'

'You always learn new things.'

'This school is special. The school helped another school.'

'This school is special because we have a reading week.'

'We have a Black History month.'

'We have a golden book to reward children who achieve their targets. They get a postcard home to say that they have done well.'

'We have a lot of activities and after-school club: tennis, street dance, freedom academy and play games.'

'Teachers, staff, TA all support us and push us. They want best for us.'

'Teacher helps us to learn.'

'You always have someone to talk to.'

'Teachers respect you and you get lots of education.'

'People come up and invite you to play if you are a new person.'

'We have buddies if you are new. Someone shows you around the school and looks after you to make sure you have some friends.'

'If someone is new you speak to them and are kind to them and make friends with them.'

'We have a lot of talented, smart people.'

'If teachers see you are struggling, they do the lesson the next day so you can learn.'

'I am new here, I feel more at home here than my other school.'

'You get chance to speak about what you have done.'

'If you really need help you get it from adults.'

The children in the case study schools are clearly very happy with their school experience and find the school they attend happy and harmonious. They have an overwhelmingly positive attitude to learning and contribute to their own excellent progress. They feel valued and fairly treated. They rated the care, guidance and support the school gave them as good during the focus group discussion. Those we interviewed saw themselves going to college or university when they leave school. They were proud of the school and the staff, felt secure at school and were happy and enthusiastic. They are confident, articulate and accomplished learners. There is a buzz of learning in the school and pupils of all social backgrounds take a genuine delight in mastering new skills.

These schools conduct a lot of pupil voice survey and consultations, seeking the students' views through school council meetings with the

SMT, pupil questionnaires, parent questionnaires, target-setting days and consultations. These views are much valued and used to inform worthwhile change in the schools. Headteachers are keen for the children to have a greater say on how the school is seen and greater involvement in their learning:

> 'Every pupil is expected and encouraged to achieve their full potential by teachers. We use pupil voice to inform the school self-review and to provide an additional targeted support.'
>
> (Headteacher, School H)

> 'We want pupil voice to be credible to the children. Pupils do feel they have an input into policies, etc.'
>
> (Deputy headteacher, School RE)

> 'We need to know what we can do better for them. We also need to know what they want from us.'
>
> (Teacher, School RE)

4.8 Summary and conclusions

The case study schools' data shows that, from their generally low starting points, these pupils reach exceptionally high levels of attainment. All the schools achieved remarkable results for all their pupils, far exceeding national average benchmarks at the end of Key Stage 2 and GCSE. From the evidence over the last twenty years we have identified the following characteristics and success factors of these schools.

The one essential feature that is shared by the most successful primary and secondary schools is the outstanding leadership of the headteachers, who focus on equality and excellence, and of the senior management teams. Each is supported by a committed team of teachers. Leaders are described as 'inspirational' and 'visionary'. Each has a strong moral drive for pupils to succeed whatever their background. Their colleagues' descriptions, such as 'brave', 'pioneering' and 'courageous', sum up the qualities of leadership. All are focused on developing the highest possible achievement of their pupils. Each of these schools has a culture of high expectations, strong collaboration with colleagues and close links with families and the community. The picture that has emerged is of schools that, while focused on their pupils and communities, are alert to the need to appoint high-quality staff and add to their repertoire of skills to sustain their interest, motivation and effectiveness. The depth and extent of teamwork, openness in sharing practice, and interest in providing new and exciting stimuli for children's learning all contribute to making these schools real learning communities. There is an exceptional sense of teamwork across each school that is reflected in the consistent and committed way managers at all levels work towards the schools' aims of raising achievement.

The high achievement is also due to outstanding teaching. The staff hold high expectations of what pupils can achieve. They deliver stimulating and enthusiastic teaching that interests, excites and motivates pupils and accelerates their learning, and well-planned lessons that meet the differing needs of pupils. Teaching assistants are well trained and highly skilled. Effective marking and assessment ensure that all pupils' learning is closely checked. Rigour and consistency characterize the schools. The inexperienced teachers are paired with outstanding teachers or work with parallel year groups of colleagues across a federation to plan optimally effective lessons. Collaborative planning, supervising and marking pupils' work offers support and challenge to the teachers too. Pupils are motivated in lessons because tasks and explanations are matched to their needs. Teachers capture the pupils' enthusiasm and make them want to succeed by showing how much they enjoy teaching them.

Evidence also indicates the excellent ways in which the governing bodies support the headteachers and senior leadership teams and hold them to account. They monitor the impact of the school's work in raising achievement and rigorously scrutinize the data on the school's performance, its intervention strategies and their impact on the performance of particular groups of children.

The study shows that amassing and applying such forensic data is fundamental to school improvement. It is a strength of this LA's schools. All use detailed, relevant and constantly updated assessment procedures and feed the findings back to the staff. Every school monitored each pupil's progress all through their school life, and connected the test and assessment data with the data on the child's ethnic background, language spoken, level of fluency in English, date of admission, attendance rate, eligibility for free school meals, EAL stage of fluency, SEN stage, mobility rate, years in school, which teachers' classes they attended, attendance rate and types of support. This data was used to set challenging targets. Early intervention and a wide range of support mechanisms – booster groups, one to one, tailoring teaching levels, mentoring – helped the pupils to achieve. Systems for monitoring the work of the pupils identify those who need additional help or extra challenge and give them appropriate additional support.

It is also evident from the research that the schools listen to their pupils' voices and respond to their feedback. In this culture the pupils can play an active role in decisions that affect their learning and well-being. Those we spoke to had specific roles on the school council or as prefects. They were unanimous in their love for their school, describing how they enjoy their lessons, playtimes and after-school activities and how they get on with each other and with the adults in the school: 'Teachers, staff, TAs, all support us and push us. They want what's best for us.' There is also strong evidence that schools are using the pupil voice and feedback for targeted support to secure improvement.

Significantly, these schools are all effective at targeting intervention and support, and all use outstanding teachers to teach English and maths and provide tailored support for individuals in the classroom, one-to-one support and booster classes delivered by the class teacher. Small groups are put in the hands of expert teachers who can focus on overcoming the gaps in their learning. Enrichment activities and funded school trips enhance the children's experiences and support their learning. The funding available from PPF is targeted on disadvantaged pupils, and this has made a dramatically large contribution to closing the achievement gap.

Notes

[1] Number Masters is a unique programme created by mathematics teachers in the case study schools, aimed at the development of number mastery and computational fluency at KS1.

[2] Springboard is additional, catch-up tuition for Year 7 pupils who achieved level 3 rather than level 4 in mathematics at the end of KS2.

[3] Mathletics is an online learning tool to improve mathematical literacy.

Chapter 5

Raising the achievement of ethnic-minority pupils

5.1 Introduction

This chapter explores the success factors behind raising the achievement of ethnic-minority pupils in schools, particularly those of Black Caribbean and Black African heritage. It presents some of the major findings reported in local publications over the last 25 years (see Demie 2005, 2017a, 2017b; Demie and McLean, 2015a, 2015b, 2016, 2017a, 2017b). Since about 1990 considerable attention has been devoted to the underachievement of Black pupils in British schools. There is now much research to show that Black Caribbean pupils are underachieving within the education system, and that they are less likely than children of other backgrounds to achieve their full potential at school (Gillborn and Gipps, 1996; Gillborn and Mirza, 2000; Demie, 2001; Ofsted, 2002a, 2002b).

The relative underachievement of Black pupils has been a concern in national education policy formulation. A government-funded inquiry committee reported on the issue twice during the 1980s: first in the Rampton Report (Rampton, 1981), which dealt specifically with the underachievement of pupils of Caribbean background. It concluded that 'West Indian children as a group are underachieving in our education system' (Rampton, 1981: 10) and identified serious concerns about whether schools were meeting the needs of Black Caribbean pupils. The concerns still persist. The final report, *Education for All* (Swann, 1985), also concluded:

> There is no doubt that West Indian children, as a group, and on average, are underachieving; both by comparison with their school fellows in the White majority, as well as in terms of their potential, notwithstanding that some are doing well.
>
> (Swann, 1985: 81)

Other research in the 1990s and 2000s reflected earlier findings that Black Caribbean-and African-heritage pupils made less progress on average than other groups of pupils (Gillborn and Gipps, 1996; Gillborn and Mirza, 2000; Demie, 2001, 2003, 2005; Education Commission, 2004).

Empirical evidence suggests that among those ending their compulsory education in the UK, Black Caribbean and Pakistani pupils were, along with Traveller pupils, least academically successful: only 47% of Black Caribbean and 51% of Pakistani pupils achieved 5 or more GCSEs at grade A* to C including English and maths. In contrast, around 75% of Chinese, 73% of Indian, 61% of Bangladeshi, 57% of Black African and 56% of White British pupils achieved 5 or more A* to C grades at GCSE (DfE, 2017c, 2017d). All the main ethnic groups achieved better than Black Caribbean pupils.

Most previous studies have focused on the reasons why Black or ethnic-minority children are underachieving. However, in recent years my research projects have looked at schools that do provide an environment where ethnic minorities such as Black Caribbean, Black African, Somali and Portuguese pupils flourish (for details see Demie, 2005, 2017a, 2017b; Demie and McLean, 2015a, 2017b, 2016, 2017a, 2017b; Demie and Lewis, 2010a, 2010b, 2010c, 2010d, 2010e; Demie and Lewis, 2015; and the present book). We identified key characteristics of successful schools that raised achievement, namely strong leadership, high expectations, effective teaching and learning, parental involvement, an ethos of respect and a clear stand on racism. This chapter asks, therefore, 'What are the reasons for such success in the case study schools?' In interviews headteachers and teachers were asked, 'What strategies does your school use to raise the achievement of ethnic-minority pupils, including EAL pupils?' The success factors in raising achievement and narrowing the gap for minority ethnic groups, including partnership with parents, an inclusive curriculum, diversity in the school workforce, valuing and celebrating cultural diversity, a clear stand on racism and effective support for pupils, are discussed below.

5.2 Partnership with parents: The overall picture

The schools encouraged and valued the active involvement of parents in their children's education, and communication between school and parents is a major strength. Schools sought imaginative ways to break down barriers, make parents welcome, and respond to parents' needs. The staff shared information with parents on achievement and development and on disciplinary issues, and established a high level of trust. The schools saw themselves as part of a community. Parents were overwhelmingly supportive of the school and appreciated what it did to provide an environment for learning. They applauded the schools' efforts to guide their children and give them a firm grounding, both academically and socially. They felt that each child was valued on their own terms and encouraged to achieve their very best. One headteacher said, 'No child is held in higher regard with comparisons made one to another. Each child is recognized as an individual. The key is confidence.' Another commented, 'The school offers a nurturing, caring environment. Children are not singled out as better but yet are told they can achieve no matter what the level.'

Parents appreciated the work of all the staff in the school. They recognized the value of the focused small groups that children across the ability range have access to. One parent observed, 'In the case of my child she needed special needs support which she got. The special needs staff really supported her. They built up her confidence. They helped her to enjoy learning. They made it fun.' Another commented, 'The staff know the children and don't allow them to slip. The reports we get on our children are very detailed. They really know our children. Those who had worked as volunteers in the school felt that each class was a small community: 'I really enjoy going out with classes on trips and to see their spirit of camaraderie. It was lovely to hear them singing.'

Headteachers in these schools meet regularly with parents, whom they regard as key partners in the endeavour. One headteacher said:

'Clearly stated, I want the parents of all pupils to feel we value and care for their children. I try to explain that explicitly when I meet parents every Monday morning. I tell them, in looking for a school, go by their gut feeling of what it stands for, and then look at the Ofsted report and then the results. When pupils have been allocated a place I meet children and parents to discuss mutual responsibilities. I try to make it clear that the school stands for fairness and high expectation for all.'

Another headteacher said:

'Every step of the way parents need to do their bit and the school tries to reinforce that. We work on the assumption that all parents want their children to do well. We try to develop strategies to sustain that. One of the practical implications of that approach is the timing of the assembly. This is held every morning at the start of the day. This gives parents who are at work a chance to drop in on their way to work and for special assemblies, and perhaps the opportunity to negotiate a later arrival. ... We try to emphasize the need for flexibility in the way support is offered. Sometimes it makes more sense for a child to read to their parents in the morning before school rather than at night when everyone is frazzled. If an older cousin or sibling is collecting a relative from school we try to involve them in helping their relative in the reading process by hearing the spelling of high-frequency words. We try to be proactive and pick up the slack.'

The classroom teachers also recognized the importance of a positive dialogue with parents to help raise the achievement of Black and other ethnic-minority pupils. A classroom teacher in a case study school said in interview:

'The parents knew the schools were worried when pupils were underachieving but they emphasized that something could and would be done. We tried to be consistent and did as we said we would do. Individual logs of pupils' work and behaviour detailing the good and the disappointing were kept and shown to parents by pupils. I really thought hard about the comments I made, as a stray negative comment could be destructive. Particularly good pieces of work were also copied so the children could take them home and keep them at home. Regular contact on the phone proved to be much better than sending notes. We could have just dwelt in our calls on the negative but decided instead always to try discussing positive developments.'

Parental support was hard won, however, when the school announced its plan to set up specific sessions for groups of five pupils to work with an external mentor. The headteacher reported:

'Although parents individually realized their children were having problems the notion of a strategy that involved external intervention with a group raised some concerns. We had a meeting of the parents to discuss the proposal and after a lot of discussion parents agreed to let the sessions proceed. In the event the group performed better in national tests than had been predicted and made a smoother transfer to secondary schools than had at one time been anticipated. Parents understood the bonus of having someone who could help their children in communicating on transfer with adults the children didn't know. The mentoring offered to the pupils helped them prepare and then cope with the transition to secondary schools. We believe what we did made a difference. The support did not stop there. After the transfer to secondary schools contact with the pupils was formally maintained for their first term. The learning mentor made regular visits and spoke with year staff and the pupils concerned. All the pupils are reported to have welcomed such continuing contact in the early stages of their transfer.'

These successful schools take the time to listen to parents and understand their aspirations for their children. They recognize that parents care deeply about their children's education and want to know about their progress, the curriculum and homework. They want information about what they can do to help. One school's positive response is summarized by its headteacher:

> 'We think listening to all parents is very important. It is a myth to say Black parents are not supportive. We try to understand their aspirations. Families want it to be straightforwardly put. I believe we should take people from where they are and realize they have high aspirations. It might not always be expressed in the same way as other groups of parents but it is there. I have learnt constant dialogue, particularly by phone, is important. You can get a bit distanced with paper.'

The schools listened to and learned from pupils and their parents, and tried to see things from the students' point of view. The schools regarded liaison with parents and the community as vital to its drive to raise standards.

Goodall *et al.* (2011) found that parenting styles improve as a consequence of receiving support and training, and that parents gain knowledge, skills, confidence and empathy. They found the most effective interventions to be those focusing on both academic outcomes and parenting skills rather than on either aspect alone, and discovered that the impact of parental engagement programmes on children's literacy greatly exceeded that for any other curriculum area.

This is certainly the case at **School V**, which incorporates the Children's Centre and offers a range of services that support families through childcare, adult learning, parenting programmes, and helping to bring a range of service providers into the community. The school makes extraordinary efforts to enable parents to support their children's learning. This is especially important as most of the parents are unfamiliar with the British education system. The school understands that simply passing information to parents without enabling them to understand what it means in practice is unhelpful. School V has overcome this by inviting parents to come into the school and to see first-hand how a phonics lesson is taught to groups of children in Years 1 and 2. They can see the materials used and can ask questions. Many ask to buy the resources they see being used in the lesson so they can use them at home. Similar demonstration lessons in mathematics are offered to parents. The Key Stage 1 co-ordinator told us, 'It is very powerful for parents to see a lesson. Staff keep encouraging parents to come to the workshops; we keep reminding them to come.'

School F takes a whole-school approach to engaging parents and adopts an outward-facing strategy that makes use of information and expertise from others. The EYFS/KS1 phase leader explained the lengths the school goes to to make sure that every parent is engaged:

> 'Having a Schools Direct student has enabled me to be more available to meet with parents. In the case of one PPG pupil, who only sees her Dad at weekends and he can't come to the school, I email him, to make sure all the family are engaged. ... Last year, the first year, we did everything we could to get parents into school. We do have EAL children, but not beginners in English. They are less confident but they get by and are picking up.'

The EYFS/KS1 leader is focusing on 'narrowing the gap' and is putting into practice some of the effective interventions identified through research.

> 'An after-school reading club has been started and children have targets for home reading. This is building confidence and a love of reading, in boys especially, and has increased their motivation. In the spring term we ran an outdoor maths explorers club, targeting PPG children. There is speech and language support from a SALT [speech and language therapist] and ChatterBugs groups for children who had low scores on the language-screening check.[1] The group helps build confidence and models good speaking and listening for children. Year 1 phonics screening check suggests that there will be a 5 per cent gap between PP children and non-PP children, so phonics interventions are taking place in the summer term. We are targeting parents to engage them in phonics, reading, developing growth mind-sets, maths and computing workshops. We have also implemented FRED [Fathers Reading Every Day]. We offer them tea and coffee and encourage them as much as possible. We have put in a lot of effort to engage parents; we are being proactive in ringing them, encouraging their attendance at meetings. We have also started a parent volunteer reading group.'

Family Digital Stories, an inspirational six-week project run by the City Learning Centre, has been offered to targeted families. The aims of the project are to increase certain parents' engagement, boost children's confidence and support parent skills. Twelve parents attended each week and feedback was very positive; a parent of a child in reception class said, 'Getting to know other parents at school was great. Doing something together with my child makes her feel important.'

At **School JE** parents and carers are pleased with how well the headteacher and staff know their children. This mirrors the teachers' view that knowing each child and building firm foundations for the relationship with home is key to the school's success. The pupils feel secure and valued, and so grow academically and socially in a warm family atmosphere, in which each is known for their individual characteristics. This generates great confidence in the pupils when they face new experiences, and enables the school to rapidly pinpoint resources and actions to meet their needs. A 'parents' forum' has long been established to facilitate listening and responding to the parents' views. It meets every half-term as a platform for parents to suggest improvements at the school, and staff take their views seriously.

A parent governor (who now has a grandchild at the school) recalled when the school was not doing well: 'Parents had stopped believing in the place; it was not a school of choice. When the new management took over a lot of teachers left', and went on to describe the challenge the new leadership faced and how the new headteacher began to transform the school:

> 'When the headteacher took over she dealt with the nitty-gritty. When she started you could see she had a vision for where she wanted the school to go. Then because she worked so hard the teachers started to work hard – she brought in the idea of teachers learning from other teachers, she brought in reward systems which made the children aspire. She did so much. Getting the parents involved no matter how much they moaned. She came back to the next meeting and told them how she had dealt with things they had concerns about. Bit by bit it started to turn around.'

Ofsted inspectors affirmed the successful partnership that the school had developed with parents:

> Engagement with parents and carers is very effective. Almost all who responded to the questionnaire say that the school helps them to support their children's learning. They attend music and mathematics workshops, parents' forums and consultation days. Parents and carers also effectively contribute to the curriculum

provision. For example, they attend lessons on 'people who help us' to describe the jobs they do.

At **School G** parental engagement with the school is outstanding, but these positive relationships did not happen overnight. As with **School JE**, it took perseverance and a genuine commitment to listen to parental concerns and commitment to address them.

School G once had a poor reputation in the community and parents were hostile and occasionally violent towards the staff. In 2002 Ofsted judged relationships with parents to be 'poor'. The newly appointed headteacher (executive headteacher, as he is now) put in place effective strategies to improve attendance and punctuality and to involve parents and the community in the process. He and his deputy would walk around the local streets before school started, encouraging parents and children to get into school before the morning bell rang. They also targeted local shops, enlisting the support of shopkeepers by asking them not to serve children if they were late for school. To encourage parents into the school and make them feel welcome, he provided a designated 'parents' room' with comfortable chairs. Parents were invited in for coffee mornings to meet the headteacher and hear what his plans were for the children. He encouraged them to come along to school assemblies and concerts. The parents' confidence increased and the school's reputation began to improve. It took genuine commitment and perseverance by the school leadership to make it happen. The headteacher reflected:

> 'We don't believe it is hard to reach parents in this school. How we engage with parents underpins pupil achievement. The way that we value people is part of our ethos, our hidden curriculum. I have to model these messages as a school leader, respecting each other, judging individuals as individuals. I have made a deliberate and conscious effort to form a relationship with these parents. I use humour, and relate to people as people. I am not frightened to talk about issues, none of my staff hide behind people; it's important to get everything out on the table. I am out there in the playground in the morning and evening. A testament to our parental engagement is the fact that parental attendance has gone up to 93 per cent from 19 per cent. We do make it a pleasurable experience for parents; we provide refreshments, music and a crèche. We are flexible; if people don't come, the class TA will contact the parents to arrange another time. If that doesn't work

the office will ring. As a last resort I will write a letter. We do all we can to get the parents in.'

Numeracy and literacy workshops are run with targeted groups of pupils in school to make games that they take home to play with their parents.

The school is very good at engaging with parents. Curriculum evenings are held annually for all year groups, with the parents, not the children. There are also parent–teacher consultation meetings, and academic tutoring days. The headteacher said:

> 'We talk to parents about feeding their children properly, regular sleeping habits, tips to support them with homework. We explore the target system with mid-term monitoring. We talk to them, like we do the girls, about aspirations, the job market.'

School E is also adept at engaging parents. One of the success factors of the school is good links with the community it serves and its good practice in developing partnerships with parents. Researchers held a focus-group discussion with the parents, who originally came from Poland and Somalia. The Polish parent we interviewed felt her children's education was of great importance; she was ambitious for her sons and daughters:

> 'Education is very important for us. I have completed university and my husband also finished university. We both finished university in Poland. We are a bilingual family and we work hard. ... I did not speak English when I came to England. The school supported me in my English-language development and socially. This is a very friendly and supportive school. ... The school employed a Polish teaching assistant and she helped Polish children and families in translation and to settle in the area. It was great to have someone who speaks Polish.'

The Somali parent we interviewed was also positive about the school, and spoke warmly of the help given to Somali children and parents:

> 'Somali parents value education highly and they have a high expectation of their children and teachers and the school meets their needs. ... All children are very proud of their origins in this school.'

The school places a high value on children's culture and home language, and the pupils benefit from its active partnership with their parents and its support of their families.

Although parents' involvement in **School RE** is strong, many parents were educated abroad and so don't know much about the British system; the school has to work hard to keep them informed. It regularly surveys parents to find out their preferred means of communication and is constantly looking to improve matters.

> 'The "Friday News" [a weekly newsletter] breaks down walls between home and school. We tell parents about school and local events. We consult with parents about, for example, the behaviour policy. We put things on the website for parents. We also survey parents regularly and have 95 per cent feedback sometimes – there's a very strong sense of parental involvement. The Catholic school ethos helps too: it's a special kind of cohesion where our faith binds us together. We invite parents in a lot. For instance, when they are new to the school, we have a Year 7 Mass for parents to bring them into our community. ... We have the support of the parents. They want their kids to do well. They appreciate that we are spending the extra time with them.'

The school does communicate successfully with parents about ways in which they can support their children. Consequently, the students told us, their parents were interested and fully involved in their learning at home.

The curriculum reflects the diverse backgrounds of the students, and the parents contribute meaningfully by attending, and taking part in, the many religious and cultural celebrations. An Ofsted inspection quoted a parent:

> 'Choosing School RE is one of the best decisions we have made as parents. We have never regretted it for a moment.' This comment reflects the high level of parental support that exists for this popular and oversubscribed school. Harmonious relationships, excellent behaviour and a strong desire to learn are features that make this an outstanding school where girls feel very happy and safe. They enjoy school because they know they are taught well and are supported to do their best.

School O is rightly proud of its positive relationships with parents and carers. The school is committed to working closely with families so that their children can succeed in school.

> 'Parents are brought into the school with the aim of making the school the heart of the community. The purpose of their continuing

education is threefold; to raise their aspirations, to support them
to support their children and to bring the community together.'

(Community education co-ordinator)

School O works together with the Community Resource Centre and Morley
College, offering courses in English for speakers of other languages (ESOL),
information and communications technology (ICT), advanced ICT, digital
photography and mathematics. The new school building provides an
impressive venue for this Saturday programme. Through the business and
enterprise specialism, the school is to launch a community project available
to 60 participants. It will bring together a range of ethnicities, including
Portuguese and Somali. Together they will decide on their focus, and learn
how to get funding and about working together. The school facilitates
people getting into work as best it can. Parents and members of the local
community who aspire to work in a school have the opportunity to come in
for 12 weeks to shadow teachers, and receive help with their CVs.

> 'We support parents and learning mentors to study for foundation
> degrees. We also have an international link with a school in Sierra
> Leone, we run a World Family Day, have Aids Awareness and
> Rights and Responsibilities.'

(Community education co-ordinator)

The school encourages and values the active involvement of parents in their
children's education and communication is a major strength. It has created
imaginative ways to break down barriers and make parents welcome, and
responds to their needs. It shares with parents information on their children's
achievement and development as well as issues of discipline. The school's
staff see themselves as part of a community. Parents are overwhelmingly
supportive and know what the school does to provide an environment for
learning. They appreciate the school's efforts to guide their children and
give them both academic and social grounding. Parents feel that each child is
valued on their own terms, and although children might perceive differences
in standards the school encourages them to do the best for themselves.
Ofsted noted: 'One parent wrote that, "I am extremely grateful for all the
encouragement, care and support my daughter gets." Care, guidance and
support are outstanding.'

Parents and carers are encouraged to be actively involved in their
children's education, especially their homework. The school exemplifies
its commitment by giving parents progress reports and discussions with
teachers at academic consultative evenings. Families are invited to share in

those glorious moments when their children are singing, acting, playing an instrument or receiving an award. These events celebrate the pupils' talents.

The school's Christian ethos has greatly contributed to links with the community it serves. The school chaplain observed: 'The school is like a family for parents and children. We are part of the community and the school has a leadership very committed to community cohesion and inclusion.'

5.2.1 Partnership with Black African parents

Black African parents value education highly. Some have themselves received a good education and gained professional qualifications, although their jobs in the UK may not fully reflect this. The schools recognize that parents, even if they have low-status jobs, can build and support a culture of achievement at home to support their children's education. Many parents are themselves continuing their studies. One said: 'My child's father is Nigerian and he is very focused on learning. He never says "I haven't got anything to do", he is always improving his skill set. This definitely is an African thing; it is like that in Jamaica too.'

All the parents see a good education as the key to their children's future success:

> 'Africans invest in education because we need it. Back home we do not have the opportunity that these children have. Education makes a way for you.'

> 'My background was such that I wasn't able to go to school due to lack of money. When I sit down with my kids I tell them I do not want them to have the life I have had. Children now have choices – education is the key.'

> 'Without an education you cannot earn a decent salary, without qualifications you cannot get a good job. The best thing is to push your children as hard as you can.'

> 'Being a Black woman, if you don't have education in this country, what job will you have to do? Clean people's toilets?'

> 'I have taught my children to get an education and you have choice. As a social worker I see children having choice in this society.'

> 'Knowledge is a lifetime investment. Money comes and goes but knowledge lasts for ever.'

> 'Behind many of the Black African students' achievement you will find some of the most dedicated parents supporting their children to ensure their children are high achievers. It is not always the school you go to, it's how strong the parental support network is behind you.'

These attitudes are the driving force behind the parents' support of their children and schools And the teachers welcome the shared values and aspirations. A teacher at School RE said:

> 'I like to teach here because I know I have the support of African parents. If I advise them what to do they will do it, whereas other parents might not. African parents may sometimes be poor, but their standards are higher ... standards regarding their aims for their children. They expect and want their children to achieve and they will do whatever they can to help them and make sure it happens. It is not so important to other groups. Because we promote this, and they already have this sense of the importance of education, we can work together. We know we have their backing so there are no behaviour issues to be resolved.'

Parents also have strong views on the importance of mutual respect and respect for authority. One parent told us that in Africa 'the teacher is an authority figure in the classroom. There is a good tradition where the start of a lesson is marked by students standing up to greet the teacher. Pupils should respect the authority of the teacher.' When asked what parents expect their children to do at school, one parent replied: 'Hard work, respect, discipline, listening to the teacher, working together. What you feed them at home is what they bring to school ... this is reinforced at school.' In short they support the authority of teachers. A teacher with twenty years' experience comments: 'parents show respect for teachers – they defer to professionalism ... they want to know what they can do to help and this plays a big part in children's success ... it is backed by action.'

One of the most frequent ways in which parents support teachers and their children is by ensuring that they do their homework. At primary age, parents often help children with their homework. One said, 'I will meet teachers at the end of the day. I want my child to get ahead and I ask for ideas about homework, especially in the holidays. I read to them even while we are away on holiday.'

At secondary level, parents check homework diaries and follow up on comments made by teachers, ensuring that work is completed.

The parent attendance rate is generally very high because parents value the opportunity to discuss their child's progress with teachers. In secondary schools, teachers share performance data with parents and include them in discussions about target setting. Thus parents feel well informed about the progress of their children and children feel that parents know of their success. A Year 9 pupil at a school where tutors and teachers regularly telephone parents said, 'When I do well they tell my parents. This reflects on me at home.'

And a Year 13 student at the same school connected the parents' and teachers' efforts: 'Parents give strong motivation from day one .... Our head of year really pushes us – he's really behind a lot of students' success.'

All the case study schools have strong links with their students' parents and communities. Each school's headteacher and senior management team have devoted substantial resources, time and commitment to this end. These schools see parents' engagement as central to the school and consequently receive good support from the parents. Staff, in turn, support the parents. Partnership with parents is a key component of a school's success. Staff involve parents early in any lapses in behaviour and the parents appreciate the school's commitment to keeping them informed. Two Black African parents confirmed this.

Parent A is the father of a girl in Year 9. He is generally supportive of the school, although it was not his first choice, but is supplementing his daughter's education with a home tutor. He also calls on his extended family. His eldest son is a graduate and is expected to help. The family take regular trips home to Nigeria to maintain traditions, and remind their children that they have an obligation to fulfil their potential.

Parent B is the father of three daughters, two of whom have already left the school. The third is in Year 10. He is very pleased with the dialogue between family and school. He believes the school shares his expectations of his daughter and is respectful of his Sierra Leonean culture. Respect and responsibility are the cornerstones of the parenting philosophy he conveys to his daughters. However, he is of the view that sanctions should be applied if his daughters 'step out of order'; then it is a case of 'tough love'.

Both these fathers feel that key features that contribute to African achievement are maintaining African traditions at home, letting children know they have an obligation to maximize the opportunities available in the school, and seeking to 'blend with the best of British society'. They consciously protect their daughters from – as they perceive them – the worst, more permissive, anti-education elements. They argue that early intervention is essential to get students back on track. Interestingly, both these men are keen to continue their own studies as well, which models family commitment to education as a transformational tool.

Many schools in this country pay lip service to notions of school–parent partnership, but it is a lived reality in this authority's schools and is demonstrable in the engagement of Black African students and their parents in co-constructing an achievement culture. It is not just the school doing all the work: Black African parents form a critical mass in the school and their commitment to education and their children's achievement is equally significant. Many students have parents who went to university, either here or in Africa. High achievement is part of the tradition of their families, and even when this is not so the parents still desire to continue their education.

The headteacher of **School H** is an active churchgoing parent herself and makes common cause with other Black parents trying to enable their children to achieve their potential. This sense of kinship is much appreciated by Black African parents. Schools know their parents well; leadership has encouraged and promoted the involvement of these parents, who are passionate about church-school education. Most of the students have two parents at home, and both parents, but especially the fathers, attend parents' evenings. Aspirations are clearly set in advance of joining the school, and their first statement is often their hope that their child can go to university.

Schools engage parents in key strategies to raise achievement. For example, one school used external consultants to teach study skills to Years 7 and 8 during the school day, and offered it as a masterclass for parents after school too. The strong faith background of families is recognized and supported, and schools conform to African notions of a church school with its formality and sense of pride. The formality of school processes reflects notions of respect and courtesy towards teachers and between students: it includes smart uniforms, lining up before entry to lessons, formal introductions, and prayers before each lesson starts. This school's ethos, its niche market, is clearly communicated and endorsed by Black African parents.

Parents' evenings at the beginning of the academic year encourage students and parents to review and evaluate the year that has passed and renew their commitment to targets for the coming year, echoing the symbolic ritual of renewal. Lots of social evenings are held at which parents and staff can interact. When the parent–school relationship does not work, it tends to be because the parent has not responded to the invitation to be part of the community and is too distant from key processes and interventions. But recovery is always available. When the school does well, the headteacher writes to parents praising them for their contribution.

One mother, a recently arrived refugee, has drawn on the school for support. She feels that support is there not just for her child but for her too, and that the school has encouraged her daughter to exceed her expectations. This engenders powerful feelings of support and gratitude towards the school. She feels the school provides opportunities and activities that 'I cannot afford to do at home', through field trips, social events and activity visits, most of which are educational. She likes the balance between social and academic and describes the school as 'helping her daughter to make up her mind to become a doctor' through its involvement in the 'Access to Medicine' programme. As a result her daughter knows she wants to be a paediatrician, but she has also taken part in drama activities sponsored by the Shell company, which is based in the authority.

For parents who have not achieved their own educational goals, the school's shared aspirations are important:

> 'To be a person in life, her education must be better than I was able to achieve. I want my daughter to achieve so many things in life so that they are a credit to you back home. I do not want to be ashamed in the future.'

A parent who came to the UK as a refugee said:

> 'I hope she becomes someone in life. She has decided to become a doctor and I was not confident since English is her third language. Miss B (a teacher) says she has made up her mind and sees that she can do it. The teachers have talked me through it and so I now believe she can do it.'

School A's success has not come without a struggle, as one teacher acknowledges: 'The school is fighting the anti-education cultures of the "street" and the "estate", which is a strong pull even for Black African students with strong backgrounds' (School A). His aspiration is to make 'educational achievement' more powerful and credible, which is no easy task. But his school is making significant inroads. Such possibilities and opportunities are reinforced in the displays on corridors and in classrooms.

The case study schools make constant efforts to maintain good motivation and have good holistic and pastoral systems to support students and their families. The parent–school partnership is of great importance in establishing and maintaining high standards for Black African students. What makes this authority partnership so strong in counteracting 'street culture' is that parents, teachers and students share the same aspirations and the same values.

5.2.2 Partnership with Black Caribbean parents

Black Caribbean parents face numerous barriers to engagement, including costs, time and transport. Some of them have low levels of literacy and numeracy, and lack confidence in supporting their children's learning or engaging with the school. But these schools place a premium on knowing all the students as individuals. If you ask students why their schools are so good, they will commonly reply 'because teachers really care'.

Some pupils find it difficult to study at home, and their parents are not in a position to support them, so these schools invest additional time in teaching and learning. Staff are generous with their time, typically running sessions at lunchtime, after school, during weekends and in their holidays. A headteacher said, 'It's a relentless struggle.' These students receive a good deal of individual help and attention. This reinforces the positive relationships that exist between students and staff, because students see that teachers 'really care'.

The staff of the LA's schools were aware that they had to draw parents in for positive reasons, and recognize that many had had negative experiences at school themselves. We asked what the key factor was in the successful and positive relationships that exist between staff and parents at **School V**. A teacher replied:

> 'I think it is down to the personal touch. Parents are invited – there is a partnership ethos. It's very warm. I know some of the parents by their first names. I care about their offspring as if they were my own and then they feel it. Building trust is important; parents appreciate someone who understands children.'

The deputy headteacher said:

> 'Our relationships with parents are definitely key. If you have built good relationships you are halfway there with the young people. If parents are on board with a plan of action, you will have success. We have got a lot of young parents in our school. A majority would say that they can relate better to Black staff. Some parents think, "You don't know me because you don't know what I've been through, so you don't get me". A lot of parents take on what their parents went through. It pours down through generations. ... A student said, "Don't you think it's true that more Black kids in our school get sent to 'Ready to Learn'?[2] I had to remind him that there are more Black kids in our school. I think he was just saying what his mum or maybe his

gran said and he's just seeing that. I had to point out particular White pupils who are sent. A lot of Black Caribbean pupils do see White authority figures as a problem – it's a cross between fear and anger at the injustice.'

Schools that want to raise the achievement of Black Caribbean pupils will go the extra mile to establish a trusting relationship with the parents. This relationship needs to be based on knowledge and understanding of a parent who might well have encountered racial discrimination and teachers who had low aspirations for them.

A group of parents from **School C** reflected on the excellent links the school has made with parents and the local community over the years:

'My grandma and grandad came here in the 1950s from Jamaica. My daughter struggled with reading but she gets more attention with phonics and she gets taken out to focus in a small group).'

'As the parent of a child with ADHD and anger problems, the school supports him by getting someone in every other week. I find it helpful getting him one-to-one. I went to my GP for help. My son came to this school in Year 1. He used to go to another local school. I attend the church so I said "Let me move him here because I am familiar with the staff here".'

A parent governor said:

'The school has a "diversity month" where pupils look at their family trees. There is also Black History Month. In Year 5 someone came in to do drama about Caribbean history and there were visits from the Black Cultural Archives. Parents come in to talk to the children about their own heroes during Black History Month. In Year 3 the children got to dress up as their heroes. There are African arts and cultural displays everywhere in the school.'

The executive headteacher at **School C** described the schools' work with parents in supporting the achievement of pupils:

'There is a lot of engagement with parents. We do home visits: the inclusion manager and teacher, or teacher and TA, would meet with the family. We try to get children into reception within the first two weeks of the autumn term. The first week is home visits and the second week they enter on a staggered basis. When they leave reception and go into Year 1 there is a similar process. The EY lead manages the transition period from YR to Year 1. We have lots of workshops for parents, showing what we can do and how they can support. We have targeted projects for hard-to-reach parents, ringing, seeing them in the playground by being very friendly. It has been invaluable to have interventions where the adults work alongside the child and parent together. The EY lead runs coffee mornings, speech and language sessions, or "how to help your child with homework".

We have a behavioural support consultant who sees any parent experiencing difficulty with trauma or a child going through a wobbly patch. The progress is between those parties, we do not intervene, and she feeds back to us though.

Most of our pupil premium funding goes on additional adults of some form or another. A small part of it we use for visits for children who wouldn't otherwise be able to go, to build social and cultural capital. It is easier to build these relationships when children come into school and the knack is to hang on to these relationships with parents. Many parents bring in their own difficulties, and they are increasing, for example mental health, housing issues, domestic abuse, things they aren't coping with on their own. They need guidance on where to go for support. The inclusion manager is doing more to signpost them. She is now doing more about EAL courses, housing benefit, etc.'

When we asked what the consequence would be if the school did not engage effectively with Black Caribbean parents, the headteacher of **School A** responded:

'It would be them and us. It's a defence. You have to break down the barriers. In my previous school we went about things the wrong way, we were on at the parents the whole time about all the things that were wrong. Communication was poor. You have got to be brave – if you do it little by little and have lots of positive things to say about children too, rather than just focusing on when the child is naughty. We have lots of events but it's not about having parents' events. At our last event two Black Caribbean mothers ended up fighting. Afterwards one of them came into the reception area and said "I'm going to tear down this school brick by brick". It doesn't matter who the parent is,

I sit them down and let them have a go. It might be serious. You have to investigate. You don't dismiss it. You need to value their opinion. When you see parents uptight, all you need to say is "Are you alright? Is there anything we can do?"'

The schools engaged parents in a range of creative ways. They arranged meetings at convenient times for parents, implemented low-cost means of bringing home-learning into school and school-learning into the home, held international evenings to which parents bring food from their country of origin, and involved parents who were already engaged with the school as ambassadors for others in the community. Home visits by teachers or other staff are particularly important in building home–school links, and they offer staff an insight into the child's background. The headteacher of School A said:

'Members of staff make home visits and then the parents and children are invited to visit the classroom before they start school. I do not know what the family story is but there is a single parent, I have not seen Dad. The visit revealed a chaotic home. The staff were ushered up to a bedroom and the discussion about the child took place sitting on a bed.'

The pupils we interviewed in the case study schools also praised their schools' engagement and communication with parents, and argued:

'Parents are invited to get feedback about our performance and to celebrate our achievement during award ceremonies.'
'The school uses texts to send information to parents.'
'They send parents information through leaflets and letters every time.'
'They have prayer meetings for parents and these are well attended and valued.'
'Our parents are very confident to talk to our teachers and staff.'
'The school is seen by our parents like a family.'
'Our school see itself as part of the community.'
'We are all like families.'
'School is a multicultural school. It is the school that values every culture, heritage and religion.'
'The school is good in breaking up cultural differences and outstanding in community cohesion. They bring everyone together.'

5.3 Using a relevant inclusive multicultural curriculum

Schools face demands from parents and children for a more inclusive curriculum, in which experience, heritage and participation in British life are more adequately acknowledged. The response by many teachers to this challenge has been impressive, but it remains a national issue to which the British education system needs to respond. The schools recognize the fact that for many Black-heritage pupils the British schools are not affirming of Black people. Teachers work hard to make sure this is not passed on, as is noted by the headteacher of School Y, a primary school:

'We are considering the implications of Black history in the curriculum and realizing that dealing with events in the past raises the issue that you often can't have Black history without White history. The interrelationships are crucial but the pain of some of those interrelationships raises broader questions about how history has been presented and mythologized. Pupils in Year 5 as part of Black History Month selected to study the biography of a famous Black person. They had to find the information using the internet. They then made their own booklets about what they had learnt. This forms the basis of a display in the school and the booklets will go into the school library. We really want to develop pupils' historical skills so that they can understand the background and development of our diverse society. It has got to be much more than one week as part of a unit on Britain in the 1930s. We have to help pupils understand the roots go much deeper than the events, say, of 1950s migration. We do, however, latch on to things. We took part in the Windrush competition and that helped us all to realize how important it is for everyone to record their personal family stories and memories. The school intends to extend the approach of studying biographies, thereby giving pupils more opportunities to study the lives of people who have broken down barriers between groups.'

The pupils spoke with enthusiasm about the work they had done as part of Black History Month. They had studied the lives of such people as Nelson Mandela, Mary Seacole, Muhammad Ali, Jesse Owens and Bob Marley. They discussed their own ethnic identities, which they considered to be complex. They took it for granted that they were British. Their discussion was rooted in an awareness of the importance of family links and associations in shaping their own sense of identity. Their definitions were as follows:

African Caribbean European, African Caribbean European American, Jamaican English with Canadian and American connections, Mauritian African European, Jamaican English with Maltese connections, Jamaican English with American connections. Their skills in debating the influences of location, family links and other factors in developing personal identify were very evident. Their confidence and maturity in these discussions was impressive.

The project schools aim to teach a multicultural curriculum that is academically robust and well resourced but also reflects pupils' heritage, culture and experience. The views of the headteacher of School Y summarized the feelings of many:

> 'There is no substitute for building the concepts that work in Black History Month into the mainstream curriculum. I see "movements of people" as a significant theme in the national curriculum, as an underpinning principle and a key learning point in our school. Conflicts and struggles based in economic developments which force upon communities movements and changes are key issues for us in London – the barometer of the world stage. This is not a secret to children, they know there are wars. The world is not a secret to children. The key is to give them the tools to understand and interpret it. Understanding the factors and forces of change and their impact are key to whether pupils are dealing with dinosaurs or volcanoes.'

The majority of our school visits coincided with Black History Month, so teachers and pupils were generally more attuned to discussions about culture and identity. The headteacher of School H confessed, 'I worry about the Americanization of Black Caribbean culture in this country. Girls appear marginalized in US culture', and he felt the key to countering this Americanization was to open up definitions of British culture and Englishness:

> 'It's back to the question of an inclusive British culture in which the contribution of Black Caribbean communities is affirmed.'

In the case study schools, headteachers see that their role is to encourage teachers to use their creative intuition to deepen the quality of pupils' learning by using a 'mesmerizing' curriculum. Many teachers, having been trained in a system in which lesson plans and schemes of work were downloaded from the internet, have found it a challenge to develop their own lessons. So these schools are engaged in curriculum development, using the richness of their local communities to enrich the foundation subjects and to bring greater relevance to the curriculum for Black Caribbean pupils.

In addition these schools have a strong sense of the contribution of the arts, drama and music to raising the self-esteem and engaging the imaginations of Black Caribbean-heritage pupils. The range of arts experiences which pupils in the case study schools have been able to access is impressive. The return of 'artists' to schools has been motivational for staff as well as pupils. In many of the primary schools the cross-curricular dimension of art was seen to have enhanced pupils' progress in literacy and numeracy. In addition the arts are seen to have a great effect on learning as a whole. The arts give children the chance to express themselves: they become less deskbound and have more opportunities to be creative, to shine and to make things happen for them. More importantly, schools combine a search for high academic standards with a determination to offer pupils and staff every opportunity to broaden their horizons. As one headteacher succinctly put it:

> 'I like to put people into a position where they do things they didn't think they could do before. Our children performed in the Millennium Dome and that gave them the message "Stick with us and we'll get you places", and that works for staff too. I succeeded in getting two of my teachers to visit the US to look at the work of gifted and talented pupils. We've got a fantastic dance company called "Wise Moves", and they are without exception the best professionals I've ever seen and governors buy them in to work with our boys and girls one day a week. That's what we learned from the US [study trip], that you have to provide the opportunities for children to be engaged and confident. Standing in front of an audience and getting applause is about as good as it gets. I ensure that every child in my school gets at least one moment of glory in primary school.'

The rich and varied range of experiences offered are not random but arise from a systematic and clearly thought-through approach by headteachers and staff. Many of the case study schools have developed links with the rich artistic and sporting communities of London such as the Royal Ballet, Royal Festival Hall, the Royal Institution and English National Opera. These links have allowed pupils to have their achievements celebrated on a variety of platforms. One headteacher said:

'We want our pupils to realize how good they are and for them to be confident in all situations so that they can develop their potential. We want to provide pupils with opportunities to achieve at the highest level. The plethora of extracurricular activities, both at lunchtimes and after school, are highly prized by pupils. They are used by the schools as a resource for enrichment and provide a platform for pupils to excel and have their achievements celebrated.'

The schools are very aware of the importance of a dynamic, innovative curriculum in signalling to the pupils a sense of belonging in the wider community. And, importantly, whatever its curriculum model, every school emphasizes the importance of linking it to the national curriculum, focusing on the core curriculum and maintaining high standards in the core subjects. Each school's curriculum is based on what kind of school it is and what the students need, but all are constantly looking for ways to improve their curriculum. They only pursue changes if they believe that these will further the students' learning, motivation, enjoyment or achievement. The schools offer an impressive range of enrichment opportunities, trips and visits that will provide cultural, artistic and sporting experiences the students are unlikely to encounter at home or in the community, thus widening their horizons and heightening their aspirations and giving them access to opportunities they may take up later in life. Furthermore, they provide opportunities for students to develop their self-confidence.

When the head of English in **School F** was interviewed, he spoke about the curriculum. He mentioned the strong sense of Black heritage that should be embraced and enjoyed in school, reflected in the choice of texts by authors who promote positive models of Black people, and in invitations to writers and poets to visit the school. A six-month intervention model is used at KS3 to enable EAL students to access the curriculum. Evening events focus on key countries and regions across the world, and are reflected in displays around the school of past evenings on, for instance, Cuba, Japan, Egypt and Portugal, and the cross-curricular, cross-departmental approach. One school is keen to extend its curriculum links with Africa, perhaps in collaboration with two other schools.

School H has developed a strong arts-based curriculum, consciously designed to broaden students' horizons and enrich both the students and the professional expertise of the school's staff. The school's curriculum is underpinned by its specialist status. Engaging more deeply with the arts, media and music, working with Creative Partnerships and being part of the pilot DfE Aiming High project (see DfES 2003a, 2003b) have given staff the confidence and tools to develop an arts-based whole-school curriculum. The school set up a working party to review the diversity of the curriculum, using INSET and curriculum-writing workshops to develop a responsive pedagogy. This increased the range of extra- and cross-curricular activities in Key Stage 3 that build students' confidence and their ability to work in project teams. This approach has strengthened relationships and students' capacity to work together in Key Stage 4. The school feels that the focus on curriculum builds an element of sustainability that surpasses mentoring programmes.

The link with Creative Partnerships has been very productive. Each term a set of arts projects and activities are provided to targeted groups across the school, as part of a strategy to raise achievement, broaden horizons and challenge students so that their aspirations are raised – but achievable. London's rich cultural life is harnessed, to include, for example, trips to the Royal Ballet School, live jazz performances at the Royal Albert Hall, dance courses at a school in another LA and participation in the Re-imagining Africa film and media project.

Other subject departments are also encouraged to be creative. The head of design and technology asked the textiles teacher to bring back ideas from the Horniman Museum for an INSET session on African materials. The music department has broadened the range of musical traditions studied in Key Stages 3 and 4.

The school is a partner in the LA link to schools in Takoradi in Ghana. In recent years staff from the school have visited their partner school in Ghana and the head of science has set up a curriculum link. His lively video of his visit to Ghana has been shown in assemblies. A Year 8 student said that it made him feel proud that he was Black because the film showed Ghanaian children asserting their pride in being Black.

All the case study schools adapt the curriculum to meet the needs of diverse school communities. For example, in a primary school in which pupils' cultural understanding is at the centre of the curriculum the children have been involved in generating questions about things they will learn about, and their questions determine the themes mapped out across the school in the teaching of the national curriculum.

> 'We wanted more visual input, especially as we have so many children with EAL and our focus is on skills and knowledge. We identify topics that can be taught with a history-, geography/ environment-, or science/health-related area. Our planning

identifies specific vocabulary and language structures. Literacy is planned on a two-week cycle, with one week the focus being on speaking and listening and one week on reading and writing. The entire curriculum has been worked out in this way. It starts with us asking the children who are going to be doing the work what they would like to find out and that question may last up to two weeks. We ensure that the national curriculum content is in there and it is underpinned with the six keys to learning which include reflection, planning, presenting ideas, and working co-operatively. At the end of every term we hold concerts and exhibitions to share our work. Children acted as curators to show parents and visitors their history work on display, confidently explaining what they had learned.'

(Headteacher, School H)

'We put a high focus on speaking and listening through role play, hot-seating, speaking and listening partners, and scaffolding structured talk and repetition of language. The make-up of the school is more diverse than it has ever been so we have developed whole-school approaches to speaking and listening for EAL.'

(Headteacher, School E)

Teachers in School E exploited opportunities to explore, and gather knowledge of, other cultures, often through first-hand experience. They understand the cultures within its community and use them as a resource for learning, drawing on the languages spoken, e.g. Somali, Urdu, Gujarati, Swahili, Arabic and Polish.

Schools use local expertise to enhance the learning of their pupils. Examples include Indian dance classes, which involve pupils learning the meaning of hand, eye and foot movements in classical Indian dance, visits to the Globe Theatre in London and trips away, study programmes including residential weekends, for example to Juniper Hall (a field centre in the North Downs) to study film making, and extended day activities to enrich the curriculum. Artists, dance groups, authors and poets feed into the curriculum in creative and innovative ways.

School E's deputy head with responsibility for the curriculum pointed out that some ethnic-minority pupils have limited experiences of life outside their immediate area and so the school organizes a residential trip out of London for pupils in Year 7. He said, 'We had a residential fairly early on. Lots of them have not had that kind of experience. We have kids who haven't even been on escalators.'

He described the impact on the curriculum when the school changed from an all-girls school to become co-educational:

> 'When we moved to co-ed we had to rethink the curriculum. The new national curriculum is narrowing, especially in English and history; you have got to be more creative now to make it relevant to our pupils. We have lead practitioners in a range of subjects. Our specialism in performing and visual arts complements and enriches the curriculum, which has been described by Ofsted as "innovative and engaging". The curriculum offers extensive opportunities for students, including established links with world-class organizations, e.g. the Young Vic, Ballet Rambert and Laban[3] and educational trips, visits and workshops with artists in residence. Collaboration is strong and I am keen that faculties do not stick to their own areas. ... With regard to enrichment, we have specialist staff and keen learners who are generally interested in their subject. The staff have helped pupils to go on to drama colleges, e.g. the Guildhall.'

School E offers many opportunities for pupils of Black Caribbean heritage to succeed, even those who are not always supported by their parents. The deputy head with responsibility for inclusion explained:

> 'When we look at the way we work with students finding an interest that engages them, gets them being part of a team or a club ... A lot of parents, even those more professional, do not spend the time to develop children's hobbies and interests. We have had a lot of kids who are good footballers and they are offered great opportunities but parents won't accompany them to West Ham or Fulham. You see their hopes disappointed and their interest wanes. This isn't only single mums. It's that importance is not placed on it. If you compare this with our basketball programme, there is full participation because the full-time coach takes them, so they don't need anyone to accompany them and they practise before and after school.'

The citizenship co-ordinator at School E told us how the school's effective teaching and rigorous curriculum had contributed to the achievement of Black and ethnic-minority students:

> 'We were one of the earliest schools to take part in Debate Mate.[4] We open it up to all students. I facilitate two undergraduate

students from LSE and they teach them how to debate. We had a Year 9 boy who was a problem – very sporty, bright boy and very involved with the debate club, he went to the Oxford Union debate – he was one of only two students from state schools. He went on to study politics and law at Liverpool University.

'We discuss things such as discrimination, reasoning and weighing up both sides of the argument. It offers students a voice and we can channel them and some of their frustrations and give them an opportunity to talk about things that affect them both inside and outside school. It broadens their horizons. There are a good number that do not travel out very far from here. We go to the House of Commons and we have workshops and they get to meet their local MP. They take part in Young People's Question Time in the Houses of Parliament with a panel of MPs. We walk along the South Bank to make it a day out. They don't always know what is available.'

The LA's primary schools offer a rich curriculum, drawing on inspiring Black role models whenever possible, to encourage pupils to aim high. One of the great strengths of **School C** is its enriched curriculum, which positively supports the aims and ethos of the school. The executive headteacher described the school's approach:

'When the new national curriculum came out in 2014, we looked at our curriculum and assessment and said they need to be based on our children. Our four key drivers are spirituality, possibilities, excellence and diversity, that the staff parents and governing body thought we wanted to preserve and develop. So we still make sure that those four elements are covered. When we got together with another school [a partner school in the federation], we formulated our values. Everything we have done has stemmed from these strong core values, articulated not only by staff and children but also by parents. It is clear in our communications and has really helped us in our journey to support our children to feel unique, to feel comfortable with who they are and with what they want to achieve. ... It's valuing each child as an individual and to be able to offer each child possibilities to broaden their experiences and motivations.'

Teachers of Years 4 and 6 at School C talked with enthusiasm about how they ensure that the curriculum takes account of the diverse range of pupils and represents them:

> 'Our key drivers of spirituality, possibilities, excellence and diversity are threaded through our curriculum. Year 5 has just been doing a project on space and last year when we were doing it, we taught about Mae C. Jemison, the first Black woman in space. We are very much aware of who our children are and we also understand what motivates them and it makes our job easier if they are motivated, so we try to weave it in. Severus, the Black Roman emperor, was a Moor. We try every way we can to link it to the pupils and to London. We visited the Windmill Project at the Black Cultural Archives and are involved in a drama project with City Heights Academy on Hiroshima. We went along the Thames when we were visiting the Globe Theatre. So many children don't go into central London and experience the amount of history there. I find it incredible that so many children never go. We walked past Southwark Cathedral, the Golden Hind and walked down by the Thames. We make an effort to do this because they just don't go there. We take children out as much as we can, even though it can be a challenge.'

Likewise, at **School A** teachers draw on the local history of the area to develop Black Caribbean pupils' understanding of their own cultural heritage:

> 'We have to do a lot to the curriculum to diversify it.'
>
> (Year 6 teacher)

> 'I try to make things interesting and relevant to them. My enthusiasms I bring into the classroom. For example, I showed the children photos of my holiday in Rome and they commented, "You have a Black friend!"'
>
> (Year 3 teacher)

> 'I took my class last year to the Black Cultural Archives. I was amazed that the Black Caribbean children had no knowledge of their history. The imagery of Black cultural history in Britain, Windrush and the signs which said "No dogs, no Irish, no Blacks" – I tried to stand in front of the sign as it could upset young children.'
>
> (Year 3 teacher)

Teachers at **School JE** have continued to develop a rich and diverse, creative curriculum, as the head of school described:

> 'We teach maths, English, science and ICT separately but use the themes to support those subjects too. As much as possible, we link the teaching and learning of subjects together through a common theme or topic. We look at our children and we ask. "What do our children need to learn about?" How can we encourage girls and boys? Our creative curriculum changes each year because we evaluate and see how effective our curriculum is. This way of working allows teachers to become more creative. We also link our homework to the whole-school theme so families become involved.'

Teachers are enthusiastic about the impact of the curriculum on the children:

> 'The curriculum offers so much flexibility in what I can do in the classroom. I can ask the children what we could do and because they are involved they take so much enjoyment from it. I can see evidence of their achievement.'

School JE's website states:

> 'The aim of all those at School JE is to ensure that the curriculum offered to the children is not only fun and enjoyable but also leads to children achieving their full academic potential.'

The school logo says 'Excellence together with our community', in the belief that it is with the 'partnership between parents and staff' that the children will be able to develop into 'well-rounded individuals'.

Each term, for every class from EYFS to Year 6, parents can access School JE's 'curriculum guides', which outline the creative curriculum and homework projects. The school's innovative and exciting partnership with London Music Masters, through the Bridge Project (which has spanned six years), has contributed to the excellence of the school's curriculum. The Bridge Project is an educational initiative that identifies and nurtures young children who might not otherwise have the opportunity to engage in classical music. It encourages children, their families and communities to develop a lifelong appreciation for classical music in all its forms. Pupils receive music tuition and participate in musical workshops and performances throughout the school year, and have performed at the Royal Festival Hall.

The rich and diverse curriculum provides many memorable experiences and brings learning to life by linking topics creatively between subjects. The writing of the boys in the school, often weaker than that of the girls, has been greatly improved by using contexts they find engaging. Whole-school topics cover EYFS to Year 6. The EYFS team leader views this spread as very positive:

> 'The EYFS in many schools are in their own little bubble. ... Here we feel more included in the whole school and so do the children. It motivates them. From my point of view it really makes a difference.'

The school's Ofsted report praised its creative curriculum:

> The creative curriculum offers a very broad range of themed activities which are developed extremely well with contributions from pupils. Consequently, the school provides rich and memorable experiences for pupils that prepare them exceptionally well for their next steps in learning. There are many excellent opportunities through the curriculum and in assemblies to promote pupils' spiritual, moral, social and cultural development. The diversity of the school is celebrated and pupils are encouraged to consider other faiths and cultures through projects such as Our Heritage. ... A very wide range of well-attended after-school clubs provides many opportunities for sports, arts and music activities.

Black History Month is built into School JE's curriculum in the autumn term; it covers influential people and groups: for example, in nursery there are Stories from Africa, in Reception Stories from America – the Obamas, in Year 1 Ride to Freedom – Rosa Parks, in Year 2 The Amazing Adventures of Mary Seacole, in Year 3 Blast from the Past WW2 (children's viewpoints), in Year 4 Aboriginal Australia – Artists, in Year 5 Windrush – Influential People, and in Year 6 From Apartheid to Peace – Nelson Mandela.

Twice a year the school invites parents to an exhibition of the children's work. Classes view each year group's work in the exhibition, and this helps them to understand what is expected of them as they progress through the school. Homework is included in the exhibition and later goes on display at the local library.

School V primary teachers have developed a broad, balanced and imaginative curriculum; a curriculum map identifies foundation subjects to be taught through topics that present a well-structured learning journey for pupils from Year 1 to Year 6. The humanities co-ordinator has taken a leading role in curriculum development and has produced exciting materials for Black History Month that feature local and national 'heroes' or role models, people from the Caribbean and Africa who have made a significant contribution to life in Britain.

Core subjects are taught systematically and the school has pioneered its own approach to the teaching of phonics and numeracy. Phonics teaching is rigorous and is taught for 25 minutes per day to children in Years 1 and 2. Because of the success of this programme (taught by teachers and instructional leaders) the school has introduced Number Masters, teaching the same pupils in small groups for 15 minutes each day to ensure that their engagement with numbers is intensive and consistent.

The teachers talk with enthusiasm about their approach to the curriculum and try to make lessons exciting and relevant to the children:

> 'We used to use the Creative Learning Journey[5] so people could become imaginative – especially in maths as it starts to make sense to children when you use real-life situations. ... We did a great maths shop last year. ... Each class came up with things they could make and sell, sandwiches, fruit shops, each class had a stall. The rest of the school came around and bought things!'

Making the connections between subjects is another strength of School V's curriculum. For example, drama was incorporated into work on food chains in science.

The school, too, affords children extensive extracurricular activities and visits to places of interest. Because of the location of the school and the excellent range of partnerships it has established, pupils are able to perform at the Royal Festival Hall and the Young Vic, and visit Tate Modern and events at the South Bank.

School C offers African-influenced art and craft work as part of the history curriculum, in which Benin is one unit of study. The outstanding quality of the artefacts stimulated the students to achieve fine work. The headteacher commented, 'The response of all pupils [to the Kingdom of Benin artefacts] was enthusiastic and it has helped to improve the attainment and the progress of Black pupils in the school.'

The schools in the study have developed an innovative curriculum that motivates ethnic-minority students. They have developed links with Africa and with rich artistic and sporting communities in London such as the Royal Ballet, the Royal Festival Hall, English National Opera, London Museums and London artistic worlds. They have created an environment in which African- and Caribbean-heritage students feel their history, culture, languages, religions and individual identities are respected and valued within the school curriculum. Black History Month is only a part of the curriculum, though celebrated in all the schools.

5.4 Links with the local communities

The schools have developed warm relationships, clear communication, networking, listening and learning so that they understand the diverse range of people and places they work with. They have learned that what may work in one area with certain people may not work as well down the road with a different set of people. There are no absolutes, no one answer to every situation, and achieving meaningful results inevitably takes time. Furthering equality and diversity – the principles of community engagement – means appreciating and understanding differences and involving each student. Diversity is about recognizing that we are all unique with our own talents, needs, ambitions and priorities.

School O's links with the business world give pupils opportunities to talk with business and professional people. Briefly, School O operates a four-step plan in which pupils become aware of business and enterprise through what they do at school in all subjects and activities. Everything has a work-related dimension. Students gain hands-on experience by putting their learning into practice. During their time at the school pupils record their business and enterprise experience in a Portfolio for Life, a valuable tool they take with them when they leave school and which leads to an Award Scheme Development and Accreditation Network (ASDAN) qualification.

The leadership development programme affords pupils an introduction to management, developing their competence in a wide range of management-oriented tasks, building their confidence and their acceptance of responsibility. Through its business and enterprise status the school has developed students' involvement to a high standard. Students can experience leadership development within and beyond the curriculum. They elect presidents and vice-presidents from their peers. They have detailed job descriptions, consult their year groups and form the school council.

The trainee leaders' programme in Year 10 is a development of the presidents and vice-presidents system in Key Stage 3. Trainee leaders help to run the school, and mentor and coach younger pupils. They lead significant programmes on higher education, college links, behaviour management, and business and enterprise. Prefects and head boys and girls in Year 11 are part of the trainee leaders' programme. This layer of pupil management often represents the school. All the above offices have detailed job descriptions, self-review and reviews. Ofsted commented: 'The school provides all students with the opportunity to visit universities and colleges including Cambridge, Imperial College and University College, London. This encourages high aspirations for their future education. Students take on leadership roles very effectively, for example as members of the anti-bullying committee, which is run by the students themselves. This helps to build a very strong school community, which thrives on its diversity.'

School V, where 73% of the pupils speak English as an additional language, reached out to make links with the community. An Ofsted inspection graded the school as outstanding in all areas. In addition to the importance of academic achievement:

> The school seeks to provide many opportunities, often in partnership with other organisations, for the children to develop talents and interests in the arts, sports and environmental education. Pupils and staff commented on the distinct 'family feel' and every member of its community refers to their 'School V family'.

School V examined its pupils' postcode areas to explore their socio-economic background and plotted them against the Index of Multiple Deprivation (IMD) (DCLG, 2011). The IMD is based on distinct dimensions of deprivations experienced by individuals living in an area. It identifies seven main types of deprivation – income, employment, health, education, housing and services, living environment and crime – and these are combined to form a measure of multiple deprivation. As a consequence of its findings, the school set up a breakfast club as a starting point, targeting pupils who were regularly late for school. Getting pupils in for breakfast improved attendance and punctuality rates. At the time of writing, over 70 pupils attend the breakfast club.

The level of skills and training in the local population is among the lowest in the UK. This confirms School V's baseline assessment of pupils. Attainment on entry to the school is below the national average. The level of home support the school can expect is low, not because of lack of parental aspiration, but because many parents are not able to help. Accordingly, the school sets out to develop basic skills. Also at issue is pupils' health. School V won its bid to become one of four pilot schools with high numbers of pupils who have FSM to receive sponsorship from Nike's 'Move It' programme. This provides physical activities (with sports coaches) for all pupils in Years 5 and 6.

School A is part of the same cluster of schools as **School V**; they share expertise and best practice with other schools. That they desire to work with other schools is a significant factor in School A's leading role in school improvement, but they also work with other Church of England schools. The headteachers of Church of England schools meet termly to discuss current issues of educational change, celebrating successes, sharing school issues and showcasing opportunities. Reflecting on why some schools manage to work together whereas others struggle, the headteacher said:

> 'To avoid the issue of people not working together, we change the "triads" [groups of three schools working together within a larger cluster] round every year – we just pull names out of a hat!
>
> 'With the church schools, there are similar issues: there is more work to do but it is very much about trust. I am quite open and honest. If things are not going well I ask for help but some might not want others to know [that there are difficulties].'

Successful bids for funding through the cluster won School A the services of a family support worker. The school also won its bid for funds to supplement pupil premium funding so that they could employ a speech and language therapist and a psychotherapist to work with children and families.

The case study schools also reach out to schools working in an entirely different context. **School C** has a well-established link with a small rural school, which has provided benefits to both. A teacher explained:

> 'We have made a link with a tiny, all-White school in Petworth, Years 5 and 6. We met up with them on the beach at Littlehampton. It was amazing. We went crabbing. When they visited us we took them to Brixton Market. We met them at Victoria and walked down to Buckingham Palace, had lunch in the park, down through Parliament Square. They were fascinated. We celebrate diversity – have multicultural picnics. We ask all the children to bring in food reflective of their heritage. We have days of national costume. To begin with they were nervous – you might not want to eat ackee and saltfish – but it's about celebration. We had a countryside day. The children did fly-fishing, forestry work, husbandry, holding a lamb. It is four years since it started. It needs to have a headteacher who wants it to work.'

The case study schools are alert to the fact that the parents and pupils who come from various countries, languages and backgrounds may have little understanding of the education system in the UK. An assistant headteacher at **School E** described some of the ways the school raises their aspirations:

'I took a group of 70 parents and pupils to Cambridge – Years 7, 8 and 9. As well as the focus being on Cambridge University, the parents got more out of it than the pupils! Someone from Oxford and the University of Sussex came to speak to pupils and every child brought a parent. We did this on a Saturday.'

No pupil is excluded from taking part in activities because parents do not understand their significance, or for financial reasons, for instance:

'For the Year 7 residential trip, I contacted all the parents to make sure no one was left behind because of lack of finance. We organize payment plans.'

School D held an event to introduce the 'Aspire to Achieve' project to parents and the community; a senior teacher described the response:

'The Aspire to Achieve evening was fantastic. It was really positive and powerful. All staff were invited and there were key speakers from the Black Caribbean community such as doctors, academics, lawyers and teachers. I have been here since 2009 and it was the most powerful event we have held. The whole hall was in tears when one of the speakers spoke. It is the fact that you are promoting it, working with targeted groups, families are onside, and we tend to sit with parents on these occasions.'

School H draws on the diversity of pupils' backgrounds and circumstances. It also celebrates several innovative activities strengthen community links, notably the gospel choir in which parents and the community play a key role.

The school has a strong link with St Martin-in-the Fields church in Trafalgar Square and the whole school goes there once every year to sing. This important tradition, started when the school was established, has been kept going. 'It is a beautiful finish to the end of the year by singing at church', says the school chaplain.

School H celebrates pupils' achievement and acknowledges the diversity of its pupil population. A teacher said, 'Displays are the reflection of our community. They are part of the community dialogue. They reflect what is going on in the school. They are part of the ethos of high expectations.' Displays celebrating events such as Christian Aid Week, the Triangle Project (see p. 000) and Poppy Day are shown around the school. A pupil responded, in earlier research, 'The pictures on the walls mean a lot to me. I am in one of the choirs and I see my face' (McKenley *et al.*, 2003: 55).

5.5 A strong commitment to equal opportunities and a clear stand on racism

As well as having strong links to the wider community, the schools recognize that race equality is crucial for all schools and all pupils. However, the school teaching workforce is predominantly White British. Some may feel out of their depth when tackling racial issues because of inadequate understanding of discrimination, racism and diversity. Research has shown that Black pupils are disciplined more frequently, more harshly and for less serious misbehaviour than their White peers, and are less likely to be praised. DfE research found 'systematic racial discrimination in the application of disciplinary and exclusion policies' (DfES, 2006). There is also evidence that 'teachers can wittingly or unwittingly affect the performance of pupils by being openly prejudiced, by being patronising or by having unjustified low expectations of the child's abilities' (Richardson, 2005: 37) based on racial background. Evidence shows that Black pupils and particularly Black Caribbean pupils are disproportionately placed in bottom sets (DfES, 2006), thus suffering from lower teacher expectations. This cycle means they often receive a less stimulating curriculum and are entered for the less challenging exams, which prevents them from gaining the highest grades.

> For example, prior to 2006 the mathematics GCSE had a three tier system; pupils entered for the higher exam were able to achieve grades A*–D. Pupils entered for the foundation tier exam could only achieve grades D–G. White students are twice as likely as Black to be placed in the top maths sets. In London in 2005 two-thirds of Black students were entered into the lowest tier, where the highest grade they could achieve was a D. In effect, they were marked out for failure before they even sat the paper.
>
> (Gillborn, 2008: 96)

We need equality education to become a key part of initial teacher training courses, to reflect the growing diversity of British schools. However, the research shows that teachers are seldom equipped, through initial teacher training or continuing professional development, to address racism or promote equality within the classroom. Most of the teachers we interviewed had received little or no preparation for tackling racism or promoting race equality during their training or teaching. Our study highlights the need for widespread training, including CPD, to equip educators in England with the skills and knowledge required to consider issues of race equality in their lesson planning and delivery, to value and acknowledge differences and similarities among their pupils.

We would argue that schools need to raise their expectations of all children and young people, fostering their potential irrespective of their race, gender, disability, religion or sexual orientation. The case study schools have a culture of respect for people as individuals and as members of particular communities. Their policies against racism and for multicultural education are unambiguous, as shown by this extract from **School Y**'s policy statement:

> The staff are opposed to racism in any form. We are committed to the principle that all children should be given equal opportunities to fulfil their potential. We condemn discrimination against people because of skin colour and cultural background because it is illegal, offensive and wrong. Our school is multicultural and multi-racial and we value this cultural diversity. Every member of the school community should feel their language, religion and culture are valued and respected. In order to achieve this we will use what children know and understand about themselves in our teaching.

Such statements of policy are not mere rhetoric: this school deals with any incidents swiftly and decisively. As one pupil said: 'Our headteacher makes sure there is no racism and is brilliant at it.'

The schools use ethnicity data to track each individual. Teachers analyse it to review student performance and to evaluate the current achievement of Black Caribbean and other minority pupils. The schools encourage and support individual teachers and TAs to complete their own teacher assessments and evidence and to review target-setting processes for all ethnic groups. Ethnic profiles are used to design interventions based on knowledge and the cultural norms and aspirations of the community. Ethnicity data is used extensively for monitoring and lesson planning to ensure accurate targets for individual pupils and to track their progress, to identify weaknesses on any topic, and to sustain high expectations of pupils. The ethos in the case study schools is open and honest: the pupils can talk about their concerns and share in the development of strategies for racial justice. Teachers and pupils at these schools clearly understand the issues:

> 'Whatever background the children come from, whether they are Black, White or speaking English as an additional language, doors should open for them, not close. It is easy to label children

and have low expectations of them. But we are a fully inclusive school and are committed to equal opportunities.'

(Headteacher, School Y)

'The school takes racism very seriously.'

(Parent, School A)

'The school promotes equal opportunity and good relations between people of different racial groups.'

(Chair of governors, School JE)

'Ethnicity data is critical in understanding how Black Caribbean and different groups in my class progress and achieve. We use it effectively.'

(Teacher, School A)

'I see ethnic monitoring as an effective method of raising achievement, to identify underachieving groups and prioritize our support systems.'

(Teacher, School B)

'This school is totally committed to inclusion in all aspects of school life. The analysis and use of ethnically monitored data are excellent and give rise to a wide range of initiatives to support Black Caribbean pupils and other underachieving groups. I work closely with Black Caribbean parents to ensure they know how their children are progressing in school. Black Caribbean parents are supportive.'

(Teacher, School C)

'The school talks to us about race and discrimination in PSHE and assembly. They deal quickly with any problem.'

(Pupil)

'Assemblies reflect different cultures and there are greeting signs in different languages about the school. Sometimes teachers try to speak with different community languages and a lot of teachers are from different cultures too.'

(Pupil)

'I like my school because all children have different backgrounds and experiences and different mix of cultures.'

(Pupil)

'In this school everyone is treated equally, no one is discriminated against based on their colour.'

(Pupil)

'I like best about this school because people are not racist here and people help other people.'

(Pupil)

'I like the education and the teachers in the school. The teachers are not racist.'

(Pupil)

'Good community links. No stone left unturned to oppose racism and support community cohesion in our school.'

(TA, School A)

The leaders of the authority's schools are strong on equality issues and tackling racism. The headteachers generally see themselves as responsible for establishing good race relations and community cohesion as a priority. Their schools have a well-developed multicultural and anti-racist curriculum that serves the community. They create opportunities for staff to reflect on the achievement of the Black Caribbean pupils in particular (as this group underachieves nationally), using data and their own experience and knowledge about individual pupils' progress. There is wide discussion about achievement, diversity and race issues in the school, and this has made a significant difference to Black Caribbean children and parents.

It was notable during our classroom observation that there was widespread in-service training designed to empower teachers and staff with the skills and knowledge they needed to address issues of race equality and diversity; this training was well attended. All the schools have a strong commitment to equal opportunities and an inclusive ethos that fosters the achievement of all pupils. Whatever a child's background, be it Black Caribbean, Other Black, White, or from the council estate, doors are open for them. The schools eat, drink, sleep and breathe inclusion. The staff show an appropriate professional affection for Black Caribbean and other ethnic-minority pupils. The members of staff we interviewed are good role models and contribute to the process of raising the aspirations of Black Caribbean pupils in their school.

5.6 Diversity in the school workforce

For many years, policy makers in England have recognized the many benefits that can accrue from having a school workforce that reflects its pupil population. As far back as 1985, it was recognized that minority ethnic teachers can play an important role in ensuring that all pupils get a more balanced view of society. The Swann report (1985) highlighted the need to ensure that the teaching ethos of each school reflected the different cultures of the communities it served and stated that the lack of ethnic-minority teachers in schools needed urgent correction.

The case study schools serve some of the most deprived wards in the LA, where many pupils come from disadvantaged economic circumstances. The school population mirrors the community in which the schools sit. Most pupils come from African, Caribbean, Portuguese and White British ethnic backgrounds and a significant proportion of pupils are of mixed heritage. The schools promote community cohesion and ensure pupils understand and appreciate others from different backgrounds, with a sense of sharing a vision, fulfilling their potential and feeling part of the community. Through the school curriculum, pupils explore the representation of different cultural, ethnic, linguistic and religious groups in this LA and in the UK. Senior managers provide strong leadership in ensuring the schools are inclusive organizations. The ethos that is developed is based on a commitment to a vision of the school that serves its pupil community in the context of diversity. The schools are multi-ethnic and multicultural. Staff are aware of the many pressures young pupils face in the wider society. They actively consider this in their approach to education. They are promoting equality and diversity in the classroom, which means, Petty argues:

> setting clear rules in regards to how people should be treated, challenging any negative attitudes, treating all staff and students fairly and equally, creating an all-inclusive culture for staff and students, avoiding stereotypes in examples and resources, using resources with multicultural themes, actively promoting multiculturalism in lessons, planning lessons that reflect the diversity of the classroom, … ensuring policies and procedures don't discriminate against anyone.
>
> (Petty, 2014)

A key success for the case study schools is leadership's ability to create a community that reflects the student population by employing a diverse multi-ethnic workforce. The quality of staff recruited, including the diversity of the staff team, is seen as crucial in the case study schools. Many schools pointed to their ability to acquire the right calibre of teaching staff, that is, staff who would buy into the explicit culture and core values as being crucial to their success in raising the achievement of all pupils. They recruit teachers who want to be in the school and who believe in real partnership with pupils and their parents. The teachers are seen to come with attributes that will enhance and help.

Table 5.1 Ethnic-minority staff in the case study schools' workforce (%)

School	Leadership WBr	Leadership BME	Teachers WBr	Teachers BME	TAs WBr	TAs BME	Other staff WBr	Other staff BME	All WBr	All BME
Y	66.7	33.3	89.5	10.6	30.8	69.2	65.0	35.0	65.5	34.5
C	100.0	0.0	50.0	50.0	33.3	66.7	36.4	63.6	45.2	54.8
JE	25.0	75.0	35.5	64.5	31.0	69.0	15.8	84.2	28.9	71.1
A	100.0	0.0	76.9	23.1	22.2	77.8	30.0	70.0	52.8	55.6
SJ	66.7	33.3	64.3	35.7	22.2	77.8	35.7	64.3	45.0	55.0
G	50.0	50.0	60.0	40.0	36.8	63.2	33.3	66.7	40.4	59.6
V	33.3	50.0	71.4	28.6	22.7	77.3	25.0	75.0	37.0	61.1
E	88.9	11.1	62.7	37.4	44.4	55.6	27.1	72.9	47.8	52.2
RE	62.5	37.5	34.1	65.9	42.9	57.1	50.0	50.0	44.7	55.3
O	50.0	50.0	16.3	83.5	14.3	85.7	30.6	69.3	24.8	75.2
F	72.7	27.3	60.5	39.4	59.1	40.9	55.8	44.1	59.6	40.4
D	66.7	33.4	41.7	58.5	23.5	76.5	50.0	50.2	43.7	56.3
H	83.3	16.7	40.9	59.0	0.0	100.0	35.4	64.8	38.0	62.0
Case study schools	61.1	37.8	48.1	51.9	26.1	74.9	36.4	63.6	40.2	59.9
LA	67.8	32.2	56.5	43.5	36.1	63.9	38.9	61.1	45.9	54.1
National	91.3	8.6	86.3	13.6	86.4	13.5	86.5	13.4	86.5	13.4

WBr = White British; BME = Black and minority ethnic group
Source: DfE (2017e).

The case study schools pride themselves on the diversity of their workforce. Table 5.1 shows the percentages of White British and ethnic-minority staff in the case study schools' workforce to demonstrate that they are more inclusive than schools are nationally. The schools have recruited good-quality teaching and non-teaching staff who reflect the languages, cultures, ethnic backgrounds and faiths of the pupils in the school. The schools also pride themselves on recruiting from the local community; this sends a strong message to the community that they are valued. This policy has helped the schools to become a central point for the wider community and has built trust. Teaching assistants are greatly valued in these schools. They play a key role in communicating with parents and supporting pupils.

Table 5.1 also shows that in England 91% of the leadership, 86% of teachers and teaching assistants, and 87% of other staff and of the workforce as a whole are White British. This national data shows a worrying picture and raises a question about the chances of headship for minority ethnic teachers; there is also an issue of representation for students. The situation limits understanding of diversity. However, in the case study schools:

- The percentage of leadership staff in the case study schools recorded as ethnic minority is 38% compared with 32% in the LA and 9% nationally.
- 52% of teachers in the case study schools are from ethnic-minority groups compared with 44% in the LA and 14% nationally.
- The percentage of teaching assistants recorded as ethnic minority in the case study schools is 75% compared with 64% in the LA and 14% nationally.
- 60% of all the case study school staff are ethnic minority compared to 54% in the LA and 13% nationally.

There is great diversity in the workforce in the case study schools in terms of range of roles, skills and ethnicity. In one outstanding secondary school 50% of the leadership team is Black Caribbean. There are also significant numbers of White British, Black African, White Other, Mixed White and Black Caribbean, Mixed White and Black African, Other Mixed Race, White Irish, Pakistani, Indian, Bangladeshi and Other Black on the staff. The school prides itself on its diversity. Overall, over 84% of teachers and 75% of the school workforce are of ethnic-minority origin and many of the languages, cultures and faiths of the pupils are reflected in the workforce. In another of the secondary schools 30% of the teaching staff are Black Caribbean.

The diversity of the staff is a striking feature of one of the outstanding primary schools. Of a reported 94 staff 71% are of ethnic-minority background, including 36% Black Caribbean, 25% White British, 8% African, 9% Portuguese, 3% Russian, 2% Mixed Race, and 2% Bangladeshi. Other staff originate from Brazil, Poland, Morocco, Colombia, the Philippines, Mauritius and Peru. These highly skilled staff make a valuable contribution to removing barriers to achievement. Among them, the staff speak Portuguese, Greek, Polish, Urdu, French, German, Spanish, Russian, Arabic and Amharic. Bilingual staff are clearly able to communicate effectively with parents and pupils whose languages they share.

Another case study primary school has a diverse multi-ethnic workforce, the staff and the leadership team including practitioners of Black

Caribbean, African and Portuguese heritage. Currently, over 75% of the 92 members of staff are of ethnic-minority origin and many of the languages, cultures and faiths of the pupils are reflected in the workforce: 34% are Black Caribbean, 25% White British, 21% Black African, 4% Portuguese, 2% Mixed White and Black Caribbean, 2% White Irish, 2% South American, 2% Romanian. There are also Polish, Hungarian, Bangladeshi, Indian, Other Asian, Other Black, Cuban and Arab staff in the school. The headteacher believes that by recruiting staff from the local community she sends a strong message to the community that it is valued. It has helped the school to become the central point of the wider community and has built trust. Pupils feel that they can relate to the members of staff from their own cultural backgrounds. Staff members can empathize with pupils; they speak the same language and understand how the systems operate 'back home'.

In another outstanding case study school, this time a secondary school, 50% of the leadership is Black Caribbean, and 25% White British. Significantly, 65% of the teachers and 71% of all the staff are from ethnic-minority groups. There is also a good number of White British, Black African, White Other, 2% Mixed White and Black Caribbean, Mixed White and Black African, Other Mixed Race, White Irish, Indian, Bangladeshi and Other Black staff. A senior manager feels that because there are teachers from the same cultures as the parents and pupils, they can be straight with parents and not give them misleading assurances about their children's performance (Demie, 2019).

The case study schools and leadership teams have some ethnic-minority staff. Five of the case study schools are run by Black headteachers, eight by White headteachers and one school by an Indian headteacher. Parents appreciate the role played by the headteachers in turning challenging schools into outstanding schools, and the contribution of White staff is affirmed too. These confident headteachers take risks and trust their instincts. They are innovative because they are focused on raising the achievement of inner-city pupils; they have emerged as strong practitioners who raise the achievement of Black African as well as other pupils. One of the Black headteachers has held the position for 14 years. Almost all are long-serving heads in the same schools and are passionate about working with the local community to raise achievement.

Four teachers from the case study schools agreed to be interviewed. Their responses summarize the views of most of those in the schools researched:

Teacher A (**School RE**) joined the school last year and was struck by the sense of community that pervades the school and into which she felt welcomed. She feels the headteacher is a community leader whose open-door approach is appreciated by both staff and students. Teacher A enjoys the diversity of the school population and has blossomed in the aspirational culture of the school community.

Teacher B (**School H**), from Ghana, is one of the longest-serving staff members, and enjoys the sense of community that permeates the school. She worked as a teacher of EAL and for the last three years has headed the EAL section and also teaches literacy. She is well qualified, experienced and knowledgeable, and praised by the headteacher for her work. She feels that the headteacher is a community leader who has high aspirations for all its pupils regardless of their background. 'I enjoy the diversity of the school population. Parents see having a diversified workforce and a Black African teacher has made a big difference for the children and they are confident that they get help for any questions. I think this school is the best school doing a lot of work for Black Caribbean and Black African and other students. A lot of this changed when the current headteacher [took over] and the school is now an outstanding school. This is highly appreciated by parents and community. I enjoy teaching in the school and supporting all pupils.'

Teacher C (**School RE**) The school has a number of Black Caribbean teachers who are confident in their work, and comfortable with being role models for the girls. 'I am a well-educated Black woman in a position of authority which helps to confront stereotypes in British culture. I bring my Caribbean background into my teaching and make common cause not just with Black Caribbean girls but also those Black Africans with a similar experience. I feel that generates a powerful discourse in a school where 75% of pupils come from minority ethnic backgrounds.'

Teacher C is using this 'insider' position to challenge assumptions and raise expectations by invoking what would be acceptable 'back home' in their countries of origin. 'I ask the girls, "How many of you have been back home and seen such behaviour?" I use this as a powerful lever around confronting negative behaviour.' They share their confidence in their own ethnicity with the girls: 'I bring the resource of living and being educated in two countries (Barbados and England), which gives me bicultural competence. If the Black Caribbean students don't have a powerful sense of identity and culture, they'll be lost. I know this approach has had a positive impact on achievement.'

Teacher D (**School RE**) 'Our school reflects the local community we serve and responds to their needs. Staff of BME heritage are represented across the school and within the leadership team. Our staff are ethnically diverse and we have a good number of African teachers from Ghana and language support assistants who speak Twi, Ga and French between them, Black Caribbean, Irish, Portuguese teachers, Mixed Race White and Black Caribbean, a Welsh teacher and two South Americans who speak Portuguese and Spanish.'

Two teachers and an SAO of Portuguese heritage agreed to be interviewed to offer their perspectives on the achievement of Portuguese pupils.

A Portuguese member of staff arrived from Madeira in 1983 and is one of the longest-serving members of staff. She admired the sense of community in the school and felt welcomed. There were only 17 Portuguese pupils when she arrived but now there are 211. She has worked as a secretary for four headteachers, and since the appointment of the new headteacher three years ago she has felt well placed to assess the school's ethos. She, too, finds the headteacher an inspirational community leader.

'I enjoy the diversity of the Portuguese school population. I am the first person to be seen because of my role as school secretary. One of my main duties is helping Portuguese parents to fill in forms, as some have difficulty with the English language. I support them during their meetings with the head, and with admission forms to the reception class and secondary transfer. Parents also come to me for help with many things not related to school. I help them and sometimes even act as a mentor. I also support the Portuguese classes. Parents saw having a Portuguese secretary as making a big difference for their children and they are confident that they get help with any of their questions. I think this school is the best school, as we are doing a lot of work for Portuguese pupils. This support has increased over the years. This is highly appreciated by parents and community. I enjoy working in the school and supporting all of the pupils.'

Another Portuguese staff member has worked in the school for the last two years as a teaching assistant and parent governor, and has felt supported by colleagues throughout. She feels:

> 'The leadership supports the Portuguese community and all pupils. The school has provided after-school classes in Portuguese twice a week for some years in recognition of the mother-tongue skills of the intake. This has helped to improve the language of the pupils. To encourage parents to attend the English classes the headteacher organizes childcare while parents are in the lesson.'

The parents often ask the Portuguese teachers for advice. There is a strong identification with Portuguese cultural norms and desire for the pupils to do well, which is reinforced by the school. The diverse staff – including the non-teachers – are happy to be seen as role models.

Diversity is also represented in the profile of school departmental teams. All the staff are clear about the importance of teachers being role models. Good relationships are observed and modelled by both staff and students. Black African teachers treat all students the same but share 'village life' stories with Black African students that reinforce the virtues of working and studying hard. There is strong identification with African cultural norms, and the desire for children to achieve is reinforced by the teachers. One Black teacher defines his teaching as 'passionate but strict'. His knowledge of Black history and experience of the African diaspora are key to his sense of himself as an effective Black teacher. He feels the school embraces the heritage of the students within the curriculum. Staff feel a professional sense of pride and reward at seeing children achieve beyond what they themselves thought they were capable of. The Ghanaian view prevails that 'every teacher is your parent'. New staff are inducted into the ways of the school that give parents confidence.

The opportunities are clear and Black parents appreciate the school's efforts. They are generally supportive of the school and try to present this approach to their children. If they do wish to challenge the school, they do so in private and not in the children's presence. Some African families struggle with the comparatively permissive nature of English education and the freedom enjoyed here is hard for those who were brought up in more disciplined and respectful and less equitable pupil–teacher relationships. In eight out of ten cases, students manage to walk that tricky tightrope of school and home expectations and remain on track, but for those one or two the freedom leads to underachievement. Routine trips home are used to reinforce the general view that the opportunities on offer in the UK are not to be squandered. The school operates a Student Learning Centre with counsellors and mentors to support the students who stray from their family's script.

If parents ask Black teachers for advice, the request has to be handled carefully so as not to contravene school procedures. There is a cultural assumption that teachers are the 'third parent' and have the children's interests at heart. The African teachers enjoy their role model status and their insider knowledge. They are also keenly aware of the sanctions parents operate in desperation when their children refuse to comply with home or school discipline, such as sending them back to Africa.

However, while there are good practices in the case study schools, some people in our focus group commented on how challenging it is to recruit more ethnic-minority teachers and leaders. Some of the headteachers who wanted to recruit more Black teachers found that there were few people of Black African and Black Caribbean origin entering the teaching profession.

> 'I am a White headteacher and most of the teachers are White. We only have one Black teacher but we have a mixed staff. Although I interview teachers for the LA schools, I have not interviewed any Black teachers and there are fewer Black headteachers in the LA now than there used to be.'
>
> (Headteacher, School A)

Another school also experienced difficulty in recruiting and retaining staff from ethnic-minority groups. One of the teachers confirmed that 'having a more mixed profile in the staffing is high on the school's agenda and has been for some considerable time – it's part of the school's positive ethos and is considered very important'.

We asked this one Black Caribbean-heritage teacher at the school why there are fewer Black teachers:

> 'I have always been curious to find out why many of my friends don't want to be teachers. It is a lot of stress being a teacher. There were not many Black Caribbean people going through the system on my course.'

Asked whether there was any correlation between lack of interest in becoming a teacher and their own negative experiences at school, she replied, 'That negativity could be expressed at home and it could put people off becoming a teacher.'

Some of those interviewed said that as pupils they were amazed when they saw a Black teacher. What is concerning is that we are hearing it again from people with recent experience of school:

> 'I went to a Roman Catholic primary school in Clapham in the 1960s/1970s where Black pupils were in the minority. At one time we had a couple of Black teachers and I was amazed that we had qualified teachers who were Black!'
>
> (Parent C)

> 'I remember a Black teacher called Miss Pink and I thought, "Wow, a Black teacher". Teachers were mainly Asians.'
>
> (SENCO, School G)

The deputy headteacher of School D, a large secondary school, felt that it is important for parents and the community to have a Black headteacher. He said:

> 'I haven't questioned it before. If parents of any background have a trust in the school then it shouldn't be a problem.'

We asked this White deputy head whether he thought White people might find it difficult to work under Black leadership and he replied:

> 'I have seen racism towards the Black staff, particularly to those who have to deliver hard messages. If that were told to White families or it came from me it might be difficult. I think it is important that the makeup of the leadership team reflects the area. We have Black members of the senior leadership team and in terms of gender and ethnicity there is a good mix across our faculties.'
>
> (Deputy head, School E)

Those interviewed were generally of the opinion that more Black teachers were needed in schools:

> 'It's about identity. If you put a young White female teacher from outside London in a class with secondary Black Caribbean boys they know that they can wind her up and she'll easily leave within a couple of weeks. If you put a mature Black teacher in there, it will be different.'
>
> (Parent H)

> 'Role models are important. We have male and female Black Caribbean teachers, teaching assistants that play a key role in supporting pupils. We need more in our schools to reflect the diversity of our school populations.'
>
> (White headteacher, School A)

> 'Being a Black headteacher I was a positive factor in Caribbean-heritage pupils' achievement. In my school I had teachers from Sierra Leone, Jamaica and an Irish male teacher. It really did pull everyone together. It should reflect the make-up of the local community.'
>
> (Headteacher, School JE)

Other headteachers are aware that 'as a Black Caribbean headteacher' they offer Black pupils in the school a strong role model, an incentive to achieve:

'I use my success in achieving the position of headteacher at the school to tell the pupils that it's about taking opportunities that are there to be taken; I tell them it's about being confident in your own abilities and about realising that we all have a lot to contribute. I hope the Black Caribbean pupils see me as someone who understands and who is providing opportunities for every single child to succeed' (headteacher, School SJ).

The headteacher thought the Black Caribbean children felt comfortable with him and that they could speak to an adult who would listen. This strongly mirrored the view of the pupils who were interviewed. The pupils were extremely positive about the school staff, but at the same time expressed the importance to them of Black staff. A Year 6 pupil said, 'When there are no Black teachers you feel uncomfortable. ... You feel they are not mixing with you. It's much better now. There is lots of support for learning.'

The Black Caribbean parents see the headteacher's appointment as a very positive step. They feel the children now have someone – a role model – who can relate to their issues, particularly around the perception of how Black children achieve. The head of School JE said:

> 'Having more Black headteachers is critical for the success of Black Caribbean and African pupils in schools. It's not about appointing Black headteachers because of their colour, though; you need Black headteachers who are equally good but with a good understanding of the local context in which the school is operating. Some headteachers come from suburban and rural areas and they really don't understand what it is like to work in a multicultural environment.'

We asked why Black Caribbean pupils do so well in these schools. These are some of the responses:

> 'This is a school where diversity is highly valued and the headteacher's leadership is strong on equality and race issues.'
>
> (Governors)

> 'The quality of leadership and planning by the headteacher, the diversity, the values-based recruitment, which leads to a high-quality teaching and support staff.'
>
> (Teacher)

> 'This is a school with high expectations for all its community. The head leads by example. She has high standards for herself

and expects the same for everyone else. She has recruited a multi-ethnic workforce that reflects the community we serve and this has helped to drive up standards in the school.'

(White teacher's comment on Black headteacher)

The case study schools all employ a representative multi-ethnic workforce, including staff of Black Caribbean heritage. The quality of the staff and its diversity is seen as crucial in these schools. So is having the right teaching staff, staff who buy into the school's culture and core values. They recruit teachers who want to be in the school and who believe in partnership with the pupils and their parents. What is special about these schools is that local communities are well represented in the school and staff speak many of the languages of the local community. Children who feel they can relate to members of staff from their own cultural background are motivated to learn.

The case study schools also illustrate that promoting equality and diversity in the classroom need not be a challenge. In every school in England, children should be familiar with diversity and multicultural education from early on. If schools actively recruit from the local community, they show loyalty to it. Most schools' staff teams are comfortable with the profile of pupils who attend and enjoy raising children's achievement. Then they can be sure that they are doing valuable and valued work.

5.7 Celebration of cultural diversity

These multicultural schools, where the diversity of ethnic origin, languages spoken and cultural heritage brings real life to learning, value the cultural heritage of each child and celebrate diversity through assemblies, the curriculum, International Day, international links and Black History Month.

Black History Month recognizes and values inspirational individuals and events within the Black communities. Introduced in the UK in 1987, it is celebrated annually. Every October the schools explore different countries and celebrate a range of activities during and outside the school day. They organize heritage days, series of lessons, activities and assemblies to focus on Black and minority achievement through the curriculum. In one headteacher's words:

'The school uses Black History Month to recognize and to value the inspirational individuals and events that have shaped the Black generation. This takes precedence in the classroom during the month to remember and celebrate the important people from the past and also those who contribute to and help our society today.'

A pupil at School O said that the school uses Black History Month as an opportunity to explore different countries and celebrate diversity:

> 'Every class studies a different country to give them a wealth of knowledge about the culture, the food, the language and people. Each class presents their country through an assembly – last year we learnt about 12 countries, this ingrains diversity in the children.'

The events during Black History Month elicited praise from parents, teachers and pupils. A parent governor observed: 'it helped our children to understand the Black history and heritage. Every culture and history is recognized and this is a great thing about this school.'

School SJ has an annual International Day for pupils, parents and neighbours that celebrates cultures from across the globe at the school. In the words of the headteacher:

> 'All the colours, sights and sounds of the world were brought to life at a buzzing International Day. The parents and pupils from different parts of Africa played colourful African dances and music in traditional dress from Ghana, Nigeria, Ethiopia, Somalia and other African countries. A Scotsman played the bagpipes in traditional dress, while elsewhere a steel band played by pupils from the Caribbean world and there was African drumming by pupils from the African continent. Many parents and students performed traditional Portuguese dance and music.'

5.7.1 International links

The case study schools link with schools in countries including Kenya, Ghana, Jamaica, Portugal, Sierra Leone, Germany, India, Cameroon, China and Russia. **School I** developed a project to link the school with Anchovy High School, St James, Jamaica and St Andrew's Anglican Complex in Sekondi, Ghana. The Sekondi project was developed in 2007 to mark the bicentenary of the abolition of the slave trade. It was named the 'Triangle Project' in recognition of the historical triangle of trade that existed between Britain, Ghana and Jamaica. The aims of the project were to increase knowledge of identity and the contribution made by people of the Caribbean, and to forge links with schools in Ghana and Jamaica. The school chaplain explained:

> 'The project has a Christian ethos of "love" of other communities and shares the resources we are blessed to have here. Many of the children's parents have a close link with the community and

value highly the school link with Ghana and Jamaica. This project not only helped to enrich the school curriculum here but also helped to improve cultural understanding and exchange between Britain and the two countries. Parents are very supportive of the school link.'

The project produced a teaching resource entitled 'The Triangle Project: Cross-curricular resources', which is widely used in the link schools to share the school and staff experience of visiting the schools in Ghana and Jamaica. The project has made a lasting impression on the school community and the link with the schools in Ghana and Jamaica remains strong. The cross-curricular material developed for classroom use is one legacy; another is the charity that was set up to raise funds to support the partner schools and sustain the links. The headteacher said:

'Working with an International Partner school is a useful way of exploring issues around identity. After all, children first need to investigate their own culture in order to explain it to an audience of international peers. They can then discover similarities and differences with their partner school's culture – and perhaps delve into deeper issues such as racism, migration and cultural stereotyping.'

5.7.2 Using assemblies and an inclusive curriculum

The celebration of diversity is embedded in school life in assemblies and the curriculum. **School RE**'s curriculum is designed to meet the needs and interests of the various groups of students as they move through the school, and offers a creative and extensive range of choices at GCSE and in the sixth form, including modern foreign languages. It is underpinned by outstanding careers guidance. The curriculum and extra opportunities contribute to the outstanding spiritual, moral, social and cultural development that prepares students for life in modern British society.

'The school has now reached the stage where it is natural for everyone to be proud of their heritage; as a community we have embraced the different languages that we have. Everyone feels they can succeed and that they have something to contribute to the community.'

(Teacher, School JE)

'We aim to ensure the cultural, religious and linguistic heritages are welcomed inside and valued within the school curriculum.'

(Headteacher, School RE)

'Everyone should be proud of their heritage; as a community we have embraced the different languages that we have. Everyone feels they can succeed.'

(Pupil, School O)

'We learn about different things and different countries. It helps us as we need to know about our language and countries.'

(Pupil, School RE)

As part of its inclusion strategy, secondary school H has introduced a Britishness project to explore what Britishness means and how to play a role in British society. It wants everyone from whatever background or heritage to feel part of British society. 'We celebrate the heritage of all groups in our school and the contribution all make to British society.' The students were given time, guidance and opportunities to research Britishness. The experiment worked well. The students came with innovative ideas and used their findings to run workshops and assemblies.

The Anne Frank Project draws on the power of this young girl, and her diary of life in hiding from the Nazis, to challenge prejudice and help foster students' understanding about citizenship, human rights, democracy and respect for others. The Anne Frank Trust supported all the KS3 students in visits to exhibitions about Anne Frank, and ran assemblies and stimulating workshops. Students became active ambassadors for the school and informed citizens.

5.7.3 Achievement Awards

The case study schools and all the others in the LA celebrate the achievement of pupils at KS1, KS2, KS3 and GCSE at the Royal Festival Hall in London each year.

The Achievement Awards ceremony celebrates both the academic achievement of around 850 young people, and the support and commitment of their families and teachers. The event has been attended by over 3,000 young people, their families, headteachers, teachers and staff across the LA's schools. It has helped to inspire pupils and to engage parents in their children's education. The parents, communities, teachers and headteachers welcome the opportunity to come together to offer encouragement to local achievers who have excelled in national examinations.

5.7.4 Attractive and informative displays

The case study schools feature numerous impressive displays that celebrate students' achievement and acknowledge the diversity of their population. School H's headteacher said:

> 'Displays in schools reflect the school community, including Black Caribbean, mixed race and African contributions to history, cultural artefacts, cultural and language background of people of Africa and historical and political maps of Africa and Black History Month activities. Displays are a reflection of our community. They are not put up to fill wall space. They are part of an ethos of expectations.'

All the evidence shows that celebrating cultural diversity is part of the LA schools' life. Together, the assemblies and Black History Month, the language of the week and the curriculum, International Days and the Achievement Awards ceremony have imbued them with a culture of acceptance and empathy. In particular, it has inspired the Black Caribbean and African students in all four case study schools.

5.8 Summary and conclusions

The schools that succeed in raising the attainment of minority ethnic pupils share broadly similar approaches to those used for disadvantaged pupils. However, in addition to the success factors outlined in previous chapters they have developed an inclusive curriculum, have established a partnership with parents and the community, actively value cultural diversity, have recruited a multicultural workforce, and have actively challenged racism (for details see Demie, 2005; DfES, 2003b; McKenley *et al.*, 2003; Ofsted, 2002; Blair *et al.*, 1998).

All the case study schools have strong links with their communities. They encourage the active involvement of parents in their children's education, and communicating with parents is a major strength. They are resourceful in employing specialists who can build trust between school and family, such as family support workers and learning mentors. Schools try to find imaginative ways to make parents welcome, and are responsive to their needs. They share information with parents on the children's achievement and development as well as any disciplinary issues. The schools see themselves as part of the community. Parents are overwhelmingly supportive: they understand that the school provides an environment for learning and feel that their child is valued on their own terms.

Another success factor is the ability of leadership to create a community ethos by employing a diverse multi-ethnic workforce at every level including leadership teams. They have recruited excellent teaching and non-teaching staff from the local community who reflect the languages, cultures and ethnic backgrounds of the students.

Valuing the diverse cultural backgrounds of the students has helped to raise the achievement of ethnic-minority pupils. The diversity of ethnic origin, languages and cultural heritage enlivens the learning. Pupils thrive because they see around them every day the living evidence of what it is to live in a multicultural world, and the schools celebrate that diversity.

In addition the study confirms that the schools have developed an inclusive curriculum that reflects and incorporates the children's heritage, culture and experience. Black experience is used to enrich the curriculum in art, dance, music, geography, history and technology. In turn, the students experience organizations such as the Royal Ballet, the Royal Festival Hall, English National Opera, the Museum of London, London's artistic worlds, the Black Cultural Archives, the British Museum and the Migration Museum, greatly widening their horizons.

Effective support to meet the needs of pupils who have English as an additional language is another strength of the case study schools. It will be discussed in the chapter that follows.

Notes

[1] ChatterBug is a type of speech and language therapy used in case study schools to help children develop their skills in the areas of maintaining attention, listening, turn-taking, and receptive and expressive language.

[2] Ready to Learn is a whole-school behaviour and learning policy aimed at eliminating disruptive behaviour in lessons.

[3] The Trinity Laban Conservatoire of Music and Dance, based in London.

[4] Debate Mate is 'an educational charity that uses the brightest university students to run after-school debate clubs in areas of high child poverty across the world' (https://debatemate.com/about/).

[5] The Creative Learning Journey is 'an online planning and assessment tool that automatically tracks the National Curriculum' (www.thecreativelearningjourney. co.uk/overview.asp).

Chapter 6

Raising the achievement of children with English as an additional language

6.1 Introduction

This chapter explores how having English as an additional language affects a child's attainment, and examines how schools help them succeed. It looks at some major findings from Inner London Education Authority schools before its abolition in 1990. Many have been reported (see for instance Demie, 2013a, 2017a, 2018c; Demie and Lewis, 2018; Demie and McLean, 2016). Details of the methodology of the research and the selection of the case study schools appear in Chapter 3 of the present book.

Children for whom English is an additional language (EAL) are learning English and using their first language. They come from a vast variety of geographical, linguistic, cultural, ethnic and educational backgrounds. They are at different stages of acquiring the English language, from complete beginner to fully fluent, and may be fluent in several other languages or dialects.

6.1.1 Children in UK schools for whom English is an additional language

English as an additional language (EAL) attracts much interest among educationalists and policy makers, and yet little is known about what works to raise EAL pupils' achievement in schools. The number of pupils in England with English as an additional language has increased over the years from 499,000 in 1997 to 1,557,511 in 2018 (Demie, 2015; DfE, 2018; Table 6.1), a rise of 161%. There are now more than 1.5 million pupils between 5 and 18 years old in England's primary, secondary and special schools and alternative provision, who speak a total of over 360 languages, and who are at varying stages in learning English.

Across both the primary and secondary phases, the number of EAL pupils has doubled since 1997, when just 7.8% of primary school pupils and 7.3% of secondary students spoke a language other than English. In 2018, of 8,109,479 pupils in English schools about 21% in primary, 17% in secondary and 15% in special schools have English as an additional language. About

19% of the school population in England and Wales now speak English as an additional language (DfE, 2018), but they are unevenly distributed. Over half of all EAL pupils are located in only 20 of the 150 local authorities (LAs) in England, and nearly three-quarters of schools have fewer than 5% (DfE, 2013: Tables 9a–c). In 2012, the DfE spelled out its policy on EAL education thus: 'The Coalition Government's priority for children learning English as an Additional Language (EAL) is to promote rapid language acquisition and include them in mainstream education as quickly as possible' (DfE, 2012: [1]). 'We believe that English should be the medium of instruction in schools' (ibid.: [5]) and that 'Classroom teachers have responsibility for ensuring that pupils can participate in lessons' (ibid.: [1]).

Table 6.1 Number and percentage of EAL pupils in primary and secondary schools in England

| | Pupils with EAL | | | | | |
| | Primary | | Secondary | | Total | |
Year	Number	%	Number	%	Number	%
1997	276,200	7.8	222,800	7.3	499,000	7.6
1998	303,635	8.5	238,532	7.8	542,167	8.2
1999	301,800	8.4	244,684	7.8	546,484	8.1
2000	311,512	8.7	255,256	8.0	566,768	8.4
2001	331,512	9.3	258,893	8.0	590,405	8.7
2002	350,483	10.0	282,235	8.6	632,718	9.3
2003	362,690	10.4	291,110	8.8	653,800	9.6
2004	376,600	11.0	292,890	8.8	669,490	9.9
2005	395,270	11.6	299,200	9.0	694,470	10.3
2006	419,600	12.5	314,950	9.5	734,550	11.0
2007	447,650	13.5	342,140	10.5	789,790	12.0
2008	470,080	14.4	354,300	10.8	824,380	12.6
2009	491,340	15.2	362,600	11.1	853,940	13.1
2010	518,020	16.0	378,210	11.6	896,230	13.8
2011	547,030	16.8	399,550	12.3	946,580	14.6
2012	577,555	17.5	417,765	12.9	995,320	15.2
2013	612,160	18.1	436,150	13.6	1,048,310	15.9
2014	654,405	18.7	455,205	14.3	1,109,610	16.6
2015	693,815	19.4	477,286	15.0	1,171,101	17.4
2016	734,355	20.1	499,061	15.7	1,233,416	18.0
2017	771,083	20.6	520,083	16.2	1,291,166	18.6
2018	998,829	21.2	539,895	16.6	1,538,724	19.3

Source: DfE, 'Schools, pupils and their characteristics 1997–2018', SFR.

The policy in England since the mid-1980s is that EAL pupils, along with all pupils, have equal access and equal opportunity, with English as the preferred school language for minority pupils. Minority languages may be valued and celebrated as worthwhile but academic attainment is only achieved through the medium of English. No detailed language curricula or assessment is provided for languages other than English.

6.1.2 Assessment of students learning EAL

In the UK, statutory assessment for pupils with EAL is the same as assessment for native English speakers, although several English-speaking countries have developed EAL standards and assessment frameworks that are linked to the mainstream curriculum. The learning of EAL takes place at the same time as learning academic content. The issue of appropriate assessment is therefore critical in the UK context.

The EAL learning needs of pupils vary greatly from beginners to advanced learners (see Demie, 2013a, 2016; Demie and Strand, 2006). The stages of English through which pupils commonly progress identified by Hester in 1990 have been widely used (see Demie 2013a, 2016; Demie and Strand, 2006). They cover aspects of bilingual children's language development in English and reflect an approach to learning in which young children acquire English language through exposure to it in a context of learning content, in a welcoming environment, for example. They are:

- Stage One – new to English
- Stage Two – becoming familiar with English
- Stage Three – becoming confident as a user of English
- Stage Four – a very fluent user of English in most social and learning contexts.

Many local authorities adapted 'Stages of English' to assess aspects of bilingual pupils' reading, writing, speaking and listening development. However, others use the Northern Association of Support Services for Equality and Achievement EAL Assessment System (NASSEA, 2001) or the Bell Foundation (2017) descriptors.

The Department for Education (DfE) recently adopted a national five-stage EAL assessment, and requires schools in England to report proficiency in stages of English language for all EAL pupils at Key Stage 1 and above, who have been recorded in the census as having English as an additional language. The schools assess the position of each of their EAL pupils at reading, writing, speaking and listening against the five-stage proficiency framework outlined below and make a 'best-fit' judgement as to the stage the pupil most closely corresponds to:

- **Stage A (New to English):** May use first language for learning and other purposes. May remain completely silent in the classroom. May be copying/repeating some words or phrases. May understand some everyday expressions in English but have minimal or no literacy in English. Needs a considerable amount of EAL support.
- **Stage B (Early acquisition):** May follow day-to-day social communication in English and participate in learning activities with support. Beginning to use spoken English for social purposes. May understand simple instructions and can follow narrative/accounts with visual support. May have developed some skills in reading and writing. May have become familiar with some subject specific vocabulary. Still needs a significant amount of EAL support to access the curriculum.
- **Stage C (Developing competence):** May participate in learning activities with increasing independence. Able to express self orally in English, but structural inaccuracies are still apparent. Literacy will require ongoing support, particularly for understanding text and writing. May be able to follow abstract concepts and more complex written English. Requires ongoing EAL support to access the curriculum fully.
- **Stage D (Competent):** Oral English will be developing well, enabling successful engagement in activities across the curriculum. Can read and understand a wide variety of texts. Written English may lack complexity and contain occasional evidence of errors in structure. Needs some support to access subtle nuances of meaning, to refine English usage, and to develop abstract vocabulary. Needs some/occasional EAL support to access complex curriculum material and tasks.
- **Stage E (Fluent):** Can operate across the curriculum to a level of competence equivalent to that of a pupil who uses English as his/her first language. Operates without EAL support across the curriculum.

(DfE, 2017a: 13–14; Demie, 2017b)

For the purposes of this analysis, pupils at Stages A–E are classified as 'EAL'. Stage A are classified as 'beginners' in English and those at Stage E are classed as 'fully fluent'. Pupils who only speak English are not assigned a stage of English proficiency and are classed as 'English only'.

The proficiency stages provide detailed information to assess EAL learners' language development from Stage A to Stage E and can be used by schools, LAs and central government as a diagnostic tool to analyse needs for future teaching, to track progress and to provide baseline information for statistical purposes.

Previous research has shown that there are more Key Stage 1 EAL pupils at low levels of English proficiency than at later key stages (Demie, 2013a, 2013b). During Key Stage 2, more EAL pupils are at proficiency stages D and E, and by the time they reach secondary school most are fully fluent in English (stage E): few are still at the early stages of English proficiency (Demie, 2013a). A recent study suggests that the majority of EAL students are between stages C and E at KS2, and at the end of secondary education are at Stage E (see Table 6.2 and DfE, 2017b). Overall, in the case study LA schools, about 8.3% are at Stage A (new to English), 16.2% Stage B (early acquisition), 23.3% at Stage C (developing competence), 23.2% Stage D (competent), and 29.0% fully fluent in English (Stage E). Fifty-two per cent of the pupils in all the LA schools are English-only speakers (Demie, Butler and McDonald, 2018a, 2018b).

6.2 The achievement of EAL students in schools: Evidence from literature

English language proficiency is the major factor influencing the performance of pupils who have English as an additional language. English is the language of instruction, so for pupils to access the curriculum fully and effectively they need to be fluent in English.

A review of the literature suggests that most of the previous studies have focused on EAL assessment and stages of English proficiency (Demie, 2013a, 2016, 2017a; Strand and Demie, 2005; Cummins, 1992, 2000; Collier, 1987, 1992), bilingualism (Murphy and Unthiah, 2015; Conteh and Meier, 2014; NALDIC, 2014; Cummins, 1992), first-language use when supporting early EAL children (Arnot *et al.*, 2014; Krashen, 1999), EAL achievement and language diversity (Demie *et al.*, 2017; Demie, 2015; Murphy and Unthiah, 2015; NALDIC, 2014; Tereshchenko and Archer, 2014), and government EAL policy (DfE, 2012; Sutton, 2017).

A number of other studies of the factors affecting EAL pupils' achievement attributed EAL pupils' underachievement to various factors, including difficulties in speaking English, ethnic background and factors such as poverty and recent entry to the country (Strand, Malmberg and Hall, 2015). However, the language barrier strongly affects EAL children's achievement. For EAL pupils to have full access to the curriculum, they need to be fluent in English. A good many studies have examined the way EAL pupils are assessed, their English proficiency and the relationship between their stage of English fluency and their attainment. Research evidence from England shows that a student's fluency in English is a key predictor of their achievement in national tests at age 11 and in public examinations at age 16 (e.g. Demie, 2013a, 2013b, 2016, 2017a, 2017b; Demie and Strand, 2006). Analyses of the KS2 test results and GCSE examination results for pupils in an Inner London LA by level of English language acquisition show that children with EAL at the early stages of English had significantly lower KS2 test scores in all subjects (see Strand and Demie, 2005; Demie and Strand, 2006). However, pupils with EAL who were fully fluent in English achieved significantly higher scores than their monolingual peers in all KS2 tests and GCSE. The association with low attainment for the early stages of competence remained significant after controlling for a range of other pupil characteristics – age, gender, free school meal entitlement, stage of special educational need, and ethnic group – although these factors effectively explained the attainment levels of the 'fully fluent' group.

In general the data shows a strong relationship between stage of fluency in English and educational attainment. The performance of EAL pupils increases as their fluency in English increases. Pupils in the early stages of English perform at low levels and EAL students not fluent in English achieve significantly below White British students who speak English only. The findings also confirm that the achievement of EAL students who were fully fluent in English far outstripped those of pupils for whom English was their only language.

The body of available literature suggests that English-language proficiency is an important factor in predicting how well children perform at the end of primary and secondary school. There is a need for more research on the way we assess these students, and on the relationship between their proficiency in English and their attainment, to improve our knowledge about how to support them in the classroom.

6.3 EAL pupils' achievement gap: The empirical evidence

Table 7.2 shows the KS2 achievement of EAL pupils in England by region. Nationally, at Key Stage 2, those with English as an additional language achieved less well in reading, writing and maths (58%) than those with English as their first language (62%). A further analysis of the achievement of Key Stage 2 EAL pupils by region also shows wide variations in performance and in the achievement gap (see Table 6.2). Inner London has the highest density of EAL pupils in England (57.5%); they perform better than EAL pupils in other parts of the country: two-thirds of EAL pupils in Inner London (66.4%) achieve expected levels or better at Key Stage 2, higher than the national average for all pupils of 61%.

Historically, EAL pupils do not perform as well as their non-EAL peers, but the gap in achievement between EAL and non-EAL pupils in Inner London was the lowest in the country, with only a 2 percentage point difference, compared to the average gap for all of England of 4%. EAL pupils in Outer London and the South East performed similarly to those in Inner London, with a similarly smaller attainment gap than the rest of the country.

EAL pupils from all regions except Inner London, Outer London and the South East were performing below the national average at Key Stage 2 (Table 6.2). EAL pupils living in Yorkshire and the Humber remain the lowest-achieving group, with only half (51%) achieving the expected standard, ten percentage points below the national average and nine percentage points below their monolingual English-speaking peers within that region.

Table 6.2 KS2 and GCSE performance of EAL pupils by region

Region	% EAL pupils	KS2 L4 (reading, writing and maths)			Region	% EAL pupils	GCSE (5+ A*–C including English and maths)		
		EAL	Non-EAL	Gap			EAL	Non-EAL	Gap
Inner London	58	66	69	–2	South East	11	66	63	3
Outer London	46	64	68	–5	Outer London	37	66	66	0
South East	13	61	63	–3	Inner London	52	64	62	3
North East	7	57	66	–9	South West	6	59	61	–2
East	14	56	61	–6	East	11	59	62	–4
South West	7	54	61	–7	North West	11	58	60	–2
North West	15	53	62	–9	West Midlands	17	57	59	–2
West Midlands	22	53	61	–8	East Midlands	11	56	60	–3
East Midlands	14	52	60	–8	North East	6	55	57	–2
Yorkshire and the Humber	17	51	60	–9	Yorkshire and the Humber	14	51	60	–10
England	20	58	62	–4	England	16	61	61	0

Source: DfE, NPD performance data for 2017.

The EAL attainment gap for students with EAL in Yorkshire and the Humber, and similarly the North East, the North West and the West Midlands is over four times as big as that in Inner London. EAL pupils in the East Midlands (52%) and the South West (54%) were also among the lowest-achieving students, even though their monolingual peers achieved close to the national average.

A similar trend appears at GCSE (Table 6.2). Nationally, the attainment gap between EAL and non-EAL pupils at GCSE was much narrower than at Key Stage 2, with EAL pupils achieving almost as well as English monolinguals.

At Key Stage 2, the South East, Outer London and Inner London have the highest-attaining EAL pupils. In 2017, Outer London EAL pupils achieved as well as their monolingual peers, while EAL pupils in the South East and Inner London outperformed English-only speakers. At GCSE, similarly to Key Stage 2, EAL pupils in Yorkshire and the Humber were the lowest-attaining EAL group: they showed a 10 percentage point difference to their peers. The East of England, the East Midlands, the West Midlands and the North East also showed EAL students underperforming when compared with their monolingual peers, but the gaps appear to be much smaller than at Key Stage 2.

It is perhaps significant that the number of EAL pupils in the regions with the poorest attainment is far smaller than in Inner and Outer London where the EAL pupil population is high. There does appear to be a positive correlation between the density of the EAL pupil population and their success, particularly at Key Stage 2. Regions with the highest proportions of EAL pupils, such as Inner and Outer London, but also the South East of England showed a higher percentage of their EAL pupils achieving expected levels than, for example, the East, North East and South West of England, where EAL numbers were much lower, which appears to have a negative impact on attainment.

It also shows that schools with many EAL and ethnic-minority pupils in London do better than other regions in England. The question is, 'Why would schools with large numbers of minority immigrant children, many of whom speak other languages before learning English in London, do better academically than similar schools catering mainly for White British pupils in other regions?' Arguably the higher attainment of EAL pupils in London is related to a London-specific effect. There are several reasons for this disparity.

A big part of the answer is that London schools have many years of experience of working with EAL and ethnic-minority communities, and as a result London schools are better at educating EAL children, providing an environment where they thrive. Because every school in London serves a linguistically diverse community, there is effective support for EAL pupils. And expertise within London schools in supporting students in learning English as an additional language surpasses other regions of England. The teaching and class support for EAL is well organized and led by EAL co-ordinators and well-trained classroom teachers. There are excellent systems for monitoring the work of the EAL pupils, identifying those who need additional help or extra challenge and then providing the appropriate support. Supporting English language acquisition for EAL students is often a dominant feature of schools' curriculum development. The schools are also analysing data to identify pupils who are at risk of underachieving. We would argue that the excellent support provided in London is one significant reason why London children do so much better than those elsewhere in England (Demie and McLean, 2015a, 2015b).

Secondly, leaders of London schools are strong on equality and diversity. They recognize the importance of cultural, ethnic and linguistic diversity in raising achievement and fostering community cohesion. The schools are highly inclusive, and strive for the educational progress, personal development and well-being of every student, whatever their background. Most London schools pride themselves on the diversity of their workforces. Teachers, teaching assistants, learning mentors and support staff are often recruited from the local communities and reflect the languages, cultures, ethnic backgrounds and faiths of the pupils. This has helped the schools to become a central point in the wider community. In addition, the school leaders appear focused upon rigorous monitoring and evaluation as the basis for school improvement. They constantly demonstrate that starting school with poor English plus economic disadvantage need not be a barrier to achievement. They recognize that proficiency in English is the key to educational success for their EAL learners and rigorously use their data on ethnicity, language diversity and language fluency to track the performance and progress of every EAL child, and apply proven strategies for improvement (Demie and McLean, 2015).

Thirdly, as Burgess (2014) argues, the composition of London's families may be a factor. It may well be that the better-educated and more aspirational immigrant families tend to end up in London. It is certainly the case that many immigrant communities take education very seriously and see it as the way out of poverty. They may even have heard from others about London's schools.

London also has one of the largest influxes of European Union (EU) immigrant families and their high educational aspirations. Timo Hannay suggests that 'the better-educated and more aspirational immigrant families tend to end up disproportionately in London than in other areas' (*TES*, 2016).

Finally, London schools are funded at a higher level than most schools in England. This additional funding has been used to employ more qualified staff and well-trained EAL teachers for targeted interventions and support (Demie and McLean, 2015a, 2015b).

Importantly, however, EAL status alone is not necessarily an accurate means of studying pupils' attainment. Pupils with EAL are a very heterogeneous group, from many different ethnic and cultural backgrounds, and likely to show a wide variation in achievement. The DfE warns us:

> EAL funding is determined on the basis of census data which records whether or not a pupil's first language is English. As such, it is not a precise measure of language proficiency at pupil-level. 'First language' is the language to which a child was initially exposed during early development and continues to be exposed to in the home or in the community. It does not mean that pupils are necessarily fluent in a language other than English, or that they cannot speak English fluently. Pupils can therefore be identified in the census as EAL when they are bilingual and have no specific need of support to access mainstream education in English.
>
> (DfE, 2016a: 27)

Other researchers have argued along similar lines:

> The NPD EAL variable clearly needs to be interpreted with some caution. It is explicitly *not* a measure of the pupil's fluency in English: pupils recorded as EAL may speak no English at all or they may be fully fluent in English. Indeed there is huge heterogeneity within the group coded as EAL. On the one hand, this might include second or third generation ethnic minority students who may be exposed to a language other than English as part of their cultural heritage but use it rarely if at all, using English as their everyday language and being quite fluent in it. At the other extreme it might include new migrants arriving in England that speak no English at all, and may have varying levels of literacy in their previous country of origin.
>
> (Strand *et al.*, 2015: 16)

Leedham (2016) noted that using EAL status, undifferentiated by levels of English proficiency and language spoken at home, has caused researchers and policy makers to reinforce a misleading picture of EAL achievement by repeating a familiar narrative. She argued that 'meaningful analysis of outcomes [of EAL pupils' achievement] is only achieved through data disaggregated by stages of fluency in English, languages and ethnic background'. Researchers are now alert to the need to differentiate a pupil's performance by their proficiency in English (Demie, 2013a, 2015; vonAhn *et al.*, 2011; Demie and Strand, 2006). More research is needed on the relationship between fluency in English and EAL pupils' academic performance in schools.

Table 6.3 KS2 and GCSE performance by proficiency in English, 2017

EAL proficiency stage	KS2 pupil number		KS2 results[1]				GCSE pupil number		GCSE results
	KS2 cohorts	%	Reading	Writing	Maths	RWM[3]	GCSE cohorts	%	5+ A*–C[2]
A (new to English)	34	1.1	0	0	12[4]	0	5	0.3	0
B (early acquisition)	98	3.3	24	20	46	12	28	1.4	25
C (developing competence)	389	13.2	65	76	81	56	106	5.4	47
D (competent)	440	14.9	75	85	82	66	217	11.1	68
E (fully fluent)	487	16.5	89	95	95	85	505	25.9	70
English only	1,381	46.7	82	82	82	71	1,076	55.1	56
All pupils	2,957	100	77	81	82	69	1,953	100	59

[1] The percentage meeting the expected standard in each subject.
[2] Including English and maths.
[3] Reading, writing and maths combined.
[4] Includes four pupils who were identified as fully fluent in their home language and with special talent in maths.

Source: Demie, Butler, Tong *et al.* (2018).

Table 6.3 also gives the average performance of EAL pupils at KS2 and GCSE by proficiency in English. The empirical findings from the attainment data, using the new national EAL proficiency stages in England, show that at KS2 no one at stage A (new to English) achieved the expected standard, compared with 12% at stage B (early acquisition), 56% at stage C (developing competency), 66% at stage D (competent) and 85% at stage E (fluent in English). The EAL pupils at stages A–D are underachieving compared with the 71% of English-only speakers who met the expected standard in RWM.

Overall the results of the KS2 analysis show that the percentage of pupils attaining expected outcomes in each subject at the end of primary education rises as the stage of proficiency in English increases. Across reading, writing and maths, those who were new to English or at early acquisition show very low attainment, but it improves as proficiency in English improves. The achievement of EAL pupils who are fully fluent in English (Stage E) continues to be high, their 2017 RWM outcome being 14% above monolingual English pupils and 16% above the test average for all pupils.

Similar findings emerged from analysis of GCSE data at the end of secondary education. The data in Table 6.3 shows that no one at Stage A (new to English) achieved 5+ A*–C including English and maths, compared with 25% of pupils at stage B (early acquisition), 47% at stage C (developing competency), 68% at stage D (competent) and 70% at stage E (fluent in English). EAL students who are fully fluent in English performed better than English-only speakers. About 70% of EAL students at Stage E (fully fluent) achieved 5+ A*–C including English and maths compared with 56% of monolingual English speakers. There is a 14% achievement gap between fully fluent EAL pupils and monolingual English speakers. The LA's GCSE data confirms that the percentage of students attaining 5+ A*–C increased as stage of proficiency in English increased.

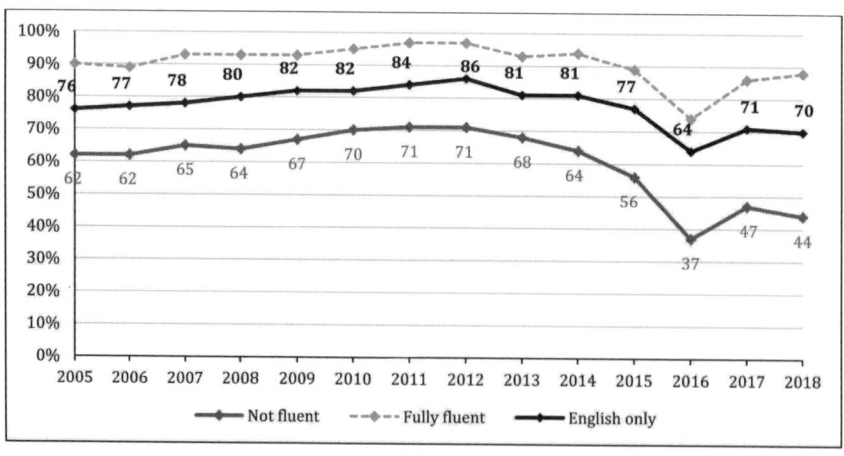

Figure 6.1 Achievement gap at KS2 (RWM level 4) between EAL pupils not fluent in English and monolingual English speakers. From Demie, Butler, Tong *et al.*, 2018

Figure 6.1, which shows the achievement gap between non-fluent EAL pupils and monolingual English students, confirms that EAL pupils overall do not perform as well as their non-EAL peers in English schools, because of English-language barriers. In particular, EAL pupils not fluent in English achieve significantly below monolingual English speakers in English schools.

Similar evidence can be seen in the secondary data (Figure 6.2). Both the primary and secondary empirical evidence shows that there is a wide variation in performance and in the achievement gap between EAL not fluent in English and monolingual pupils. What is even more worrying is that low achievement of EAL pupils not fluent in English, has been masked by the failure of government statistics to monitor and distinguish EAL pupils by stages of proficiency in English.

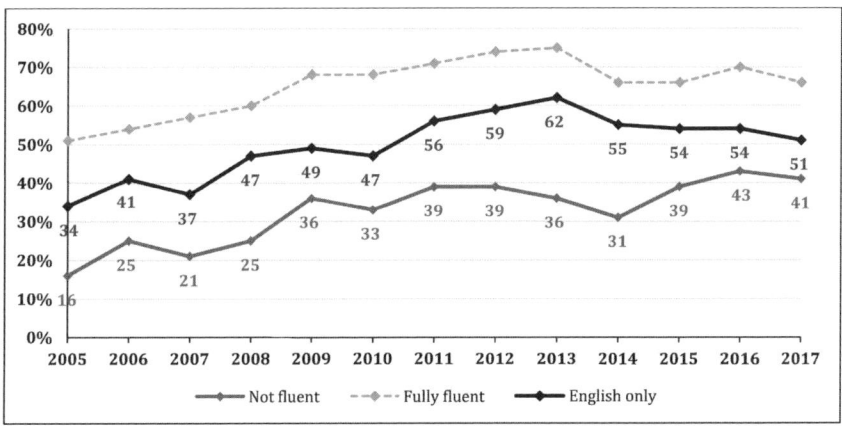

Figure 6.2 Achievement gap at GCSE (5+ A*–C including English and maths) between EAL pupils not fluent in English and monolingual English speakers. From Demie, Butler, Tong *et al.*, 2018

The analysis of the attainment of EAL pupils by stage in English proficiency at KS2 and GCSE produced three key findings.

First, 49% of pupils in primary schools and 47% in secondary schools in the case study LA were classed as EAL pupils. The empirical evidence shows that more Key Stage 1 EAL pupils are at low levels of English proficiency than at later key stages. During Key Stage 2, more achieve proficiency stages C, D and E, and by the time they reach secondary school most are fully fluent (stage E) and far fewer are at stage A or B.

Second, data using the new national EAL proficiency stages found that EAL pupils at stages A or B had low achievement, whereas EAL pupils who were fully fluent in English far outstripped the achievement of pupils for whom English was their only language (Demie, 2013a, 2017a). Overall, the research confirms the strong effect of stage of English proficiency on the children's educational attainment: the number of pupils attaining expected outcomes at KS2 and GCSE increased as their English proficiency rose. These findings support previous research (Demie, 2013a, 2016; Demie, Lewis and McLean, 2006; Goldfeld *et al.*, 2014; Halle *et al.* 2012; Prevoo *et al.*, 2016; Strand and Demie, 2005) that suggests that the academic attainment of EAL pupils is dependent on their proficiency in English.

6.4 Schools' strategies for raising the achievement of EAL pupils

The literature suggests that there is a paucity of research on what works to raise the achievement of EAL pupils (DfES, 2006; DfE, 2012; Sutton, 2017; Demie, 2013a). However, there is research that identifies the reasons for schools' success in raising achievement, namely the quality of teaching and learning, effective leadership at all levels, effective use of an inclusive curriculum, diversity in the school workforce, high moral and academic values and high expectations, and the effective use of assessment data to monitor and track EAL children's performance and target support accordingly (see Demie, 2017a; Demie and McLean, 2016; Ofsted, 2009a). These success factors are about driving school improvement for all groups of pupils. The key challenge for this study is therefore to establish what strategies schools can use to raise the achievement of pupils with EAL.

There are various reasons for the vast improvement in the achievement of EAL pupils in the case study schools compared with schools elsewhere in England. We asked the headteachers and teachers, 'What strategies does your school use to raise achievement of EAL pupils?' They identified a range of common factors, which included effective EAL teaching and learning, an understanding of what pedagogy best supported pupils with EAL, targeted support towards their progress, an inclusive curriculum that recognized children's cultural heritage, and the use of performance data for school improvement, tracking each child's progress and achievement. These good practices are discussed below.

6.5 Effective EAL teaching and learning in the classroom

One significant reason for the excellent performance of pupils for whom English is an additional language and the huge improvement in the schools as a whole, over time, is strong leadership towards equality. The headteachers set high standards for their senior team and staff. The headteachers are proud of their schools' focus on developing the EAL department, which is 'critical for schools with large numbers of pupils with EAL'.

The expertise available to support students in learning English as an additional language in the schools studied is outstanding. All the staff are trained in specific techniques promoted by the 'Raising the Achievement of EAL Learners in Primary Schools' project. The project included:

- planned opportunities for speaking and listening
- use of the first language
- talk partners
- pre-teaching, and application of these techniques across the curriculum.

These elements of support were based on the use of rigorous scrutiny and analyses of students' performance data to target resources towards specific individuals or groups. The outcomes of these interventions were evaluated candidly, and informed future planning. Overall, these schools have a strong culture of self-evaluation. The views of pupils, parents and students have been sought regularly and are much valued; they are used to inform worthwhile changes. One of the headteachers summed it up: 'We are very good in using data and monitoring progress and this has been useful in identifying pupils with EAL who are underachieving.'

All the members of staff interviewed felt well supported by senior managers and knew who to go to for help. The emphasis was on collective responsibility: the senior and middle leaders had their own areas of responsibility for the pupils' progress. Staff discussed possible strategies for addressing issues about specific pupils. The exemplary relationships within the staff teams enabled the schools' performance to be monitored in a positive, supportive and constructive way, and identified priorities for future development. Most importantly, in the words of a headteacher, 'equality of opportunity is at the core of school life'. The schools' systems ensured that all groups of pupils achieved optimally.

All the staff, including senior managers and teaching assistants, took responsibility for the achievement of EAL pupils and understood that quality teaching for all pupils was synonymous with best practice for EAL learners. In the words of one headteacher, 'Whatever we do, everything is done from the EAL perspective. ... The EAL strategies are a good starting point with any child.'

On entry to school all pupils with EAL were assessed in English, using the Stages of English and national curriculum descriptors. In addition, pupils' literacy skills in their first language and their numeracy skills were assessed to ensure that teaching was pitched at the appropriate cognitive level. On the basis of these assessments, individual targets were set. Interventions ran alongside the EAL provision: they consisted of tailored

EAL talks for small groups of pupils, one-to-one support, booster sessions, and mentoring by bilingual teaching assistants. The staff were aware of the pupils' developing English and planned accordingly.

The staff took a holistic approach that incorporated strategies known to be effective for learners with EAL, such as collaborative learning, a focus on talk and vocabulary development through the curriculum, an experiential curriculum and promotion of pupils' first languages in the classroom as a tool for learning. Planned talk and drama sessions gave pupils the chance to use their home languages, but also to develop and rehearse their English in a non-threatening environment before contributing to a larger audience or writing. Teachers created supportive learning environments in which the children felt safe to take risks when speaking their first language and English. As one teacher, who described herself as an EAL learner, observed, 'If I don't feel safe, it's putting me off speaking. I need to be able to make mistakes.' This, she said, should be the same for pupils in the classroom.

Each school had a focus on talk throughout the curriculum, facilitating language development through adult modelling, talk partners, talk frames and the general expectation that pupils would respond in full sentences. The role of collaborative learning in both cognitive and language development was emphasized by the teachers, who also understood their own roles as providers of good models of English language. The pupils were aware of the value of collaborative work for their English development. One pupil said, 'Your partner has words and knows the language and you put your ideas together and learn the language and become better.' Teachers ensured that the pairings and groupings encouraged the use of pupils' home languages but afforded good English-language models and scaffolding for the EAL learners. A pupil said, 'When I say a word wrong he corrects me and says "Try again", and every day I learn a couple more words.'

Talk frames were used to scaffold pupils' language in order to move them towards the written form. Having talk partners enabled pupils to discuss and rehearse language. One school developed a focus on drama and oral rehearsal after modelling, which was supported by experience, visuals and objects. Planned opportunities for talk underpinned all learning, to the point at which one new arrival observed, 'Everyone was talking so I could learn the word from them.'

Teachers recognized the importance of supporting pupils orally with sentence structures, requiring pupils to respond in full sentences and recasting sentences that were grammatically incorrect. An EAL co-ordinator told us:

'I encourage teaching of language structures through talk partners, with a focus on response. They must respond in the correct way – in whole sentence answers. We rehearse the question together – I model first, they repeat, say it to their talk partner and then we focus on the response. In the planets work, for example, we rehearsed the request, "Tell me a name for your planet and explain why it is a good name for it". The response was scaffolded for them but they needed to use the structure and the conjunction "because" – "My planet is called … because …".'

This practice began in the nursery, in which a project called 'Responding to Talk' supported adults to refine pupils' responses into academic language and whole sentences during class discussion or in small groups. In the early years, pupils learnt English through a programme of carefully planned opportunities to both hear and use it in meaningful activities and experiences. Adults scaffolded pupils' learning through role play, songs and rhymes, and circle activities, developing contextual understanding and providing essential repetition of the language focus. We observed a teacher reading the story 'Dear Zoo' to her class, in preparation for a visit to the zoo. The teacher and the children told the story together, exploring each page through questioning and modelling, and focusing on the names and the body parts of the various animals. The class storytelling was supported with toy animals in a story sack, gestures, actions and pictures on a board. The pupils had to use their newly acquired vocabulary independently in a song; this gave them opportunities to rehearse new vocabulary in meaningful contexts and add it to their language repertoire.

KS1 and KS2 teachers described how they focused on vocabulary development, especially when teaching reading: modelling it in context, repeating it throughout the day and deliberately choosing texts that included academic language, not just 'everyday' language. The pupils said that the teacher's strategy of modelling and contextualizing words helped them to do well. One explained, 'She [the teacher] does it first on the board, on a different subject so we don't copy it, and then [we] do our own', and another, 'The teacher explains clearly to us and if we don't understand they draw it and give us examples'. The teacher told us, 'You have to constantly read faces for understanding; repeat, pair and group pupils so they can listen and understand.'

Home languages were given priority in classrooms and used as a tool for learning. Pupils with the same language were encouraged to support each other in class, and encouraged to use their first language through talk partners, drama and Talk for Writing,[1] where they could develop and rehearse their English before either speaking to a bigger audience or writing. Pupils were encouraged to maintain and develop their home languages so that the skills learnt in their first language were transferred to English. An example of this was a school's class prayer books. Children were encouraged to write a prayer in their home language with their family, and to share them at school so they would 'hear the melodies in the languages. We are helping them to transfer their skills in their first language into English.' The role that developing their first language played in developing their English was clear: reflecting on the grammatical differences, a child observed, 'In English there is one way – "How are you?" But in Tigrinya there is one way for boys and one way for girls.' It was evident that in all the schools children were happy to use their first language in the classroom in learning and social contexts.

6.5.1 Giving effective targeted support

We saw evidence in our observation and interviews that it was teamwork that underpinned support for pupils with EAL. At termly learning assessment meetings, headteachers, deputy heads/inclusion managers and EAL staff discussed the needs of each child in the light of their stage-appropriate EAL targets, put interventions in place and monitored them regularly for effectiveness. Designated EAL teachers, together with EAL support staff, many of whom were bilingual, supported teaching and learning. For example, in one school the bilingual teaching assistants were placed in the early years foundation stage and Year 1, to help build EAL pupils' confidence, encourage them to develop their first language and support their English. This also helped build sustainable partnerships with the parents and engage them in their children's learning in the long term.

We learned from discussions with an assistant headteacher (inclusion), and with teachers, teaching assistants, learning mentors and the leadership team in one school, that the schools implement change and improvement through clear induction processes, interventions to improve EAL proficiency in English and attainment, one-to-one support, and interventions in English and maths. How targeted support raised achievement is clear from this example of outstanding school practice. This case study school provided the following targeted support:

- Induction support: the school has an induction process for new arrivals, which incorporates assessment of both English and (where possible) their literacy and numeracy skills in their first language, to ensure that teaching is pitched at the appropriate cognitive level;

- settling in, implemented by learning mentors;
- in-class EAL support programmes and resourcing, such as dual-language dictionaries;
- differentiation by class teachers, monitored by the senior management team (SMT)
- teachers working with the inclusion manager to develop differentiated resources, and planning learning support;
- visual resources to support learning;
- Talk for Writing and maths;
- clear tracking of progress and monitoring via provision mapping.

The teachers' knowledge and understanding of EAL pedagogy and strategies were clear to see. We noted how EAL teaching principles inform classroom pedagogy and are incorporated into lessons. The teacher used talk partners, sentence starters, speaking frames, collaborative working and other strategies. As a result, the achievement of EAL pupils is considerably better than that of their peers nationally. The school uses three teaching assistants who are designated EAL assistants for part of their time. All have attended whole-school training and specialist training by an EAL consultant, and so can deliver intervention programmes designed to develop the academic language EAL children need: Talking Maths[2] and guided writing units. They join weekly team meetings after school, reporting back and contributing to planning. They emphasize their role in helping children to apply in the classroom what they have learnt from the group work, and they model for and support children to use the key vocabulary and sentence starters, rephrasing questions and supporting them to structure responses.

Our analysis of individual EAL pupils in **School A** reveals remarkable progress in their levels of fluency in English and their attainment at the end of key stages. For example, a Portuguese-speaking child who was assessed as Stage 1 (new to English) when she joined the school in Year 1 made huge progress. With the additional support outlined above, her level of fluency improved from beginner stage to fully fluent by the time she started Year 6. Significantly, in her KS2 tests she achieved level 5 in maths and level 4 or above in reading, grammar, punctuation and spelling. Such excellent achievement by a pupil who had no English when she joined the school highlights the effective targeted support she received in this primary school.

The schools emphasized the importance of distinguishing between EAL needs and SEN and described how progress through the stages of English is monitored and unpicked to identify any learning difficulty. Where there is concern, staff assess the child through their first language, and interpreters are employed for meetings and assessments with outside agencies. Clearly, then, there are protocols for differentiating between needs arising from learning EAL and those related to SEN, and this informs the educational provision.

6.5.2 Targeted support provided by EAL co-ordinators and EAL teachers

Many schools have a dedicated EAL co-ordinator who has been a class teacher or assistant head, and now has oversight for EAL provision throughout the school. In one case study school, in which 20% of the pupils spoke Portuguese, the co-ordinator herself was of Portuguese origin and originally came to the school as a Portuguese support teacher. Her promotion to senior manager enabled Portuguese parents (many of whom had hesitated to enter the school before) to see that their culture and heritage were valued there. She raised the profile of EAL provision at a strategic level and brought to the school a detailed understanding of the needs of the Portuguese community, the political climate in Portugal, the legacy of dictatorship, the changing nature of the community surrounding the school, and how these issues affected the pupils and their parents. This understanding enabled her to devise a detailed action plan to empower Portuguese pupils, parents and staff to raise the achievement of the Portuguese pupils at the school.

She regularly observed class teachers from an EAL viewpoint, discussed targets with teachers and TAs in order to improve their practice, updated the EAL registers, and oversaw target setting for individual pupils. Many subject co-ordinators also managed the TAs who worked under the EAL co-ordinators' and class teachers' direction. They trained assistants in specific strategies for EAL learners and were accountable for enhancing their learning.

Thorough data analysis informed the EAL teachers' work across the schools. The EAL teacher allocated to a year group attended planning meetings and identified new vocabulary and areas of challenge for pupils with EAL. One co-ordinator 'identified unfamiliar vocabulary for the new story "Traction Man" and sourced objects for the teacher to use when introducing the story'. Furthermore, she identified the language demands of the lesson and set language targets to move pupils from stage B to Stage D of the LA stages of English fluency. These language targets were additional to their class targets and known by all the members of staff. EAL teachers ensured that these aspects of language were modelled by the class teachers and used by the pupils throughout lessons. Any withdrawal work was linked closely to the class work. This way of working had become ingrained across the schools. In the afternoons EAL teachers often worked with new arrivals, especially those who were at an early stage of learning English, in groups of no more than three.

6.5.3 Targeted support from EAL support staff

The supporting adults had a unique role in raising the achievement of pupils with EAL. Like the teachers, they had received specific training in routine practices and specific interventions to raise the achievement of pupils, such as encouraging children to use their first language, talk partners and pre-teaching specific concepts, and then applying these techniques across the curriculum. Teachers and support staff planned and delivered lessons together. While the teacher led the lesson, the support staff modelled the English language for pupils, using visuals. They supported the pupils with EAL in drama, using activities such as hot-seating. One teaching assistant explained, 'It is now an automatic process; we know what is needed, so we embed it automatically.'

The support staff in one school worked on a special science project with pupils with EAL needs. Growing seeds, for example, afforded plenty of opportunity for adult–child interaction, as there were two adults and eight children. The TAs taught the children age-related academic vocabulary relating to seeds.

While pupils might move quite quickly from Stage A, new to English, to Stage B, early acquisition ('becoming familiar with English'), they often needed additional support to develop more demanding language for learning, for example in written activities. Much one-to-one work was done to support this. A teaching assistant and a teacher discussed how Stage A learners were 'chatty' in the playground but lacked the confidence to take part in classroom talk; they planned a series of short regular slots centred on group work, for four pupils, which developed talk around a picture trigger supported by adults modelling sentence starters. This was followed by supported writing. The pupils were then encouraged to use this learning in the classroom.

Similarly, TAs led a 'Talking Maths' programme for EAL pupils, which was closely linked to classwork in which they used their learning in a whole-class setting. The TAs supported small groups of EAL learners with grammatical issues within EAL-guided writing groups. They tailored the input of sessions to what children might need in their whole-class sessions. Many of these TAs evaluated, monitored and recorded pupils' progress. They commented on how group work developed the pupils' confidence in speaking in class.

Key adults, usually TAs, were assigned as 'buddies' to newly arrived pupils who had no knowledge of English, especially when they shared the same language. Newly arrived pupils in one school were given visual prompt keys to aid communication in their first days, such as 'the magic words "please", "thank you", "hello", "I am sorry"'. Many of the TAs also ran language clubs, taught their mother tongue as a foreign language, and interpreted when necessary. One of the TAs ran after-school clubs in Spanish twice a week, taught Spanish as a modern foreign language to Year 3 during the day, and supported new arrivals with EAL needs. Often, the content of the language clubs mirrored the content of the curriculum, which enabled the children to learn both in English and in their home language.

6.5.4 Using assessment data to monitor EAL pupils

The use and analysis of EAL data by the case study schools was one of the most significant drivers for raising achievement and narrowing the gaps. Individual teachers used data to inform their teaching and learning, including lesson planning, to set accurate targets for individual students and for specific gender and ethnic groups, to arrange groupings for teaching and learning for tracking progress of pupils, and to set high expectations. We asked staff, 'How effective is the school in using EAL data for improving the quality of teaching and learning? To what extent is the English proficiency assessment data used for tracking the progress of pupils with EAL to identify support needs and target interventions?' These are some of the replies:

> 'The school has a good system for assessing and mapping the progress of pupils with EAL at individual and group level. A wide range of data on English levels of fluency and national curriculum levels are analysed by ethnicity, levels of fluency in English, and gender, enabling the school to identify support needs and organize the deployment of resources appropriately, whether for pupils with EAL or for underachieving groups.'
>
> (Deputy headteacher, School C)

> 'The school assessment-tracking spreadsheet strongly supports the school's main business of teaching and learning. The system can identify "threshold" pupils and so trigger targeted interventions. Teachers record progress as points linked to national curriculum levels or predicted GCSE grades. Using red, amber and green to indicate "actual" against "expected" levels of progress and attainment is clear and easy to grasp, which is useful in discussions with parents.'
>
> (Data manager, School H)

'There is a strong focus on learning in the school to make sure no student with EAL falls behind. Through detailed monitoring and tracking, students with EAL who fall below the expected level or are at risk of falling behind, are quickly identified and individual needs are targeted. All students are assessed carefully using the LA's stages of fluency in English to ensure that they receive the appropriate provision and are making the required progress.'

(Head of EAL department, School H)

These responses confirmed similar findings in other case study schools and indicated that the schools have effective, well-developed pupil-tracking and -monitoring management information systems. All the teachers had tracking sheets for pupils, which identified types of support, previous school and favourite subjects. In particular, the EAL department's sheet included detailed background information data, such as date and place of birth, date of arrival in the UK, ethnic background, home language, stage of fluency in English, date of admission, attendance rate, eligibility for free school meals, SEN stage, mobility rate and years in school, to track the progress of groups and individuals, and to ensure that no pupil became 'invisible'. Data can be retrieved in many combinations and at any time, and this makes the assessment database a valuable management tool, for example for reviewing the impact of provision for those with English as an additional language.

The schools are particularly forensic in monitoring the progress of particular groups, for example boys, those receiving free school meals, those with special educational needs, or those with English as additional language. Where data analysis highlighted issues to be addressed, the school employed interventions such as one-to-one support and making the teaching programme more personalized or differentiated. As a result, children with EAL make rapid progress and achieve outstanding results at KS2 and GCSE, as the stories below illustrate:

Case study A (School F): 'Pupil A speaks Urdu as his mother tongue and came from India. He was at beginner [Stage A] level of fluency in English when he started his primary education here. Through targeted support, which included one-to-one support and booster classes, his language fluency improved fast. At GCSE he achieved A* in chemistry, English language, English literature, Spanish and design and technology – textiles technology, and A grades in biology, geography, mathematics, physics, religious studies, citizenship, plus C in applied ICT and study skills.' The secondary school has made a big impact on Pupil A. He is one of the high-flying students with EAL. In addition to excellent performance in threshold results, his value-added progression between KS2 and GCSE was also excellent and topped the national league table.

Case study B (School F): 'Pupil B is Black African of Somali heritage. She attended primary school in the LA and was assessed as Stage B (early acquisition) when she took the KS2 tests, that is, she required considerable English support to access the national curriculum. As a result, her results at KS2 showed that she achieved no level in English, level 2 in mathematics and level 4 in science. However, through one-to-one, booster classes and in-class support, her level of English fluency improved to stage E (fully fluent) by the time she took GCSE examinations. The school's support helped her to achieve B in history, mathematics, religious studies, science, C in English language, English literature, French, citizenship and sociology.' This is a remarkable achievement for a child who had only six years in the English education system.

Case Study C (School G): 'Pupil C came from Portugal and previously attended primary school in another London LA. She speaks Portuguese at home and was fluent in English by the time she completed Key Stage 2, gaining level 4+ in English, maths and science. Through targeted support of booster classes, one-to-one tuition, and in-class intervention, she achieved As at GCSE in French, mathematics and Portuguese, B in English literature, C in English language, business studies, economics, religious studies and science, D in arts and design (textiles). What is particularly special about Pupil C is that her value-added score tops national expectations and she has shown excellent progress between KS2 and GCSE.'

Case Study F (School C): 'Pupil F started school in 2003 in the nursery with no previous experience in English. He speaks Tigrinya, a language that is spoken in Eritrea and northern Ethiopia. However, following one-to-one and additional support in the school, he was assessed as Stage 4 (fully fluent in English) in Year 6 and was a high achiever at KS1 and KS2. His KS1 data shows that he achieved level 3 in reading, 2A in writing and maths. At KS2 his performance was as predicted and he achieved level 5 in both English and maths. This is an excellent achievement for a child who spoke no English when he started school.'

On the whole, schools in the LA have excellent systems for monitoring the work of the pupils: they identify those who need help or extra challenge and provide them with appropriate additional support. In all the case study schools, a high priority is placed on supporting language acquisition among EAL students not fluent in English. This often appeared to be a dominant feature of curriculum development in these schools. The teaching and class support for EAL is well organized and led by EAL co-ordinators. In general, pupils in these schools who are in the early stages of fluency perform at very low levels, whereas bilingual pupils who are fully fluent in English perform better, on average, than English-only speakers. We conclude that the case study schools are highly effective at analysing data in order to identify pupils who are at risk of underachieving. The excellent range of support they provide has had a positive impact on the achievement of EAL pupils and those whose circumstances have made them vulnerable.

6.6 Implications for policy and practice

This chapter looked at the achievement gap of EAL pupils and examined the factors behind their successful achievement. The main finding from the empirical data was that EAL pupils perform below their non-EAL peers in English schooling because they lack command of English. In particular, EAL pupils not fluent in English achieve significantly below the national average. The empirical evidence shows wide variation in performance and in the achievement gap between EAL pupils not fluent in English and monolingual pupils. What is even more worrying is that low achievement of EAL pupils not fluent in English has been masked by the failure of government statistics to monitor and distinguish EAL pupils by their stage of proficiency in English.

The empirical evidence also suggests that EAL pupils in the early stages of English proficiency performed poorly, while the achievement of EAL pupils who were fully fluent in English far outstripped that of pupils for whom English was their only language. The findings confirm that there is a strong relationship between stage of proficiency in English and educational attainment.

The case study schools closed the achievement gap by improving EAL pupils' language skills to the point at which they can access the national curriculum. Teaching and learning were excellent, and informed by assessment. These schools recognized that proficiency in English was the key to educational success for their bilingual learners and acted to help children acquire fluency in English as soon as possible. All the schools chose their staff with care from a wide range of ethnic-minority backgrounds, so that teachers and TAs, as well as other school staff, provided good role models and showed understanding of their pupils' difficulties. The level of expertise was excellent, the EAL co-ordinators well qualified, experienced and knowledgeable. Consequently, the EAL pupils' needs were met in lessons and targets for their literacy needs were regularly set.

The use of performance data for school improvement was a great strength of the case study schools. All the schools had effective pupil assessment procedures, which were detailed, relevant and constantly updated to reflect staff feedback. Each school focused on tracking and monitoring EAL pupils' progress and achievement throughout their school life and collected test and assessment data alongside background data such as ethnic background, language spoken, level of fluency in English, date of admission, attendance rate, eligibility for free school meals, EAL stage of fluency, SEN stage, mobility rate, years in school, which teacher's classes have been attended, types of support, and postcode. This data was used to set challenging targets for attainment.

Overall, the evidence presented here enables the conclusion to be drawn that the schools in this study demonstrate the many ways in which they work to support pupils from all EAL backgrounds through a wide range of imaginative inclusion strategics. The most effective practice was evident where EAL teachers conducted robust assessments with pupils and kept a register of detailed information, concerning pupils' first language, level of fluency in English and other relevant data, all regularly updated. Moreover, communicating these assessments to teachers and support staff enabled the children's learning to be effectively supported.

It was clear from our research that EAL was at the heart of each school's culture. As a headteacher put it:

> 'The key thing about EAL is that it permeates everything that we do. It is not an add-on. It has to be part of the school culture. … The provision for pupils with EAL is the responsibility of everyone. As a staff we don't see it as a challenge, we see it as an opportunity. We have all these children with EAL – what a wonderful opportunity to share our languages and our cultures.'

This empirical evidence of children's stages of English proficiency has far-reaching implications for policy and practice. The government uses the data on the English proficiency of EAL pupils to inform policy:

> 'The information will help the department understand how effective the education sector is for EAL pupils and will provide valuable statistical information on the characteristics of these children and, together with their attainment, will allow us to measure whether the individual pupils, or the schools they attend, face additional educational challenges.'

> (DfE, 2017a: 65)

The new national five-stage assessment framework is similar to the four-stage proficiency assessment model that the case study LA has successfully employed in its schools since 1990. They can be used to highlight the broad needs of EAL learners, to inform pedagogical and administrative planning and to measure broad progress over time (Demie and Strand, 2006: 227).

There are resourcing implications for national policy makers. In England the government uses EAL as an additional factor to fund schools through the national schools funding formula. The national education policy guideline states:

> Research suggests that EAL status increases costs for schools and that there is a strong relationship between a pupil's fluency in English and their educational attainment. … [The Government believe that allocating funding] on the basis of those pupils with EAL who entered the state education system at any point during the [previous] 3 years … would target funding to schools likely to have pupils in need of targeted support to increase language proficiency.
>
> (DfE, 2016a: 27–8)

The EAL factor could be included in local funding formulae to enable schools in England to meet the needs of EAL pupils. This factor is limited to bilingual pupils who have been enrolled in English schools for a maximum of three years at present, despite research evidence that suggests it takes five to seven years to acquire English proficiency in a UK context (see Demie, 2013a). A new EAL policy agenda is needed, to review the funding formula to ensure that EAL pupils receive additional support for five to seven years.

Notes

[1] Talk for Writing is based on 'developmental exploration, through talk, of the thinking and creative processes involved in being a writer' (https://webarchive.nationalarchives.gov.uk/20130323063703/https://www.education.gov.uk/publications/eOrderingDownload/DCSF-00467-2008.pdf).

[2] Talking Maths is a 10 week intervention programme which targets speaking and listening skills in the context of mathematical language' (www.educationworks.org.uk/what-we-do/mathematics/talking-maths).

Chapter 7

What works

7.1 Introduction

This final chapter brings together the key findings of the research into the schools in one local authority where the students excel, and identifies the lessons that can be learned by all those involved in statutory education. We consider the part policy makers and school improvement practitioners have played in making certain schools effective by drawing lessons from what has been learned over the last two decades and its significant implications for educational policy and practice nationally and internationally. This book shows that the gap between groups who have underachieved for decades and their peers can be closed, and so the achievement of all schoolchildren raised.

7.2 Conclusions

The substantial body of research into how to make our schools more effective in raising attainment has offered a valuable background and useful insights for improvement (Edmonds, 1982; Hopkins *et al.*, 1994; Sammons, Hillman and Mortimore, 1995; Reynolds *et al.*, 1996; Mortimore, 1999; Mortimore *et al.*, 1988; Rutter *et al.*, 1979; Mortimore, Sammons and Thomas, 1994; Stoll and Fink, 1994; Muijs *et al.*, 2004; Blair *et al.*, 1998; Demie and Lewis, 2010a, 2010b, 2010c, 2010d; Demie and McLean, 2015a, 2015b, 2016, 2017a, 2017b). Some researchers attempted to study schools that were successful in educating students of all backgrounds, regardless of the students' socio-economic background. However, Thrupp (1999, 2001) and Mortimore and Whitty, 1997) argued that research into school effectiveness and improvement has taken insufficient account of socio-economic context and has contributed to making schools and teachers the focus of blame for educational failure and underachievement. Others (Gillborn, 2002, 2008; Gorard, 2018; Mongon and Chapman, 2008; Clifton and Cook, 2012; Demie and McLean, 2015a, 2015b) suggested that school improvement research looked at the significance of social factors and race, including the colour blindness of recent education policy. Researchers have now accepted that much of the difference in pupil outcomes is due to the social background of the children, their socio-economic situation and the neighbourhood in which they live (Mortimore and Whitty, 1997; Sammons, 1999; Gorard, 2000; Clifton and Cook, 2012; Ofsted, 2014). However, we are still some way from having a clear understanding of why some schools in disadvantaged areas perform so much better than others. So researchers started to look at schools that provide an environment in which pupils flourish against the odds (Mongon and Chapman, 2008; Ofsted, 2009a, 2009b; Demie and Lewis, 2010a, 2010b, 2010c, 2010d, 2010e; Demie and McLean, 2015a, 2015b, 2016, 2017a, 2017b).

Building on past research that suggested significant differences in performance between disadvantaged pupils and their peers, this study explores the remarkable story of how schools in one London local authority defy the association between poverty and low achievement, through targeted interventions that close the gap between the achievement of pupils who are disadvantaged, from an ethnic minority, or with EAL, and their peers. It is underpinned with quantitative and qualitative methodology that included longitudinal data analysis, case studies and focus groups that explored children's performance and gathered the views of teachers, governors, parents and students.

First, we collected detailed national KS2 and GCSE data and analysed it by the children's entitlement to free school meals. Second, we examined eight primary and six secondary schools, observing lessons and holding discussions with headteachers, staff, governors and pupils. And we gathered evidence on how well disadvantaged pupils in the schools were achieving and on the factors that contributed to this achievement. Third, we held focus group interviews to ascertain the views of teachers, parents and children on what works in schools and the impact of the pupil premium grant.

The longitudinal KS2 and GCSE NPD data reveals the attainment pattern by social and ethnic background and region. The evidence from the data confirms:

- Closing the gap in academic achievement between disadvantaged pupils and their peers is the greatest challenge faced by education policy makers in England.
- There remains a significant attainment gap between FSM and non-FSM pupils, which is wider for Black Caribbean, White British and Mixed White and Black Caribbean groups than for other ethnic groups and widens further at the end of secondary education.

In successful schools, students from these ethnic groups, and those eligible for FSM, buck the national trend.

Chapters 3 to 6 detail the success factors behind outstanding achievement and how one LA's schools, which serve disadvantaged inner-city areas, have achieved remarkable academic success and enriched their communities. The chapters carry discussions and interviews with headteachers, staff, governors and children to present a range of perspectives on these schools. The findings from successful case study schools show that the students reach exceptionally high standards at KS2 and GCSE despite their generally low starting points. These schools demonstrate outstanding practice in all areas of their work. Their contexts differ, but their approaches to raising achievement have common features. All have bucked the national trend through a range of highly effective strategies for tackling educational inequality and closing the customary achievement gap:

- strong leadership on equality and diversity
- consistently excellent teaching
- effective use of data
- effective use of pupil voice
- effective targeted support through intervention strategies such as:
  - small-group additional support
  - one-to-one tuition
  - feedback
  - directing the best teachers to teach English and maths
  - booster classes using class teachers
  - enrichment activities
  - early intervention.

These approaches have a positive impact on the achievement of all groups of pupils. However, the research also identified success factors that are particularly critical for ethnic-minority students, bilingual students and students from families that are socially and economically disadvantaged. We argue that schools that are effective in one respect tend to be effective in others, although the factors that lead to successful outcomes may differ. In the case of ethnic-minority and EAL pupils the studies suggest, in addition to the above common success factors, the importance of a number of other factors that were found to raise the achievement specifically of ethnic minority and bilingual children:

- engaging parents in school and classroom activities
- links with the community
- celebrating cultural diversity

- an innovative curriculum that reflects and meets the needs of the community
- targeted support from teaching assistants, EAL teachers and learning mentors
- home language classes
- diversity in the school workforce.

What is special about these schools is that local communities are represented in the school. Staff members are able to speak many of the community languages. Headteachers make deliberate efforts to recruit a multi-ethnic workforce, often from the community the school serves. As a result children feel that they can relate to staff from their own cultural background, so they feel well supported and motivated.

Core principles of respect, fairness and social justice therefore inform the schools' daily practice, and there is open debate with parents and the community about barriers to achievement. Above all, these schools have confident leaders who take risks and trust their instincts. They are innovative because they are focused on the moral purpose of raising the achievement of Inner London pupils; through the experience accumulated during a turbulent decade of educational change, they have emerged as strong advanced practitioners in raising the achievement of disadvantaged, ethnic-minority and EAL students.

Our findings are in line with other studies (see for example Ofsted, 2009a, 2009b; Demie and McLean, 2015a, 2015b; EEF, 2019). The improvement made by students in the case study schools is exceptional by all measures, and central government, local authorities and school governing bodies and leaders can learn from it. The research findings also contain important messages for policy makers and school improvement practitioners.

7.3 The lessons to be drawn from these outstanding schools

Backed by sustained empirical research, this book tells the remarkable story of how one disadvantaged LA's schools have successfully addressed educational inequalities and bucked national trends. The wide range of effective strategies to raise educational attainment at KS2 and GCSE consistently featured the following:

1. Strong school leadership and excellent teaching tailored to each child's abilities, which raises the achievement of all schoolchildren.

2. Building close links with the community, giving extra support to disadvantaged pupils, minority ethnic pupils and pupils who are learning the English language. This approach enables children to reach a high level of educational attainment, which closes the gap between the groups that underachieve nationally and their peers.
3. Developing an inclusive and broad curriculum that engages the students because it reflects and values cultural diversity and has relevance to their lives.
4. Robust tracking and monitoring of each individual student's progress and achievement through the effective use of data and good-practice research. Effective data can generate both optimism and urgency about where improvement is most needed to tackle underachievement and inequalities in provision.

The stories of how case study schools have succeeded in closing the achievement gap are of local and national significance. Our study confirms, beyond doubt, that the excellent education provided in the schools is the reason they are bucking national trends and closing the achievement gap. Effective schools that have been dealing with these issues over a number of years hold the key to the way forward. The decades-long research has proved what works and identified the factors that make a difference. This good practice needs to be widely disseminated.

The successful schools offer hope to school improvement practitioners and policy makers. Whatever the challenges and experiences of schools that succeed against the odds, what this book documents and describes points to ways forward for schools in which children are struggling to reach their potential. These success stories have implications for schools, central government, local authorities, multi-academy trusts, school governors and the research community.

7.4 Implications

7.4.1 Implications for schools

The implications for schools are many and varied. The case study schools show that schools can and do make a difference to the life chances of young people. They demonstrate outstanding practice in all areas to support disadvantaged pupils. Many approaches are not new or different but they require leadership teams and staff across the school to ensure that every member of staff is aware of which children are disadvantaged and that they take clear and accountable action to accelerate those students' progress. The methods used by the case study schools can be used elsewhere. The key ingredients are, as we have seen, strong leadership on equality and diversity, high-quality teaching, the effective use of data to monitor performance and deliver an inclusive curriculum, and targeted support interventions. These can be replicated in schools nationally and internationally.

An important messages for schools and policy makers is that there is no pick-and-mix option. An effective school will seek to develop all the approaches, underpinning them with practical data that monitors the achievement of the target groups in order to pinpoint and tackle underperformance. To help raise the achievement of disadvantaged, ethnic-minority and EAL pupils, these schools:

1. develop leadership capacity. As a matter of good practice the school should audit the current workforce and pursue diversification at all levels, including senior management and teachers, to ensure that it reflects the school population.
2. use data to identify underachieving groups and to improve teachers' and management's understanding of how and why some students underachieve and what teachers can do about it.
3. audit the curriculum to ensure that it reflects the diversity of the school community and the needs of all pupils. In the light of this audit, the schools map provision across years and subjects. They ensure that coverage is coherent and addresses the needs of ethnic-minority children and the disadvantaged.
4. promote community cohesion so that all pupils understand and appreciate others from different backgrounds and develop a sense of shared vision, fulfil their potential and feel part of the community. Through the school curriculum, they explore the representation of the different cultural, ethnic, linguistic and religious groups in the area.
5. openly discuss issues of ethnic diversity and race within lessons. These issues are an integral part of the professional development of all school staff.
6. celebrate cultural diversity through effective use of International Day, Black History Month and, above all, an inclusive curriculum that meets the needs of a multicultural society.

7.4.2 Implications for central government

The government needs to recognize that tackling the underachievement of certain ethnic groups is an important part of raising standards for all in schools. Although national projects like Aiming High proved effective, their replacement with a 'colour-blind' approach has again put these groups at a disadvantage, while the current national curriculum fails to reflect the reality of a diverse, multi-ethnic society – to the detriment of all students. All recent Acts and White Papers on education reform have neglected to explore the specific needs of ethnic-minority and other new immigrant communities.

To tackle underachievement the central government and schools need to develop targeted initiatives to identify and address the needs of pupils of ethnic minorities. In the past the Ethnic Minority Achievement Grant (EMAG) was introduced by the government as a means of supporting the attainment of pupils from ethnic-minority groups and ending the shocking underachievement of ethnic-minority pupils in comparison with their White British peers. The EMAG funding given to schools by government was designed to provide greater resources for schools with a high proportion of ethnic-minority students. Ending it in 2011 was a political decision that has undermined statutory education.

It appears that government has become ineffective in using evidence to tackle inequality and race issues. Our data shows clearly that the achievement gap has widened nationally. Our evidence confirms that the performance of some ethnic-minority groups consistently lags behind that of their peers. And it shows what can be done to address educational inequality. We need to take action to tackle the problem at the national level. The recommendations for central government that emerge from the present study are:

1. The DfE needs to recognize the fact that schools and local authorities need targeted funding to support pupils from underachieving minority ethnic groups, and pupils learning English as an additional language. The DfE needs to reintroduce ring-fenced targeted funding to schools in which ethnic-minority pupils are underachieving, to provide the foundation for an education system that values social justice.

2. Building on the lessons learnt from the present research, earlier proven national initiatives for raising the achievement of Black Caribbean pupils and the lessons learned from the London Challenge, the DfE needs to establish a national project for raising the achievement of ethnic-minority children, to be applied where ethnic-minority students are being failed by their schools.

3. The national data indicates that teachers in England tend to be from White British monocultural backgrounds. Fewer than one in seven come from an ethnic-minority group. Government needs to encourage schools to employ a workforce that reflects the community and the area they serve. All schools in England need to be aware of diversity and of multicultural education.

4. The DfE should ensure that every school develops a curriculum that reflects this nation's rich cultural diversity.
5. The DfE should work with the case study schools to disseminate their good practice to all schools in England and Wales.
6. Educational inequalities should be tackled at national and local-authority level.

7.4.3 Implications for local education authorities and multi-academy trusts

Our research findings have implications for local authorities. Since about 1990 successive governments have seized powers and functions from local education authorities and have weakened local government and democracy (Benn, 2011; Lane, 2013; Mortimore, 2014), and educational provision has suffered as a result. From the 1990s on, local authorities were the middle tier between school and central government in the education system. However, central government's academy and free school programmes have taken some schools out of local authority control. At present, academy chains and free schools do not have local accountability, and nor do they represent the local community. They are not responsible for allocating school funding, planning school places or ensuring special educational needs are met across an area; neither do they have local responsibility for community cohesion and the safeguarding of children within their area. Parents need access to a single, local body responsible for holding their children's schools to account, however it is governed. Some functions need to be performed by area-based and democratically legitimate bodies. This, we believe, will end the muddled and confusing structure of the current English school system. We argue that school improvement and area-based school systems cannot be driven successfully from central government, for a number of reasons. Central government lacks local knowledge and the capacity to provide oversight to meet local needs and to monitor performance so as to identify problems early (Muir and Clifton, 2014; Mortimore, 2014; Demie and McLean, 2015). This is best carried out by democratically elected bodies that serve the local area. More importantly, the LAs know the local context – its culture, languages, ethnicities and degree of community cohesion.

The case study LA's determination to hold schools in a local 'family' of education providers despite the fragmentation of the education system is a success story. Successful LAs have always fostered collaboration between their schools, including academies. The case study LA has ensured that the needs of all local children are met by providing an effective school improvement and data service to the schools in the area it serves, regulating fair access, providing sufficient school places, managing services for children with special educational needs, maintaining strong partnerships and school-to-school support, and fostering community cohesion. Importantly, it has used public authority to push its school improvement agenda, to challenge complacency and to intervene when schools fail to address inequality or their students underachieve.

Although recent legislation has diminished the power of LAs, they remain accountable to their communities and are uniquely placed to provide key school improvement services such as monitoring, challenging, supporting and intervening in schools to ensure they meet statutory requirements, and providing performance data to support school improvement by identifying underachieving pupils and prioritizing areas for development. Successful local authorities have developed their education provision in various ways by strengthening and refocusing their school improvement service or creating schools partnership services as autonomous departments. Government itself has developed multi-academy trusts (MATs) to run schools that have no geographical boundary. In particular, LAs play a key role in promoting community cohesion and valuing diversity so that all pupils understand and appreciate others from different ethnic and linguistic backgrounds in the area they live in.

Our recommendations for local authorities and multi-academy trusts are:

1. Continue to gather and use data effectively to support school improvement, identifying underachieving groups early and targeting interventions accordingly.
2. Audit the workforce in the school and develop a workforce that reflects the local community.
3. Provide schools with programmes of centrally based training to share good practice for raising attainment and narrowing the achievement gap.
4. Value and celebrate cultural diversity.
5. Invite the local authority featured in this research to work with the case study schools to share good practice with other schools.

7.4.4 Implications for school improvement practitioners in the use of data and research

The English education system has accumulated rich data on each pupil. Since early in this century (Rudd and Davies, 2002; Demie, 2003, 2013b) there has been a revolution, thanks to the increase in national curriculum assessment data at pupil level, including FSP, phonics, KS1, KS2, KS3 and

GCSE. All this plus pupil data from the school census gives us sophisticated information about the progress of different groups of pupils at each key stage. Schools also have more information about their own pupils than they once did, for example optional and individual pupil targets and results from their own assessment and monitoring. The overall evidence about the use of data in the case study schools confirms that data is used effectively to support school improvement, by, for example:

- identifying pupils' achievement and informing target setting
- supporting the allocation of staffing and resources
- challenging the aspirations of staff, pupils and parents
- supporting school self-evaluation
- tracking pupils' performance and progress
- identifying underachieving groups
- narrowing the achievement gap
- celebrating good news.

The recommendation from this study is that schools, LAs, MATs and school improvement practitioners should attach great importance to the use of data and evidence from research on good practice to raise standards and close the school achievement gap.

7.4.5 Implications for the research community

Policy makers and schools need more evidence on what works in schools, yet our review of literature found little research about what constitutes good practice. The government, Ofsted and the Education Endowment Fund have spelt out the value of such research (see EEF, 2019; Cabinet Office, 2014, 2018; Ofsted, 2002a, 2002b, 2009a, 2009b). The EEF offers teachers evidence of what has worked best to boost the attainment of disadvantaged pupils. More research of this type, that challenges preconceived notions of underachievement, will encourage and assist educationalists and policy makers to strive for greater academic success, and enhance the evidence on what the most promising ways of closing the attainment gap appear to be.

Our research also suggests possibilities for future research. While we do not want to make generalizations from our case studies, we point out that our case study-and-focus group approach is an established research design that is used in various disciplines, particularly in the social sciences, to extend the range of information and evidence (see Carey and Asbury, 2016; Bassey, 1999; Stake, 1995; Bell, 1993). The design is useful for obtaining detailed in-depth information about personal and group feelings, perceptions and opinions, in a way that observation, one-to-one interviewing and questionnaire surveys cannot reveal on their own, and because the findings are so accessible they can serve a variety of audiences, not only policy makers, school managers and teachers.

Little ethnographic research can be found elsewhere in the UK that addresses educational inequalities and measures the effect of targeted interventions to eliminate or reduce them. Additional longitudinal studies, carried out by other schools, local authorities and regions, would provide a wider picture of the learning opportunities offered to schoolchildren in the UK. Meanwhile, however, this book offers a regularly replicated model of research that shows indisputably what works.

References

Andrews, J., Robinson, D. and Hutchinson, J. (2017) 'Closing the gap? Trends in educational attainment and disadvantage'. London: Education Policy Institute. Online. http://tinyurl.com/ybc3poe8 (accessed 8 February 2019).

Arnot, M., Schneider, C., Evans, M., Liu, Y., Welply, O. and Davies-Tutt, D. (2014) 'School approaches to the education of EAL students: Language development, social integration and achievement'. Cambridge: Bell Foundation.

ASCL (Association of Schools and College Leaders) (2014) 'Supplementary written evidence submitted by the Association of Schools and College Leaders'. House of Commons Education Select Committee', *Underachievement in Education by White Working Class Children: First report of session 2014–15*. London: The Stationery Office, 68, WWC 05.

Atherton, J.S. (2011) 'Learning and teaching: Experiential learning'. Online. www.learningandteaching.info/learning/experience.htm (accessed 29 October 2018).

Barber, M. and Mourshed, M. (2007) 'How the world's best-performing school systems come out on top'. London: Mckinsey and Company. Online. http://tinyurl.com/yd2p6fux (accessed 8 February 2019).

Barber, M. and Mourshed, M. (2009) 'Shaping the future: How good education systems can become great in the decade ahead: Report on the International Education Roundtable, 7 July 2009, Singapore'. London: McKinsey and Company. Online. www.eurekanet.ru/res_ru/0_hfile_1906_1.pdf (accessed 1 March 2019).

Bassey, M. (1999) *Case Study Research in Educational Settings*. Buckingham: Open University Press.

Behnke, A.O., Gonzalez, L.M. and Cox, R.B. (2010) 'Latino students in new arrival states: Factors and services to prevent youth from dropping out'. *Hispanic Journal of Behavioral Sciences*, 32 (3), 385–409.

Bell, J. (1993) *Doing Your Research Project: A guide for first-time researchers in education and social science*. 2nd ed. Buckingham: Open University Press.

Bell Foundation (2017) 'EAL Assessment Framework – Version 1.1'. Cambridge: Bell Foundation. Online. www.bell-foundation.org.uk/eal-assessment-framework-version-1-1 (accessed 4 April 2019).

Benn, M. (2011) *School Wars: The battle for British education*. London: Verso.

Berliner, D.C. (2009). 'Poverty and potential: Out-of-school factors and school success'. Boulder, CO, and Tempe, AZ: Education and the Public Interest Center, and Education Policy Research Unit. Online. https://nepc.colorado.edu/sites/default/files/PB-Berliner-NON-SCHOOL.pdf (accessed 28 March 2019).

Blair, M. Bourne, J., Coffin, C., Creese, A. and Kenner, C. (1998) *Making the Difference: Teaching and learning strategies in successful multi-ethnic schools*. Sudbury: DfEE Publications.

Bourdieu, P. (1987) 'What makes a social class? On the theoretical and practical existence of groups'. *Berkeley Journal of Sociology*, 32, 1–17.

Burgess, S. (2014) 'Understanding the success of London's schools'. Working Paper no. 14/333, Centre for Market and Public Organisation, University of Bristol. Online. www.bristol.ac.uk/media-library/sites/cmpo/migrated/documents/wp333.pdf (accessed 3 April 2019).

Cabinet Office (2014) 'What works? Evidence for decision makers'. London: Cabinet Office. Online. https://tinyurl.com/yd772brw (accessed 9 February 2019).

Cabinet Office (2018) 'The What Works Network: Five years on'. London: Cabinet Office. Online. http://tinyurl.com/y96auafh (accessed 8 February 2019).

Carey, M.A. and Asbury, J.-E. (2016) *Focus Group Research*. London: Routledge.

Cassen, R. and Kingdon, G. (2007) *Tackling Low Educational Achievement*. York: Joseph Rowntree Foundation.

Cassen, R., McNally, S. and Vignoles, A. (2015) *Making a Difference in Education: What the evidence says*. London: Routledge.

Clifton, J. and Cook, W. (2012) 'A long division: Closing the attainment gap in England's secondary schools'. London: Institute for Public Policy Research.

Coleman, J.S., Campbell, E.Q., Hobson, C.J., McPartland, J., Mood, A.M., Weinfeld, F.D. and York, R.L. (1966) *Equality of Educational Opportunity*. Washington, DC: US Government Printing Office.

Collier, V.P. (1987) 'Age and rate of acquisition of second language for academic purposes'. *TESOL Quarterly*, 21 (4), 617–41.

Collier, V.P. (1992) 'A synthesis of studies examining long-term language minority student data on academic achievement'. *Bilingual Research Journal*, 16 (1–2), 187–212.

Conteh, J. and Meier, G. (eds) (2014) *The Multilingual Turn in Languages Education: Opportunities and challenges*. Bristol: Multilingual Matters.

Cummins, J. (1992) 'Language proficiency, bilingualism, and academic achievement'. In Richard-Amato, P.A. and Snow, M.A. (eds) *The Multicultural Classroom: Readings for content-area teachers*. White Plains, NY: Longman, 16–26.

Cummins, J. (2000) *Language, Power and Pedagogy: Bilingual children in the crossfire*. Clevedon: Multilingual Matters.

Day, C. and Sammons, P. (2014) *Successful School Leadership*. Reading: Education Development Trust. Online. www.educationdevelopmenttrust.com/EducationDevelopmentTrust/files/a3/a359e571-7033-41c7-8fe7-9ba60730082e.pdf (accessed 4 April 2019).

Day, C., Sammons, P., Hopkins, D., Harris, A., Leithwood, K., Gu, Q., Brown, E., Ahtaridou, E. and Kington, A. (2009) *The Impact of School Leadership on Pupil Outcomes: Final report* (Research Report no. DCSF-RR108). London: Department for Children, Schools and Families.

Day, C., Stobart, G., Sammons, P., Kington, A., Gu, Q., Smees, R. and Mujtaba, T. (2006) *Variations in Teachers' Work, Lives and Effectiveness* (Research Report 743). London: Department for Education and Skills.

DCLG (Department for Communities and Local Government) (2011) *The English Indices of Deprivation 2010*. London: Department for Communities and Local Government.

DCSF (Department for Children, Schools and Families) (2008) 'The extra mile: How schools succeed in raising aspirations in deprived communities'. Nottingham: Department for Children, Schools and Families. Online. https://tinyurl.com/y6x64l8k (accessed 9 February 2019).

Demie, F. (2001) 'Ethnic and gender differences in educational achievement and implications for school improvement strategies'. *Educational Research*, 43 (1), 91–106.

Demie, F. (2003) 'Raising the achievement of Caribbean pupils in British schools: Unacknowledged problems and challenges for policy makers'. *London Review of Education*, 1 (3), 229–49.

Demie, F. (2005) 'Achievement of black Caribbean pupils: Good practice in Lambeth schools'. *British Educational Research Journal*, 31 (4), 481–508.

Demie, F. (2013a) 'English as an additional language pupils: How long does it take to acquire English fluency?' *Language and Education*, 27 (1), 59–69.

Demie, F. (2013b) *Using Data to Raise Achievement: Good practice in schools*. London: Lambeth Research and Statistics Unit. Online. https://tinyurl.com/y828qyaa (accessed 7 February 2019).

Demie, F. (2015) 'Language diversity and attainment in schools: Implication for policy and practice'. *Race Ethnicity and Education*, 18 (5), 723–37.

Demie, F. (2016) 'Stages of proficiency: The implications for national data collection'. *EAL Journal*, 1 (Autumn), 28.

Demie, F. (2017a) *Raising Achievement of English as an Additional Language Pupils in Schools: Good practice*. London: Lambeth Research and Statistics Unit.

Demie, F. (2017b) *English as an Additional Language: Good practice to raise achievement in schools*. London: Schools Research and Statistics Unit, Lambeth LA.

Demie, F. (2018a) *A school survey of factors that contributed to improved school performance, 2014 and 2018*. London: Schools Research and Statistics Unit, Lambeth LA.

Demie, F. (2018c) 'English as an additional language and attainment in primary schools in England'. *Journal of Multilingual and Multicultural Development*, 39 (3), 210–23.

Demie, F. (2019) 'Raising achievement of black Caribbean pupils: Good practice for developing leadership capacity and workforce diversity in schools'. *School Leadership and Management*, 39 (1), 5–25.

Demie, F. and Butler, R. (2018a) *Primary School Profile: Making figures speak for themselves*. London: Schools Research and Statistics Unit, Lambeth LA.

Demie, F. and Butler, R. (2018b) *Primary Contextual Report: FSP, phonics, KS1 and KS2*. London: Schools Research and Statistics Unit, Lambeth LA.

Demie, F., Butler, R. and McDonald, J. (2018a) *Primary Value Added Report: KS2 to GCSE*. London: Schools Research and Statistics Unit, Lambeth LA.

Demie, F., Butler, R. and McDonald, J. (2018b) *Secondary Value Added Report: KS1 to KS2*. London: Schools Research and Statistics Unit, Lambeth LA.

Demie, F., Butler, R., Tong, R., McDonald, J. and Hau, A. (2018) *Education Statistics*. 21st ed. London: Schools Research and Statistics Unit, Lambeth LA.

References

Demie, F. and Lewis, K. (2008) *Raising the Achievement of Portuguese Pupils: Good practice in Lambeth schools*. London: Lambeth Research and Statistics Unit.

Demie, F. and Lewis, K. (2010a) *Outstanding Secondary Schools: Good Practice*. London: School Research and Statistics Unit, Lambeth LA.

Demie, F. and Lewis, K. (2010b) *Raising Achievement: A study of outstanding secondary schools*. London: Schools Research and Statistics Unit, London Borough of Lambeth.

Demie, F. and Lewis, K. (2010c) 'Raising the achievement of Portuguese pupils in British schools: A case study of good practice'. *Educational Studies*, 36 (1), 95–109.

Demie, F. and Lewis, K. (2010d) *Raising the Achievement of White Working Class Pupils: School strategies*. London: Lambeth Research and Statistics Unit.

Demie, F. and Lewis, K. (2010e) *White Working Class Achievement: A study of barriers to learning in schools*. London: Lambeth Research and Statistics Unit.

Demie, F. and Lewis, K. (2018) 'Raising achievement of English as additional language pupils in schools: implications for policy and practice'. *Educational Review*, 70 (4): 427–46.

Demie, F., Lewis, K. and McLean, C. (2006) 'The achievement of African heritage pupils: Good practice in Lambeth schools'. London: Lambeth Research and Statistics Unit.

Demie, F. and McDonald, J. (2018a) *Secondary School Profile: Making figures speak for themselves*. London: School Research and Statistics Unit, Lambeth LA.

Demie, F. and McDonald, J. (2018b) *Secondary Contextual Report: Year 7 and GCSE*. London: School Research and Statistics Unit, Lambeth LA.

Demie, F. and McLean, C. (2006) *The Achievement of African Heritage Pupils: Good practice in secondary schools*. London: Schools Research and Statistics Unit, London Borough of Lambeth.

Demie, F. and McLean, C. (2007) 'Raising the achievement of African heritage pupils: A case study of good practice in British schools'. *Educational Studies*, 33 (4), 415–34.

Demie, F. and McLean, C. (2013) *Outstanding Primary Schools: A study of successful practice in Lambeth*. London: Schools Research and Statistics Unit, Lambeth LA.

Demie, F. and McLean, C. (2015a) *Narrowing the Achievement Gap: Good practice in schools*. London: Lambeth Research and Statistics Unit.

Demie, F. and McLean, C. (2015b) 'Tackling disadvantage: What works in narrowing the achievement gap in schools'. *Review of Education*, 3 (2), 138–74.

Demie, F. and McLean, C. (2015c) *Transforming Education: The Lambeth story*. London: Lambeth Research and Statistics Unit.

Demie, F. and McLean, C. (2016) *What Works in School Improvement: Examples of good practice*. London: Schools Research and Statistics Unit, Lambeth.

Demie, F. and McLean, C. (2017a) *The Achievement of Black Caribbean Pupils: Good practice*. London: Schools Research and Statistics Unit, Lambeth.

Demie, F. and McLean, C. (2017b) *Black Caribbean Underachievement in Schools in England*. London: Schools Research and Statistics Unit, Lambeth.

Demie, F. and Strand, S. (2006) 'English language acquisition and educational attainment at the end of secondary school'. *Educational Studies*, 32 (2), 215–31.

DfE (Department for Education) (2010) *The Importance of Teaching: The schools White Paper 2010*. London: Department for Education.

DfE (Department for Education) (2011) National Pupil Database. London: Department for Education.

DfE (Department for Education) (2012) 'A brief summary of Government policy in relation to EAL learners'. Online. www.naldic.org.uk/Resources/NALDIC/Research%20and%20Information/Documents/Brief_summary_of_Government_policy_for_EAL_Learners.pdf (accessed 24 May 2019).

DfE (Department for Education) (2013) 'Schools, pupils and their characteristics: January 2013', Local authority and regional tables, SFR21/2013. Online. www.gov.uk/government/statistics/schools-pupils-and-their-characteristics-january-2013 (accessed 24 May 2019).

DfE (Department for Education) (2014) 'Pupil premium: funding and accountability for schools'. London: Department for Education. Online. www.gov.uk/guidance/pupil-premium-information-for-schools-and-alternative-provision-settings (accessed 4 April 2019).

DfE (Department for Education) (2015a) 'National curriculum assessments: Key stage 2, 2015 (revised)', National tables: SFR47/2015. Online. https://assets.publishing.service.gov.uk/government/uploads/system/uploads/attachment_data/file/522817/SFR47_2015_KS2_National_FinalData_Tables.xlsx (accessed 9 April 2019).

DfE (Department for Education) (2016a) 'Schools national funding formula: Government consultation – stage one'. London: Department for Education. Online. https://tinyurl.com/jylfnwu (accessed 9 February 2019).

DfE (Department for Education) (2016b) National Pupil Database. London: Department for Education.

DfE (Department for Education) (2017a) 'Collection of data on pupil nationality, country of birth and proficiency in English: Summary report'. London: Department for Education. Online. https://tinyurl.com/y4ataewu (accessed 9 February 2019).

DfE (Department for Education) (2017b) 'School census autumn 2017 to summer 2018: guide for schools and LAs'. London: Department for Education. Online. www.gov.uk/government/publications/school-census-2017-to-2018-guide-for-schools-and-las (accessed 9 February 2019).

DfE (Department for Education) (2017c) *NPD GCSE Performance Data 2017*. London: Department for Education.

DfE (Department for Education) (2017d) *National and LA KS2 and GCSE Performance Table 2005–2017, SFR*. London: Department for Education.

DfE (Department for Education) (2017e) 'School workforce in England: November 2016', SFR 25/2017. London: Department for Education. Online. www.gov.uk/government/statistics/school-workforce-in-england-november-2016 (accessed 2 April 2019).

DfE (Department for Education) (2017f) 'Schools, pupils and their characteristics: January 2017', Local authority and regional tables, SFR28/2017. www.gov.uk/government/statistics/schools-pupils-and-their-characteristics-january-2017 (accessed 5 April 2019).

References

DfE (Department for Education) (2018) 'Pupil premium: Conditions of grant 2018 to 2019', October. London: Department for Education. www.gov.uk/government/publications/pupil-premium-conditions-of-grant-2018-to-2019/pupil-premium-2018-to-2019-conditions-of-grant (accessed 14 March 2019).

DfES (Department for Education and Skills) (2003a) *Aiming High: Raising the achievement of African Caribbean pupils: Guidance for schools*. London: Department for Education and Skills.

DfES (Department for Education and Skills) (2003b) *Aiming High: Raising the achievement of minority ethnic pupils*. London: Department for Education and Skills.

DfES (Department for Education and Skills) (2006) 'Getting it. Getting it right. Exclusion of black pupils: Priority review'. London: Department for Education and Skills.

Duncan, G.J. and Magnuson, K.A. (2005) 'Can family socioeconomic resources account for racial and ethnic test score gaps?' *The Future of Children*, 15 (1), 35–54.

Edmonds, R.R. (1982) 'Programs of school improvement: An overview'. *Educational Leadership*, 40 (3), 4–11.

Education Commission (2004) 'The educational experiences and achievements of Black boys in London schools 2000–2003: A report by the Education Commission'. London: London Development Agency.

Education Policy Institute (2017) 'Key findings'. Online. https://epi.org.uk/publications-and-research/closing-gap-trends-educational-attainment-disadvantage/ (accessed 30 March 2019).

EEF (Education Endowment Foundation) (2019) 'Teaching and Learning Toolkit: An accessible summary of the international evidence on teaching 5–16 year-olds'. Online. https://tinyurl.com/yagghs79 (accessed 9 February 2019).

Full Fact (2015) 'Is the performance of disadvantaged pupils improving?' *Full Fact*, 8 September. Online. https://fullfact.org/education/performance-disadvantaged-pupils-improving/ (accessed 10 February 2019).

Gewirtz, W. (2002) *The Managerial School: Post-welfarism and social justice in education*. London: Routledge.

Gillborn, D. (2002) *Education and Institutional Racism*. London: Institute of Education.

Gillborn, D. (2008) *Racism and Education: Coincidence or conspiracy?* London: Routledge.

Gillborn, D. and Gipps, C. (1996) *Recent Research on the Achievements of Ethnic Minority Pupils*. London: HMSO.

Gillborn, D. and Mirza, H.S. (2000) 'Educational inequality: Mapping race, class and gender: A synthesis of research evidence'. London: Ofsted.

Gillborn, D. and Youdell, D. (2000) *Rationing Education: Policy, practice, reform and equity*. Buckingham: Open University Press.

Goldfeld, S., O'Connor, M., Mithen, J., Sayers, M. and Brinkman, S. (2014) 'Early development of emerging and English-proficient bilingual children at school entry in an Australian population cohort'. *International Journal of Behavioral Development*, 38 (1), 42–51.

Goodall, J., Vorhaus, J., Carpentieri, J.D., Brooks, G., Akerman, R. and Harris, A. (2011) 'Review of best practice in parental engagement: Practitioners summary. London: Department for Education. Online. https://tinyurl.com/pjv86hk (accessed 10 February 2019).

Gorard, S. (2000) *Education and Social Justice: The changing composition of schools and its implications.* Cardiff: University of Wales Press.

Gorard, S. (2018) *Education Policy: Evidence of equity and effectiveness.* Bristol: Policy Press.

Halle, T., Hair, E., Wandner, L., McNamara, M. and Chien, N. (2012) 'Predictors and outcomes of early versus later English language proficiency among English language learners'. *Early Childhood Research Quarterly*, 27 (1), 1–20.

Harris, A. and Chapman, C. (2002) 'Leadership in schools facing challenging circumstances'. *Management in Education*, 16 (1), 10–13.

Hattie, J. (2009) *Visible Learning: A synthesis of over 800 meta-analyses relating to achievement.* London: Routledge.

Hester, H., Ellis, S. and Barrs, M. (1993) *Guide to the Primary Learning Record.* London: Centre for Language in Primary Education.

Higgins, S., Katsipataki, M., Villanueva-Aguilera, A.B., Coleman, R., Henderson, P., Major, L.E., Coe, R. and Mason, D. (2016) *The Sutton Trust–Education Endowment Foundation Teaching and Learning Toolkit.* London: Education Endowment Foundation.

Hopkins, D., Ainscow, M. and West, M. (1994) *School Improvement in an Era of Change.* London: Cassell.

Hutchinson, J., Dunford, J. and Treadaway, M. (2016) *Divergent Pathways: The disadvantage gap, accountability and the pupil premium.* London: Education Policy Institute. Online. https://tinyurl.com/y6gl9lcc (accessed 10 February 2019).

Iniesta-Martinez, S. and Evans, H. (2012) *Pupils Not Claiming Free School Meals* (Research Report 235). London: Department for Education. Online. https://tinyurl.com/y3gdyu4u (accessed 9 February 2019).

Krashen, S. (1999) 'Bilingual education: Arguments for and (bogus) arguments against'. In Alatis, J.E. and Tan A.-H. (eds) *Language in Our Time: Bilingual education and official English, ebonics and standard English, immigration and the Unz initiative* (Georgetown University Round Table on Languages and Linguistics). Washington, D.C.: Georgetown University Press, 111–27.

Lane, G. (2013) *How Different Governments Have Weakened Local Government and Democracy.* Amersham: Iris Press.

Leedham, D. (2016) 'Nobody puts EAL in the corner'. *Schools Week*, 23 April 2016. Online. https://schoolsweek.co.uk/eal-learners-in-schools-how-the-government-could-help/?utm_content=buffer5a4af&utm_medium=social&utm_source=twitter.com&utm_campaign=buffer (accessed 3 April 2019).

Leithwood, K., Day, C., Sammons, P., Harris, A. and Hopkins, D. (2006a) *Seven Strong Claims about Successful School Leadership.* Nottingham: National College for School Leadership.

Leithwood, K., Day, C., Sammons, P., Harris, A. and Hopkins, D. (2006b) *Successful School Leadership: What it is and how it influences pupil learning* (Research Report 800). Nottingham: DfES Publications.

References

Leithwood, K. and Louis, K.S. (2012) *Linking Leadership to Student Learning*. San Francisco: Jossey-Bass.

Lewis, K. and Demie, F. 2015. 'Raising the achievement of white working class pupils: good practice in schools'. *Review of Education*, 3 (1). Online. https://researchgate.net/publication/273390211_Raising_the_achievement_of_white_working_class_pupils_good_practice_in_schools (accessed 24 May 2019).

Macleod, S., Sharp, C., Bernardinelli, D., Skipp, A. and Higgins, S. (2015) *Supporting the Attainment of Disadvantaged Pupils: Articulating success and good practice*. Research report. London: Department for Education. Online. https://tinyurl.com/yyypsq2e (accessed 9 February 2019).

McKenley, J., Power, C., Ishani, L. and Demie, F. (2003) *Raising Achievement of Black Caribbean Pupils: Good practice in Lambeth schools*. London: Lambeth Research and Statistics Unit.

Mensah, F.K. and Kiernan, K.E. (2010) 'Gender differences in educational attainment: Influences of the family environment'. *British Educational Research Journal*, 36 (2), 239–60.

Mongon, D. and Chapman, C. (2008) 'Successful leadership for promoting the achievement of white working class pupils'. Nottingham: National College for School Leadership.

Mortimore, P. (1999) *The Road to Improvement: Reflections on school effectiveness*. Lisse: Swets and Zeitlinger.

Mortimore, P. (2014) *Education under Siege: Why there is a better alternative*. Bristol: Policy Press.

Mortimore, P., Sammons, P., Stoll, L., Lewis, D. and Ecob, R. (1988) *School Matters: The junior years*. Wells: Open Books.

Mortimore, P., Sammons, P. and Thomas, S. (1994) 'School effectiveness and value added measures'. *Assessment in Education: Principles, Policy & Practice*, 1 (3), 315–332.

Mortimore, P. and Whitty, G. (1997) *Can School Improvement Overcome the Effects of Disadvantage?* London: University of London, Institute of Education.

Muijs, D., Harris, A., Chapman, C., Stoll, L. and Russ, J. (2004) 'Improving schools in socioeconomically disadvantaged areas: A review of research evidence'. *School Effectiveness and School Improvement*, 15 (2), 149–75.

Muir, R. and Clifton, J. (2014) *Whole System Reform: England's schools and the middle tier*. London: Institute for Public Policy Research.

Murphy, V.A. and Unthiah, A. (2015) 'A systematic review of intervention research examining English language and literacy development in children with English as an additional language (EAL)'. University of Oxford, Department of Education.

NALDIC (National Association for Language Development in the Curriculum) (2014) 'The national audit of English as an additional language training and development provision'. Online. https://tinyurl.com/yxbmg8au (accessed 10 February 2019).

NAO (National Audit Office) (2015) 'Funding for disadvantaged pupils'. Online. www.nao.org.uk/wp-content/uploads/2015/06/Funding-for-disadvantaged-pupils.pdf#page=19 (accessed 9 April 2019).

NASSEA Assessment Working Group (2001) 'NASSEA EAL assessment system'. Dukinfield: Northern Association of Support Service for Equality and Achievement. Online. www.wigan.gov.uk/Docs/PDF/Council/Schools-Portal/n/nassea20booklet.pdf (accessed 14 March 2019).

Ofsted (2002a) *Achievement of Black Caribbean Pupils: Three successful primary schools*. London: Ofsted.

Ofsted (2002b) *Achievement of Black Caribbean Pupils: Good practice in secondary schools*. London: Ofsted.

Ofsted (2009a) *Twelve Outstanding Secondary Schools: Excelling against the odds*. London: Ofsted.

Ofsted (2009b) *Twenty Outstanding Primary Schools: Excelling against the odds*. Manchester: Ofsted. Online. https://tinyurl.com/no9m6x2 (accessed 10 February 2019).

Ofsted (2013) 'Unseen children: Access and achievement 20 years on: Evidence report'. Manchester: Ofsted. Online. https://tinyurl.com/yyuk3ccj (accessed 10 February 2019).

Ofsted (2014) 'Supplementary written evidence submitted by Ofsted'. House of Commons Education Committee, *Underachievement in Education by White Working Class Children: First report of session 2014–15*. London: The Stationery Office, 68, WWC 37.

Petty, L. (2014) 'How to promote equality and diversity in the classroom'. *Hub*, 1 September. Online. https://tinyurl.com/y8vwn5ka (accessed 10 February 2019).

Prevoo, M.J.L., Malda, M., Mesman, J. and van IJzendoorn, M.H. (2016) 'Within- and cross-language relations between oral language proficiency and school outcomes in bilingual children with an immigrant background: A meta-analytical study'. *Review of Educational Research*, 86 (1), 237–76.

Rampton, A. (1981) *West Indian Children in Our Schools: Interim report of the Committee of Inquiry into the Education of Children from Ethnic Minority Groups*. London: HMSO.

Rasbash, J., Leckie, G., Pillinger, R. and Jenkins, J. (2010) 'Children's educational progress: Partitioning family, school and area effects'. *Journal of the Royal Statistical Society: Series A – Statistics in Society*, 173 (3), 657–82. Online. https://research-information.bristol.ac.uk/files/63296556/rasbash2010jrssa.pdf (accessed 28 March 2019).

Rea, S., Hill, R. and Sandals, L. (2011) *System Leadership: Does school-to-school support close the gap?* Nottingham: National College for School Leadership.

Reynolds, D., Sammons, P., Stoll, L. Barber, M. and Hillman, J. (1996) 'School effectiveness and school improvement in the United Kingdom'. *School Effectiveness and School Improvement*, 7 (2), 133–58.

Richardson, B. (ed.) (2005) *Tell It Like It Is: How our schools fail Black children*. London: Bookmarks.

Robinson, V., Hohepa, M. and Lloyd, C. (2009) *School Leadership and Student Outcomes: Identifying what works and why: Best evidence synthesis iteration (BES)*. Wellington: New Zealand Ministry of Education. Online. https://tinyurl.com/y2knmrkf (accessed 11 February 2019).

Rudd, P. and Davies, D. (2002) *A Revolution in the Use of Data? The LEA role in data collection, analysis and use and its impact on pupil performance* (LGA Research: Report 29). Slough: National Federation for Educational Research.

References

Rutter, M., Maughan, B., Mortimore, P. and Ouston, J. (1979) *Fifteen Thousand Hours: Secondary schools and their effects on children*. London: Open Books.

Sammons, P. (1999) *School Effectiveness: Coming of age in the twenty-first century*. Lisse: Swets and Zeitlinger.

Sammons, P. (2007) *School Effectiveness and Equity: Making connections: A review of school effectiveness and improvement research – its implications for practitioners and policy makers*. Reading: CfBT Education Trust.

Sammons, P., Hillman, J. and Mortimore, P. (1995) *Key Characteristics of Effective Schools: A review of school effectiveness research*. London: Ofsted.

Sharp, C., Macleod, S., Bernardinelli, D., Skipp, A. and Higgins, S. (2015) *Supporting the Attainment of Disadvantaged Pupils: Briefing for school leaders*. London: Department for Education.

Sharples, J., Slavin, R, Chambers, B. and Sharp, C. (2011) 'Effective classroom strategies for closing the gap in educational achievement for children and young people living in poverty, including white working-class boys'. Schools and Communities Research Review 4. Centre for Excellence and Outcomes in Children and Young People's Services (C4EO), London.

Slater, H., Davies, N. and Burgess, S. (2009) 'Do teachers matter? Measuring the variation in teacher effectiveness in England'. Working Paper 09/212. Bristol: Centre for Market and Public Organisation.

Stake, R.E. (1995) *The Art of Case Study Research*. Thousand Oaks, CA: SAGE Publications.

Stoll, L. and Fink, D. (1994) 'School effectiveness and school improvement: Voices from the field'. *School Effectiveness and School Improvement*, 5 (2), 149–77.

Stoll, L. and Fink, D. (1996) *Changing Our Schools: Linking school effectiveness and school improvement*. Buckingham: Open University Press.

Strand, S. (2010) 'Do some schools narrow the gap? Differential school effectiveness by ethnicity, gender, poverty, and prior achievement'. *School Effectiveness and School Improvement*, 21 (3), 289–314.

Strand, S. (2014) 'School effects and ethnic, gender and socio-economic gaps in educational achievement at age 11'. *Oxford Review of Education*, 40 (2), 223–45.

Strand, S. and Demie, F. (2005) 'English language acquisition and educational attainment at the end of primary school'. *Educational Studies*, 31 (3), 275–91.

Strand, S., Malmberg, L. and Hall, J. (2015) 'English as an additional language (EAL) and educational achievement in England: An analysis of the National Pupil Database'. University of Oxford, Department of Education. Online. https://tinyurl.com/y6hxzvcd (accessed 10 February 2019).

Sutton, D. (2017) 'Setting the EAL agenda'. *EAL Journal*, 2 (Spring), 29.

Sutton Trust (2011) 'Improving the impact of teachers on pupil achievement in the UK: Interim findings'. Online. www.irisconnect.com/us/wp-content/uploads/sites/3//2014/08/sutton-trust-teachers-impact-35.pdf (accessed 18 February 2019).

Swann, M. (1985) *Education for All: The report of the Committee of Inquiry into the Education of Children from Ethnic Minority Groups*. London: HMSO.

Tereshchenko, A. and Archer, L. (2014) 'New migration, new challenges: East European migrant pupils in English schools'. King's College London, Department of Education & Professional Studies.

TES (2016) 'UK schools with large numbers of EU migrant pupils "achieve better results"'. *TES*, 2 June 2016. Online. www.tes.com/news/schools-large-numbers-eu-immigrant-pupils-achieve-better-results (accessed 3 April 2019).

Thrupp, M. (1999) *Schools Making a Difference: Let's be realistic!* Buckingham: Open University Press.

Thrupp, M. (2001) 'Sociological and political concerns about school effectiveness research: Time for a new research agenda'. *School Effectiveness and School Improvement*, 12 (1), 7–40.

vonAhn, M., Lupton, R., Wiggins, R., Eversley, J., Sanderson, A. and Mayhew, L. (2011) 'Using School Census language data to understand language distribution and links to ethnicity, socio-economic status and educational attainment: A guide for local authority users'. Institute of Education, University of London.

Williams, B. (ed.) (2003) *Closing the Achievement Gap: A vision for changing beliefs and practices*. 2nd ed. Alexandria, VA: Association for Supervision and Curriculum Development.

Index

Index